K/137

$\frac{}{8^{00}}$

D1020038

Also by Molly Picon

So Laugh a Little
(*with Ethel Rosenberg*)

MOLLY!

AN AUTOBIOGRAPHY

BY MOLLY PICON

WITH JEAN BERGANTINI GRILLO

SIMON AND SCHUSTER • NEW YORK

Copyright © 1980 by Molly Picon
All rights reserved
including the right of reproduction
in whole or in part in any form
Published by Simon and Schuster
A Division of Gulf & Western Corporation
Simon & Schuster Building
Rockefeller Center
1230 Avenue of the Americas
New York, New York 10020

Designed by Edith Fowler
Photo editor: Vincent Virga
Manufactured in the United States of America

1 2 3 4 5 6 7 8 9 10

Library of Congress Cataloging in Publication Data

Picon, Molly
  Molly! : An autobiography.

  Includes index.
    1. Picon, Molly. 2. Kalich, Jacob,
1891–1975. 3. Actors—United States—
Biography. 4. Theater—Jews.
I.   Grillo, Jean Bergantini, joint author.
II.   Title.
PN2287.P53A28 792'.028'0924 [B] 79-21067

ISBN 0-671-24016-1

Reading a few pages of this book is enough to reassure one that here is not another theater story of the struggles to the top and the inevitable triumphs of a theater poster figure. This is a real-life story of a whole, complete woman. In the round. True, the career is there—of the Molly Picon treasured by thousands all over the world as a rare and gifted entertainer. But that Molly has to move over now to make room for Molly the writer. On paper she makes her points, be they funny or sentimental or even terrifying, with the same unerring precision and timing she displays on stage.

And, Molly the woman. There is something else again. One falls in love all over again with her humor, her honesty, her charm, and her capacity for loving her Yonkel. Why can't more wives be like that nowadays? I feel sure they would be happier.

Then, there is Molly the Jew—with compassion for the few who have let the terrible struggle to survive taint their lives—and Molly the proud Jew, glorying in and thrilling us with stories of the courage, the grandeur, of the many.

We first met in her dressing room after a performance of *Milk and Honey*. I had barged in because she had given me such a treat and I wanted to tell her so. Molly said to me, "People have called me the Jewish Helen Hayes. I hope you don't mind." To which I replied, "Not if they'll allow me to be the shiksa Molly Picon."

After reading this book, I think I had a nerve.

Blessed Molly!

HELEN HAYES

CHAPTER 1

WHENEVER YONKEL AND I (let me explain in case someone doesn't know the name Yonkel—Yonkel is the Yiddish for Jacob and Yiddish is the Jewish for Jewish—I hope that's clear, for Yonkel always said all his Gentile friends called him Yonkel and all his Jewish friends called him Jack) whenever Yonkel and I were with people and held forth our stories and anecdotes about our life in the Yiddish theater, everyone would say, "You ought to write a book—you should write a book—you *must* write a book."

So I asked Yonkel, who was a brilliant writer, a former Talmud student, and, not so incidentally, my husband for over fifty years, "How do you write a book? Where do you begin?" And in typical Yiddish fashion, he answered my question with a question. "Where do you begin? You begin at *berayshet,* as in the Bible, which means you begin at the beginning."

So: "In the beginning," on my mother's side, there were Grandpa and Grandma Ostrovsky (later, of course, Ostrow). For generations, they and their ancestors lived in Rizshishtehov, a small village near Kiev, Russia. Grandpa was in the grain business with a big farm and an even bigger family.

One night a neighbor came running into Grandma's kitchen to warn her that the Cossacks were coming and all the Ostrovskys would be murdered. Jews were being slaughtered in pogroms all over Russia, and this was all Grandma had to hear. She gathered her children, her samovar and *perrina* (warm bed quilt), some bread and tea, Grandpa took his prayer shawl and Bible, and they started to run. Miraculously, they made it all the way to Philadelphia, where Grandpa's brother had run just a few years before.

They settled there. Grandpa became a trunk maker and my mother, who was thirteen years old, went right into a shirtwaist factory. All the other children went right out to work—selling papers, shining shoes, each somehow making a few pennies a day.

I never knew my father's people. Actually, I scarcely knew my father. Louis Picon was born in Warsaw, Poland, and had once studied to become a rabbi. But he came to America instead. He never told us why, or anything else about his background. All we knew was he met Mama here and they married. Shortly after my sister Helen and I were born (I first, in 1898), Mama discovered—I don't know how—that our father was already a married man with a wife and three children in Warsaw, and no divorce. So actually Helen and I are *mamzarim* (the Jewish word for bastards).

Of course, this was not an unusual predicament in the days of heavy immigration. Our newspaper, *The Jewish Daily Forward,* regularly ran a column called *A Bintel Brief* (A Bundle of Letters), a kind of "Dear Abby" of the times, and all too often the letter writers were wives who had been deserted when their husbands left them to go to America with promises they would send for the family as soon as they had earned enough money to bring them to the *goldeneh medine* (Golden Land). Perhaps this is how Mama found out, but as soon as she knew, she began sending money to them. They never corresponded, however, because neither of them could write.

Many years later, in 1936, Yonkel and I went to Warsaw to make the film *Yiddel Mit'n Fiddle* (Yiddel with His Fiddle), which, incidentally, is still being shown here (especially in Miami), and in Israel.

One day, while we were shooting on the lot, a strange man with a heavy black beard approached us and in Yiddish said, "I am your brother." And he resembled me, especially his eyes. His mother, whom our father deserted when he came to America, had heard about me, and before she died she told him if ever he needed help to write to Mama. All he said to me then was, "I have a daughter who wants very much to go to Israel, and I can't afford to send her." Naturally, Yonkel gave him the money he needed.

As for Papa—well, Papa was disdainful of life in general and, I think, of me in particular. He never worked. He was too "educated" to do menial labor. Basically, he was just "anti": anti-capitalist, anti-religion, anti-labor and anti-girls. He stopped speaking to Mama for one whole year after I was born, and then moved out completely when she failed to heed his fury and presented him with Helen. He barely managed to bring home packages from the sweatshop for Mama to sew while he sat and studied—philosophy, astronomy and Greek. He read continuously and found fault with his three females. Theirs was not a happy marriage, but no one ever mentioned divorce, especially Mama. What would the neighbors say?

In his last years, Papa was on our payroll, and every week he would come to the theater to collect his annuity. Once in a while he would even watch me perform at the Second Avenue Theater. However, it was beneath his dignity to praise or even comment on what I did—despite the fact it was providing him with a salary. The last time he came for a check he wanted a raise, and he threatened Yonkel that if he didn't give it to him, he would actually go to work! But he never did. He just faded out of our lives until he died in 1943. Never did he ever hug or kiss Helen or me. I was and still am sorry we never really knew Papa.

But Mama—ah, Mama. She was everything Papa wasn't. She was born Clara Ostrovsky but everyone called her Mama Picon. She was small and dark and always neatly groomed. All her life she worked hard and never complained. She smiled and sang and could make *yom tov* (a holiday) out of thin air. Trained as a seamstress, she'd buy buttons and make dresses around them. Often she made identical ones for Grandma (*Bubbe*), herself, Helen and me. She was always ready to dress up and go out. She loved people, and although not the world's greatest cook, she would regularly orchestrate our pajama parties so she could bake dozens of cookies.

Mama was not a disciplinarian. She neither complained nor scolded. And she never discussed Papa. When he would periodically leave home, I never worried about his absence because Mama didn't worry. She had an inner joy, loved people and made a home out of any shabby room we lived in.

Her greatest delight was having company; she'd serve cookies and tea, and we all sang. Mama and I had a special duet
we used to sing at the drop of a hat (or the first visit of a
guest). Looking back on it, I can appreciate the truth she
must have found in its poetry:

ME: Why are you sad, Mother my darling?
    Why are those tears falling today?
    Why do you look at me so sadly?
    Have I done wrong? Tell me, I pray!

MAMA: No, no, my child, thou art an angel;
    There's not a soul purer than thine!
    That's why I fear some day you'll leave me
    Just as your father did—there'll come a time.

BOTH: There'll come a time some day
    When I am far away
    There'll be no mother to guide you from day to
      day.
    Think of the words I have said;
    Honor the man you wed.
    Always remember my story—there'll come a
      time.

Mama loved amusement parks—the rides, the shoot-
the-chutes, the noise and clamor. She was also attracted to
the freak show and the man who had a baby growing out of
his stomach. He explained it was supposed to have been his
twin. I found it horrible to look at; but Mama talked to the
man at length and told him how brave he was to do his act
and show people how lucky they were to have normal children. Then she would give him a quarter and promise to send
all her friends to see his act.

She always shared the little she had and taught us "You
never go with empty hands." Even when she went to the
Italian bakery, she brought the baker cookies. And in Italian
bakeries, there was often a priest in the store. The baker
would say, "Mama Picon, I want you to meet Father." And
Mama answered, "Hello, Father, how is Mother?"

Clearly, she had her own perspective on things. When

her contemporaries started dying, she said, quite seriously, "You see Malkale (little Molly)—people are dying who never died before."

One of her most memorable remarks came in Schwartz's Funeral Parlor on Second Avenue. Edelstein, my first producer, after ten years of almost dying, finally really gave up the ghost. Our Yiddish theater union (actually, the Yiddish theaters were the first to create an actors' union in New York) called all its members to pay their respects to Edelstein, who definitely was dead. We all put on our mourning clothes and walked solemnly by the casket. Mama was the last one. In a voice clear as a bell, she said. "Yes, Edelstein, there's a first time for everything."

Once, when Yonkel and I were living at One University Place on the fifteenth floor, we found Mama sitting by the window and sighing "Oy, veh is mir" (Oh, woe is me). From our window she could see the Empire State Building, which Governor Smith had just built. It was evening and only half the lights in the building were on. "Poor man," she said, "he'll go broke. Only half the place is rented!"

Mama's philosophy and approach to life were succinct: If it's good it's not forever, and if it's bad it's not forever. Once we took her to a Romanian cabaret on Allen Street on the lower East Side. Sadie Banks, who called herself the Yiddish Sophie Tucker, was singing the kind of fractured bawdy songs you sing in a Romanian cabaret on Allen Street when you bill yourself that way. Knowing Mama was with us, she came to our table and said apologetically, "You know, Mama Picon, it's a different world here; you have to cater to them." And Mama answered, very sweetly, "That's all right, Sadie—I take it where it comes from."

However, even after many years backstage with actors, she was still naïve enough to be shocked when she heard there was some hanky-panky going on between an older actress and a young actor. Of course, she wouldn't say "sleeping together," so she sputtered, "You mean . . . he *caters* to her?!"

Mama had no anger or jealousy in her, but there was a bit of bigotry. A black woman came to clean my apartment once

a week, and she and Mama got along fine. They worked together, ate together, sang together. But whenever something
was missing, Mama would say, "The *shvartzeh* (black person) took it." We'd argue with her, but she was adamant: The
shvartzeh took it. Later, when the missing article would turn
up and we'd say, "You see?" Mama would just shrug and
answer, "And if I didn't find it, who else would take it?"

When asked how she was feeling, she'd reply, "Fine,
only I'm suffering from odds and ends. A little diabetes, a
little arthritis, a hyena hernia." When we corrected her—
"You mean a hiatus hernia"—she'd come right back. "Hiatus,
hyena, my enemies should have it!" To Mama, a condomin-
ium was always a "pandemonium," and sometimes I think
she was right.

Despite such naïveté, however, Mama had a sense of
elegance. Everything had to match, and even when we ate
on a trunk, there would always be a tablecloth (in those days
it was an oilcloth). As we became more affluent, it was fine
linen. Later, wash and wear. And, finally, plastic ones, to
close the circle. Nevertheless, Mama went for the finer
touches. She was forever scolding Helen, my sister, who was
sometimes careless about her clothes, and would threaten,
"I'd like to come back after I die just to see if your petticoat
isn't showing!"

Everyone loved her for her simple, uneducated, completely honest and unspoiled self. She never let us down.
When she died, the Yiddish Theatrical Alliance chose her
tombstone and engraved it simply "Mama Picon" with her
birth and death dates.

As for me, I was a small, skinny kid who loved to kibbitz
with the neighbors. I don't remember much of my first five
years—only what Mama would sometimes reminisce about.
How, for example, whenever the rent was due, we'd move.
Or how she would sit and consult with me to help her figure
out whom we could go to for a loan. She often shared her joys
and problems with me, for I always had an *alter kop* (old
head) on my young shoulders.

In Philadelphia we lived with Grandma and Grandpa.
"We" included all my cousins (eight or nine of them), Mama,

Helen and me. Once in a while Papa joined us and then vanished into thin air. Everyone was working, but when the little two-story house was chokingly overcrowded, Mama would send me to Mamie Emanuel, who lived down the street. Mamie was an old maid (all of seventeen) and *nebech* (poor thing), not married. She loved children. We sat on the stoop, and she taught me song and dance routines. I acquired quite a repertoire.

We lived on Orianna Street, and around the corner, on Third and Green Streets, was the Columbia Theater. A Jewish company played there with Mike Thomashefsky, the brother of the famous Boris Thomashefsky, whose grandson is the famous symphony conductor Michael Tilson Thomas. The actresses from the Columbia Theater came to Mama to have their costumes made, and one day Fanny, Mike's wife, came for a fitting. There I was, singing and dancing and doing somersaults—practically the same routine I did sixty years later on Broadway in *Milk and Honey*.

Fanny was quite impressed with my act, and she told Mama to put me on the stage, that I had talent. Mama thought it over, decided it was a good idea, made me a fancy party dress and took me on a trolley car to the Bijou Theater. The Bijou was a burlesque theater, and every Friday night they had amateur night for children, complete with a "get-the-hook man" standing by.

On the trolley car there was a drunk, and he said, "Hey there, kid, whatcha all dressed up for like Mrs. Astor's pet horse?" In my tiny child's voice I said, "I'm an actor, and I'm going to sing in the Bijou Theater and win the first prize, a five-dollar gold piece." And he said, "She's gonna sing? You can't sing!" And Mama said, "Molly, show him."

So I got up in the car and did my whole act that Mamie had put together for me. Then the drunk took off his derby and passed it around to the people in the car and collected two dollars in coins, which he gave me. So I consider that my first professional performance.

We went to the Bijou, and I did my act. But the master of ceremonies said Molly Picon wasn't a fancy enough name for the theater. Nobody would ever remember it. So he changed it to Baby Margaret. I won the five-dollar gold piece, and since, in those days, people threw coins up on the stage, I gingerly picked these up too, while I was dancing.

We came home to Grandma and plunked down ten dollars on the kitchen table. Grandpa had never earned more than fifteen dollars a week, so when Grandma saw all that money she cried "*Oy, ich chalesh!*" (*Oy,* I'm fainting!)—*Oy* is *Oy* in any language. "Tell me, how did she do it?"

Mama told her the story of the trolley car, the drunk and the amateur night at the Bijou Theater, and she ended by saying, "Mama, I'll take Molly every week to another amateur theater, and she'll win the first prize, and we'll be able to move into our own flat." Grandma nodded her head and quietly said, "Clara, there are maybe five or six theaters in Philadelphia. Better you keep her on the trolley cars!"

And that's how my career began—from the all-American amateur nights in which sometimes my little sister, Helen, would also appear (and always insist on sharing the prize that I got) to the trolley cars to the Columbia Yiddish Theater.

Mama took on the job of wardrobe mistress, and since there were no baby-sitters in those days, she took Helen and me with her. We'd watch the show backstage or sometimes sleep on a rickety couch or in an old trunk, until Mike Thomashefsky put on *Uncle Tom's Cabin.* He engaged Helen to play Little Eva, since she was so beautiful. In one of her scenes she was supposed to be dead, lying in bed face up with the spotlight on her. She blinked at the light and simply turned over, and that was the end of her career as an actress.

I played Topsy, and I imagine it must have been quite an experience hearing all of us speaking Yiddish with a Southern accent. But I was a big hit with Topsy's song, "Shoo Fly, Don't Bother Me; I belong to the Company B."

Of course, I finished with a "Yeah, man!" And I did a little jig, my first time step, and a somersault, to a big round of applause which was music to my ears.

The only trouble I had was getting to school in the morning. Our shows had four and sometimes five acts and finished well after midnight. Then to have to get up at 7:00 A.M. to go to school was not easy. But we needed the fifty cents that I got for each performance, so, as Yonkel said many years later, "Leave it to Molly—she can do it." It had to be done, so I did it. I even did Topsy in German. Between the Columbia Theater and the *Turngemeinde* and Mama's dressmaking, we managed.

Other outlets for child actors in those days were the nickelodeons, where they showed you a two-reel silent film and an act. My act was very good for them, because the audiences were mostly children, and by now I was "Baby Margaret, the International Comedienne." The manager gave me the International Comedienne title because in my act I did an English song, a Dutch recitation and a Russian dance. The English song was "I'm Afraid to Go Home in the Dark"; and I've been asked by so many people to send them a copy of the Dutch recitation since I performed it on "The Mike Douglas Show" that here it is for free (if you buy my book, of course):

I am a puzzled Dutchman wot's filled mit grief und
    shame;
I'll tell you vot der trouble iss: I does not know mine
    name.
You tink dot's very funny, but ven you der shtorey
    hear,
You vill not vunder den so much it vas so strange und
    queer.

Mine mudder had two little twins; dey vas me und
    mine brudder;
We look so very much alike, no one knew one from der
    udder.
One of der boys was Yakob, und Hans der udder's
    name;
But den it made no diff'rence, we both got called der
    same.

Well, one of der boys got dead—Yah, mine herr, dot is
    so;
But whether Hans or Yakob, mine mudder she don't
    know.
So now I am in trouble, I can't get through mine head
Whether I am Hans wot's living or Yakob wot is dead!

By this time a new Yiddish theater opened, the Arch Street Theater. Most of the Columbia Theater actors went touring, for there were Yiddish theaters all over the country, from coast to coast. But we stayed in Philadelphia, where Mama got her job as wardrobe mistress.

I began watching the actors. We had visiting stars from New York: the famous Adlers (Jacob and Sarah), Boris and Bessie Thomashefsky, David Kessler and others. Whenever there was a part for a child, they called for the Picon's daughter—me. I watched and I learned and imitated the greats of our theater, and for the first time began to feel that I wanted to be an actress. Not so much for the fifty cents, but for the joy of making people laugh and cry. And for the applause!

And for the traveling. Philadelphia had blue laws then. We were not allowed to perform on Sundays. Everything was closed dead on Sundays. So we traveled to Baltimore, and sometimes to Washington. On one trip there was great excitement. We, of course, traveled by coach, but there was a special parlor car, and Sarah Bernhardt and her entire company were on it. I don't know whether her much publicized coffin was with her, too. Mike Thomashefsky, never inhibited by anyone, took me by the hand and said, "Come, Molly, I'll introduce you to the greatest actress in the world." And he took me right to the great Sarah. He introduced himself as the King of the Yiddish theater and then turned to introduce me. But I was way up front in the parlor car looking at the little girl who played with the French troupe. She had lovely long blond curls, her coat was trimmed with ermine and she wore patent-leather buttoned shoes.

Thomashefsky took me back to our coach car, explaining as he went along, "Some day you'll realize that you were once in the presence of royalty, and you stopped to play with a little nothing."

He must have been clairvoyant, for in 1946, right after the Holocaust, Yonkel and I went to Europe to entertain in the displaced persons camps. Our first stop was Paris, and since we were giving concerts free for anyone who had survived, a Jewish committee was formed, which prevailed upon the management of the Sarah Bernhardt Theater to give them the theater for one concert. And for the first time since her demise, they opened her dressing room for us. Thirty-six years before I had missed an opportunity to meet the Divine Sarah because I was too dazzled by a pair of shiny patent shoes. Now I had to settle for a snapshot taken standing under her picture.

Life was very exciting for us back in those days, with Papa in one day and out the next. Helen grew prettier every day, and Mama used to say, "Molly, if ever, please God, you have a beau calling to see you, we'll have to put Helen in the closet."

I didn't seem to grow. In gymnasium, when the teacher measured us, she'd call: "Mary Smith, five feet two inches; Amy Greer, five feet three inches; Molly Picon forty-five inches." I never made the five-foot line, and I'm still only four feet eleven if I stand on my toes.

But I kept working, and so did Mama. She bought me a piano, an old upright I thought was beautiful, to be paid for in installments. We found a teacher who charged fifty cents a lesson, and I started to learn to play.

By this time I was going to the William Penn High School. It was quite a distance from where we lived on Nevada Street in a little two-story house with four rooms. Two were upstairs, one with a tin bath (this was Helen's and mine); the other was Mama's—and Papa's, when he came home. On the ground floor were the two other rooms, a kitchen and a parlor, where we had a velvet-covered mahogany couch, two chairs and the piano. To which Mama added another goody for me: a bicycle, so I could ride to the William Penn High School on Broad Street and back to our mansion with a front stoop, which I had to scrub twice a week with sand soap. And when I wasn't traveling on Sundays, all the boys we knew would come visiting. We'd sit on the stoop and sing—"*Yip Ei Yadi Ei Aye*," a nonsense rhyme, along with "And a Little Child Shall Lead Them," "Pony Boy" and others, until Mama called us in for cookies and hot chocolate. Then she and I would sing our famous duet for the company.

Seems to me we sang more in those days than we do now —at home, that is. Just little parties, but they were real get-togethers, and there was the security of being with friends and neighbors. We were, in fact, very poor, but we never felt poor or underprivileged or poverty-stricken. There was a home, humble as it was, there were holidays with the family, and sometimes even a ride in the open trolleys to Strawberry Mansion for a picnic.

On my bike I often pedaled all alone to the park, where I picked violets and sat under a tree, trying to imagine myself as the little girl with the lovely curls in Sarah Bernhardt's company. But my hair was straight and I was just plain skinny. Still, something inside me shone bright and clear, and I *knew* I would stick to the theater all my life. Perhaps if I had been Louis Picon's son I would have had a classical education and been a scholar. Instead, as the wardrobe mistress' daughter, I got a love of the stage because there I could make believe I was all the things I could never be in real life.

CHAPTER 2

MY LOVE FOR PERFORMING was fated to clash with my love for learning, and after my second year in high school I had to leave in 1915. I wasn't making enough money to pay the installments on the piano, the bike and the rent for our four-room mansion. For the next few years, I played various local variety shows, but I still wasn't making ends meet. So I went to Ted Riley, who put on acts for vaudeville theaters, which had become very popular in 1917. Riley asked me what I could do, and I modestly answered, "Everything! I sing, dance, play the piano and ukulele, and I do somersaults." I sat down at the piano in his cheerless office and sang "There's a Long, Long Trail A-winding." He stopped me after the first line and said, "You're hired, kid. Come in to-morrow and I'll have an act lined up for you."

And he did. Three girls and me, to be called "The Four Seasons." I would be Winter, because I could do a *kezatzke*, a Russian dance. The soprano was Summer, even though her name was Alice Blizzard. I don't remember Spring's name, but Autumn was Margaret Newell. She came straight from Billy Watson's Beef Trust, a burlesque show with all the females two-hundred-pounders and over. There she had been the comic relief, weighing about one hundred pounds and standing five feet eight. In our act she was the eccentric comedienne, as well as the manager of our quartet. She was probably over fifty years old, and, because she was consumptive, always had a room to herself, while the three of us slept together in another room.

Marge, as we called her, carried a crocheted grouch bag pinned to her chemise (she didn't wear a bra, didn't need one), and in it were her jewels, which she had earned the hard way as she went through life clowning, crying over her wasted life, and coughing. For three hundred and sixty-five days (we toured that long), she ate roast beef, mashed potatoes and stewed tomatoes for dinner. She claimed that was the only kind of food you could trust in the beaneries we ate in. At night she had her Thermos bottle filled with coffee, ready to enjoy with doughnuts for breakfast.

Marge laid down the law for us about keeping the act up, our clothes clean, and our makeup sexy (Cupid-bow lips, plenty of rouge). She would sit for half an hour putting mascara on her eyelashes so heavily she could barely open her eyes. She was bittersweet and kind and very protective toward the three of us, who were just kids to her. Mama had no advice for her daughter's first road trip. She knew I was a good girl, a pure girl—and so I stayed till the day I wed.

On this tour (or "time" as it was called), we traveled for three months with the same acts—usually an acrobatic act, a male singer, a magician and The Four Seasons. By the time we'd finished the Gus Sun circuit, Riley had us booked for the Ackerman-Harris circuit, for which we opened in San Francisco. There was a trained-seal act on the show with us, and the seals were kept in a tank of water in the basement. They had already done their act when we opened ours, singing "There's a Long, Long Trail A-winding," after which I ripped off my long skirt, revealing a short, fancy-spangled costume, took a ukulele off the piano and sang and danced to "Yaka Hula, Hicky Dula" and made my exit to a nice round of applause. I looked down as I exited, and there in the wings was one of the seals, shaking himself dry and me wet, and blocking my way. So I went back on for a bow, danced off again, and there was the seal, still flapping his flippers. On I went for another bow—but the applause had already died down, so I danced off again, and when I saw I couldn't get past that shaking seal I went back on stage *again,* did a quick somersault and exited at the other side of the stage.

After that the rest of our act didn't do so well, and the manager came back to tell us we were canceled. When I told him about the seal, he said, "Go tell it to the big boss, Mr.

Ackerman." Of course Marge wanted to "tell him off" (as she put it), but I thought . . . Ackerman? Sounds like a Jewish name. Maybe he'll be more sympathetic to my story, which I decided right there and then wasn't going to be exactly honest. The other three girls were devout Catholics, I the only Jew. I put my coat on over my fancy pants (and fancier hula bra) and strode right into Mr. Ackerman's office. Before he could say a word I declaimed in my best Jacob Adler style, "Mr. Ackerman, you can't do this to four nice Jewish girls!" Then I told him the story of the seal, and by the time I was finished I had him laughing. He invited me to lunch, to which I went with Alice Blizzard, and we were back in show business again.

The same acts were on the bill with us for the whole tour. Billy Knight's rooster, the famous rooster of Pathé Films, was one of them. This rooster did a drunk act with a stovepipe hat on his head. He crowed and swayed and the audience ate it up. There was also an all-Arab acrobatic act. They rehearsed every morning in every town we played, and I often joined them to loosen up and practice my high kicks and Russian dance. One morning, while watching the Arabs warming up, I jokingly said to one of them, "I'd like to try that." "Okay," he said, and lying flat on his back he began to balance me while I stood straight up on his feet. Then suddenly he rolled over into another position with me still standing on his feet. The other Arabs all got a great kick out of this, and from then on, every morning, I worked out with them.

Their acceptance of me was more than professional, however, for then I got a big surprise: the star of their act asked me to marry him! My first proposal. And when I asked him why, he answered, "Because you have a *perfect* back— and," he added, "I like that." I've often thought, had I accepted his proposal, I might be in Iran or Syria now, with twelve children and a very strong back. Maybe even an oil well! Instead, fate and the weather intervened.

The Ackerman circuit took us all the way to Boston, only to find when we arrived there that everything was closed down. It was the winter of 1918 and the first big epidemic of influenza had broken out. People were dying all over the

city. The schools and stores—and all the theaters—were shut
tight. Except one. The old Grand Opera House on Washington and Dover Streets, under the El, had somehow escaped
the ban.

Although now a parking lot, in its day it really had been
a grand opera house. All the famous American stage stars had
played there: the Barrymores, the Drews. They said that
even Caruso had sung there.

But in 1918 it found itself in the wrong part of town.
Saloons and brothels had sprung up around it, and the entire
neighborhood was in disrepute. The once great house now
had wrestling matches on Tuesdays, second-rate fights on
Thursdays and Fridays, and Jewish theater on Saturdays.

When I heard there were Yiddish actors there, I felt sure
I would know someone in the company who had played with
me in Philadelphia and might lend me money to get back
home. I had been earning thirty dollars a week with The
Four Seasons, but half of that went home to Mama every
week and the other half paid my bills. Unlike Marge, I had
no grouch bag to fall back on. In fact, I was flat broke.

And that was how and where I met my Yonkel. Although
barely in his twenties, he had finagled himself into the thank-
less position of manager, director, producer, prompter and
general referee to a company of has-beens and third-rate actors. When I asked him why the city hadn't shut him down
when all the other theaters were closed, he answered, "Because nobody knew we were open." That was my first laugh
with Yonkel, the beginning of our fifty-eight years together.

I always said influenza was our matchmaker. But, despite
its having been overlooked by the Board of Health, Yonkel's
company wasn't so bad. Paul Muni (then Muni Weisen-
freund) was in it, and Menashe Skulnick, who later did very
well on Broadway in Sylvia Regan's play, *The Fifth Season*.
Herschel Bernardi's parents, two very capable character actors, were also in the company along with Dinah Feinman,
one of the famous Jacob Adler's several wives. But they
needed a *flaam*, a *feierdig soubrettin*, a flaming, fiery soubrette who could sing, dance, look young, and who was Jewish, too. Needless to say, there weren't many applicants.

Yonkel felt I fit the bill. He had seen me perform at a benefit in Philadelphia and remembered me as a talented little girl. I surely wasn't very pretty then, had no single, special talent. I didn't even sing well. But I was versatile. I did funny little songs, funny little acts, and poignant recitations. Yonkel had come backstage and complimented me after the benefit. Now he was offering me a contract for thirty-five dollars a week, more than I got in the *goyish* (non-Jewish) circuit. He was also very good-looking: perhaps a mite skinny (one hundred and eighteen pounds), but fair-haired and fair-skinned and with big brown eyes. In addition, he was kind and very polite, and didn't, as we used to say then, try to get fresh. I thought it over on the spot and grabbed his offer. He advanced me fifteen dollars in cash and told me where I could find a boardinghouse where actors lived. I rushed back to the other three Seasons, and told them of my good fortune. We said good-bye, cried a little and promised to keep in touch. My commitment to both Yonkel and the Yiddish theater had begun.

Yonkel, otherwise known as Jacob Kalich, had been born in Galicia, Poland, in 1891. An only child, and the last in a long line of rabbis, he was quickly enrolled in a series of rabbinical schools in Romania, Poland, Austria and Hungary. It was his rabbinical attire, in fact, which was responsible for his theatrical career.

When Yonkel was fifteen and studying for the rabbinate in his hometown of Rymanow, he became friendly with a traveling acting troupe. They, in turn, were equally admiring of his *kapote*, a long caftan worn by orthodox Jewry. They desperately needed his fine wardrobe for costumes and Yonkel willingly obliged. When the costumes moved on to Bucharest, Yonkel went with them, leaving the rabbinate far behind. In Bucharest he joined the famed Zshignitza Theater, the birthplace of the Yiddish stage. He eventually toured London and Paris before slipping into America (unauthorized) in 1914. He had no money, no passport and no English but he somehow made it to manager of Boston's Grand Opera House.

When we met in Boston, I was the All-American Girl full

of hurdy-gurdys and absolutely illiterate about Jewish culture. Yonkel, on the other hand, was the complete intellectual who knew not only classic Yiddish but its plays, theaters
and writers. He was my mentor who spoke to me in Polish,
Russian, German, Yiddish and fractured English. I would
chuckle when he talked to me about "always *klibing* mountains" instead of climbing them.

In truth, despite my awe of his knowledge and grace,
there was also a great deal about him that smacked of the
greenhorn. Especially to Miss Winter, late of *vodvil,* who saw
herself as pretty hotsy-totsy. When I first set eyes on Yonkel
in Boston, I didn't stop to notice he was charming, intelligent, and industrious. I first noticed that heavy accent and
the fact that his clothes looked like the ones he had worn
over on the boat. Indeed, they were. He hadn't bought a
thing since Poland, and he looked it. As we began courting,
he spruced up my performing and I worked on his wardrobe.

But first, I had to get through my first show, in which
Yonkel wanted me to sing, dance and do all the *shtik* (tricks)
I did with The Four Seasons. He called rehearsal after the
show, where I met all the actors, most of whom I knew from
the Arch Street Theater. We rehearsed until two in the morning, then went to a really shabby café for a late snack. Madame Feinman, who was the star of the company and also
partner in the business, took me under her wing, saw to it
that I got to my room and advised me to go to sleep right
away because she and Yonkel had decided I would open the
very next day. If I forgot a line, Yonkel would be in the
prompter's box in front of the stage to help me.

I was a quick study in those days. (Many years later,
when Jack Benny was asked how long it took him to memorize a script, he replied, "When I was young, I took minutes
to make up and hours to memorize my script; but now I take
minutes to memorize my script and hours to make up.") Instead of going to sleep, I stayed up all night and memorized
my part. We rehearsed before the matinee and I didn't miss
a line. The actors all applauded me and gave me my own spot
in the dressing room. I unloaded my makeup and clothes (we
supplied our own things then), and instead of going out to

lunch, had a sandwich and tea, which Yonkel brought me. I relaxed, ran through my part (half in English, half in Yiddish), and in my heart I prayed I would make good.

Actually I prayed to make good not so much with the audience as with Yonkel. I sensed he believed in my ability, and I didn't want to let him down. I think now, all through our wonderful years together, I always wanted to make good with Yonkel. His faith in me kept me going when I was high, and even more so when I was low.

So . . . I went on—and was a big hit. The Bernardis bought a bottle of *schnapps* (slivovitz) and some cake, and we celebrated after the show. It was one of the most exciting opening-night parties I have ever had.

From then on Yonkel started to groom me for stardom. He wrote one of my most famous parts for me—"Yonkele," which is the diminutive for Yonkel. Actually, Yonkele was a kind of Peter Pan role, with a slight difference: whereas Peter Pan doesn't want to grow up, Yonkele wants desperately to grow up and make a better world for our people and all people.

I was twenty years old then and weighed ninety-five pounds. The actors scoffed at the idea of a ninety-five-pound star when the stars then were big, buxom, luscious ladies like Lillian Russell and Trixie Friganza. But Yonkel argued that a ninety-five-pound star would be a novelty, something different. He also wrote a part in the play for Paul Muni. Muni was twenty or twenty-one when I first met him at Grand Opera House; he was already doing character parts. He played my father in the first version of *Yonkele,* a cross, crotchety old man who went around and *burtchet* (a sort of grumbling and growling—it sounds funnier in Yiddish). Muni never enjoyed his success. He was never good enough for himself, and was always digging into himself for more and more. I don't know why he couldn't get more joy out of acting but I suspect he was physically impotent. I know he had problems in that area, and I feel it made him strive all the more to be an absolutely perfect performer on the stage or screen. He was such a perfectionist that the first time he saw himself on film, he vomited. He had overacted in his close-ups and the results literally sickened him. He was to be just as overcritical of himself the rest of his life. When I look back to our performances together and in my mind hear the laughter and applause, I realize how brilliant Yonkel was to start me off in the kind of a role no one had ever played in the Yiddish theater. Later, when Mama joined us in Boston, she gave the right evaluation: "It's different!" and that was enough.

We remained in Boston for two years, and Yonkel and I began to fall in love in our fashion. He began to write more starring roles for me and I began hinting to him he wasn't stylish enough for the manager of the Grand Opera House, even though he did have a cutaway coat and striped pants with a fancy vest which he wore at every performance. He always went on between acts to speak to the audience and explain the play to them. (I often thought those talks were much better than our plays!) Yonkel took my hints, and three days in a row he appeared onstage in a different brand-new suit. He walked to my boardinghouse under the elevated train with me, and as the cars roared by he proposed to me, each time in a different language. By the end of the week I accepted his proposal, and we advertised our engagement party onstage at the Grand Opera House. (Business was slow and we were desperate for publicity.) Over fifteen hundred guests came (and, of course, paid for their tickets) and shouted "Mazel tov" (good luck) after the show. Even now, in 1979, I meet people who tell me they were at our engagement party onstage at the Grand Opera House.

By this time Mama had come to Boston to see what was going on. I had written her about Yonkel, and she came to make sure he had honorable intentions. She moved into my room with me, and from then on we all ate together. Mama found a big old trunk, put an oilcloth cover on it, went to the five-and-tenny (as we called it then), bought dishes, cutlery and a Sterno stove, and made a home for us.

The flu had died out, and many hundreds of people along with it. Then there was a police strike, which Governor Coolidge managed, after much bloodshed and damage, to end. He later became President of the United States.

The Yiddish theater was thriving all over America. Yonkel often went to New York to find new plays and music and to try to convince the Second Avenue managers (our Broadway) that he had a find, a new star. But they all laughed at him—the Picon's daughter a star? Who ever heard of her? And how could such a skinny little nothing compete with Sarah Adler, Bessie Thomashefsky, Madame Kenni Liptzin and Bertha Kalish?

So we stayed in Boston until the summer of 1919. Yonkel and I were married in Philadelphia on June 29th. My whole family still lived in Philly and Yonkel had bought Mama a little grocery store there so she could make a living (and maybe Papa would come back and help out). Besides, as Grandma used to say, "Who gets married in Boston?"

The day before the wedding, we had to get a marriage license at City Hall. Yonkel paid two dollars for it. (Many, many years later, we drove into Philadelphia in our new Chrysler convertible to do "The Mike Douglas Show" and drove through the same City Hall area. Lo and behold, we didn't recognize a stick. When we got our license, there had been no skyscrapers, no giant office complexes or luxury hotels. Yonkel looked up at all the new buildings and said, "My God, Molly—look what they did with my two dollars!")

Our little religious ceremony took place in the room behind Mama's new store. I wore a wedding dress Mama had made from a curtain she "acquired" from the Arch Street Theater. There were also musicians and a cantor (courtesy of Grandpa), and we all sang and danced and ate.

The only hitch was when the ceremony began and the bride had to walk around the groom under the canopy. The bride was not in the room. Panic set in, but Yonkel calmly walked outside into the backyard and found me playing hopscotch with my little cousins. He took my hand and said gently, "Miss Picon, you're on! Don't ever keep an audience waiting."

We made our entrance with my veil off (when it should have been hiding my face from the groom's sight) and my dress rolled up to my knees (so it shouldn't get dirty). Grandpa was momentarily stunned, but Grandma quickly pulled my veil over my face as Mama struggled to get my wedding gown down over my knees. Then, majestically, we were on. The benedictions, the ceremony, the sermon and glass-breaking, all went smoothly. I was Mrs. Jacob Kalich, with a thin golden wedding ring and a love-full heart and, as I write this, nothing has surpassed that shabby little wedding in the back room of Mama's store.

We honeymooned in Niagara Falls (naturally), and for the first time in his life, Yonkel played baseball with me. He was brought up in the strict Orthodox Jewish tradition and had never, as a child, had a toy of any kind. But on our honeymoon, we frolicked. I taught him how to throw and catch a ball and even got him to walk under the falls, a very scary thing. Once you're in line, there's no turning back as that tremendous downpour thunders over you. It's a wonder he didn't divorce me then and there.

It was all such a funny situation. I was trying to make him a real American guy, and he was trying to make me a little *Yiddishe* Mama. But it was fun. After a week we took a boat trip home. Yonkel left his trousers on the stateroom door knob and in the morning all his money was gone. But he wasn't dismayed, just angry that he'd been so careless. "Well, live and learn," he said, "sometimes what to do, sometimes what not to."

When we got back to Mama's store, Yonkel had to borrow two dollars from her to pay the taxi fare. He included a fifty-cent tip, which was quite a lot in 1919. "You see, Malkale," he said to me, "Rockefeller only tips a dime, but with a future star I have to put on a show, yes?"

Our second season at the Grand Opera House in Boston was even more successful than our first. Yonkel began giving me my first dramatic roles, expanding my range, pushing me farther than I thought I could go. And always, he tried to sell me to Second Avenue, but they still weren't buying. So we rented a little house on Florence Street in Boston and furnished it with theatrical odds and ends including an upright piano and a majestic red velvet throne—I don't know what for. Mama was back with us, her store bankrupt. My sister Helen went to live with a girlfriend and Papa, again, was we didn't know where.

It was the three of us once more. Mama even got into the

act briefly. Yonkel had tied up all of New England with our Hebrew Actors Union to avoid competition. However, he had only ten actors, and one holiday we had performances due in three theaters. Yonkel cut characters out left and right until he was minus only one actress. The part required two or three lines—Mama could fill in. She agreed, they rehearsed the part and Yonkel himself sat in the prompter's box just in case Mama got stage fright.

The show started with Mama rarin' to go. When she made her entrance and saw Yonkel in the prompter's box, she promptly recited her lines from all four acts to show him she still knew her part. That was her debut and farewell performance.

We were so busy studying new parts, making new costumes, learning new songs and dances that I hardly noticed my menstrual periods had stopped. It eventually dawned on me that I was pregnant, and wow! I ran to tell Yonkel. He was thrilled and immediately began making me sit still and not overdo it, etcetera, etcetera. But when I got on stage, all the king's horses and all the king's men couldn't keep me from doing my best, giving 100 percent. Because I was in love, not only with Yonkel, but with the theater and especially our audiences. It's a love that's true for many performers. I have seen them bent over in physical pain or thoroughly distracted by emotional pain, yet when they hear their cues, they straighten up, go on and do their show, bow to the applause, exit and collapse.

Since I had no pain and my condition didn't show, I went on performing and even doing somersaults until the seventh month of my pregnancy. By that time it began to be quite evident, so Yonkel rented a bigger house in Sharon, a resort near Boston. We all moved in to await the baby's arrival.

At that time, we had a few bids from actors who wanted to take over the lease on the Grand Opera House. Yonkel still had no offers from Second Avenue for his ninety-five-pound star and he had begun to think I might have to achieve official stardom somewhere else. We began to talk about going to Europe, making my name abroad and then coming back truly internationally known. But now, with a child on the way?

Well, there was never a question but that I would go back to my career; Mama was there to baby-sit, but maybe for now we would stay in Boston. After all, wasn't childbirth just a normal part of things, to be gotten over and done with? I felt neither great expectancy nor trauma about having the baby. Oh, we delighted in buying baby things and preparing the nursery, but we were in fact planning beyond it, thinking up new skits and routines. Our only problem was whether to postpone Europe or not.

The problem was solved in a tragic way. I had never gone to a baby doctor, and we were strangers in Sharon, so when I went prematurely into labor, Yonkel called the only doctor in town, a lung specialist. He had delivered several babies, nonetheless, and he told us to call when the spasms began to come more frequently. At one o'clock in the morning I was really in pain. Since I was born in a room on the fourth floor in the back, and Helen was also born at home, it never dawned on us to go to a hospital. The doctor didn't suggest it either; and when he got the call at one o'clock, he took his time before finally arriving to begin preparations. He worked and sweated, I screamed, and finally he gave me an anesthetic. He called a specialist in from Boston, who came at 4:00 A.M., took one look and realized the baby was dead. He delivered the child, a little girl, and told Mama to keep me in bed for a week, no sitting up or getting up, just rest and quiet.

I can only imagine those hours from one to five, with Yonkel walking up and down outside my room and the doctors noncommittal until it was all over and Mama told him what had happened. I was still under ether and didn't know until I awoke in the morning and saw that the crib and all the things we had prepared for our baby were gone, that the baby was gone, too. When Yonkel finally pulled himself together and came in to console me, all he could say was, "Don't worry, Malkale, we'll have other children some day. Now all I want is for you to get well again. I'm turning the theater over to a new management, and I'm taking my little star to Europe, where she will become a big star."

I was numb to Yonkel's flattery, however. He always had

had me believing I could do anything. "Leave it to Molly—
she can do it!" Yet I had failed him so dismally in what all
women do so naturally. In addition to my sadness at the loss
of the baby, there was the severe blow to my vanity. When
my doctor told me months later that I had an infantile pelvis
and could never bear another child, the blow was severer
still. Never again would I be so sure of myself when Yonkel
said, "You can do it, Molly."

I tried to cover my gloom by throwing myself into preparations for our trip to Europe. Yonkel and I never brooded
about the past, and I am not one to cry. I'm sure, to everyone
else, I appeared to recover quickly. However, in going
through my many yearly diaries while writing this book, I
realized just how long the pain remained.

On Friday, August 13, 1920, I wrote: *My baby came into
the world dead. Peculiar that a perfect love should bear dead
fruit—a girl it was—and one must believe it's for the best.*

They were the only words I could write for the rest of
that year.

CHAPTER 3

YONKEL'S DECISION to take me to Europe was the incentive
I needed to get well quickly. I had never been abroad, and I
attacked the venture by rapidly filling seven old-fashioned
iron steamer trunks full of plays, music, orchestrations, costumes and wigs. I even bought a few evening dresses in a
thrift shop. These I carried aboard ship in a bag, along with a
home-baked *challa* (a braided loaf we eat on the Sabbath)
from Grandma and a bottle of Manischewitz wine from
Grandpa.

I had always thrown myself into new things head first
without ever worrying about the outcome. I had no sense of
fear—a characteristic I inherited from Mama. Yonkel immediately began writing new plays and I worked equally fu-
riously on new songs. And off we went to conquer Europe!

I can't remember the liner we sailed on (second class),
but Yonkel immediately made a sailor of me. No matter how
bad the weather was or how much the ship tipped up and
down and from side to side, he walked me on deck around
and around—before meals, after meals and between meals.
That was the beginning of a walk that took us around the
world, to South America, Africa, Egypt, Israel, all of Europe,
Japan, Korea, the Arctic Circle and most of the U.S.A. (In fact,
when we were doing Sylvia Regan's *Morning Star* at the
Longacre Theater in 1940, the shopkeepers would tell us
they knew exactly what time we would be walking past their
stores—and they set their watches accordingly.)

We arrived in Le Havre, took the boat train to Paris, left
the trunks to be delivered when we knew where we would
be working, and went immediately to the Yiddish theater in

Paris, which was located on rue Lancry in the Jewish section. The theater itself, also called the Lancry, was a dinner theater with the audience up close to the stage. Once, when a comedian pulled off his wig, it slipped out of his hand and landed in someone's soup.

In Paris, the *Vilna Trope* were the classical Yiddish dramatists who did Shaw and Shakespeare while our music-and-comedy group was referred to as the *shund* branch, the "shameful" one. But then, the origins of the Yiddish theater itself grew out of the very desire to condemn it.

The beginning of the Yiddish theater movement dates back to the Jewish Enlightenment, a movement beginning in the 1700s led by Moses Mendelssohn, which disparaged Yiddish as a jargon of the streets, unworthy to be a literary language like Hebrew.

At first, Mendelssohn's group did have a crushing effect on the Yiddish tongue; but eventually his movement unified the lovers of Yiddish who were determined to make it the true Jewish folk language. They began by creating scenes from home and religious life and acting them out in Yiddish (the Purim Festival story was a favorite). Then Mendel Levin, Yisrael Aksenfeld, Solomon Ettinger and others began writing other, original stories and plays in Yiddish. By the late 1800s, this expressive language had been welded into a distinctive literary form full of satire, humor and unique idiomatic expressions. The largest Yiddish-theater center, in Jassy, Romania, was the training ground that eventually led to the Adlers, the Thomashefskys and the Kesslers bringing Yiddish theater to the *goldeneh medine* itself, America. Yonkel had been fortunate to work on both continents. I, however, was a Yiddish illiterate. The Yiddish I spoke was completely bastardized, and part of our plan was for me to learn correct Yiddish with its soft, guttural European accent. Here in Paris, I would start my education.

We took a taxi, and Yonkel, in his Romanian version of the French language, made it perfectly clear where we wanted to go. Suddenly we were backstage greeting old friends, to whom Yonkel introduced me. He immediately began negotiating for me to appear in *Yonkele*. The impresario objected. "What kind of a name for a play is *Yonkele?* A one-name play?" To which Yonkel countered, "How about Shakespeare's *Hamlet?*" The impresario fired back, "*Mais oui,* but he protected himself with a subtitle: *Hamlet, or the Prince of Denmark.*"

So we humored the impresario and opened at the Lancry in 1921 in *Yonkele Geht in Shul Arein* (*Yonkele Goes to the Synagogue*). However, the ticket buyers demanded *Yonkele,* and no one seemed to care whether Yonkele went to the synagogue or not. So *Yonkele* it has remained, and as *Yonkele* I have played it all over the world—more than three thousand times.

The trunks arrived, we settled in a little hotel on rue Rivoli and went to work. Paris in 1921 was still suffering the ravages of World War One. There were no white bread, milk, sugar or soap to be had, but plenty of champagne. For the first time in my life, I saw dinner guests taking home the leftovers of their meals—even in exclusive restaurants. There was no destruction of the city, however, so Paris looked elegant, at least on the surface, and I began to study French. I read Colette and loved her description of Parisian women: "They carry their behinds on their ankles."

Although Yonkel took me to every theater in the city so I could see and hear French plays, we never mingled with people outside the Yiddish theater. Yiddish was our center, our link, and I never felt like a complete stranger in Europe because I was always in the midst of a familiar language and heritage—the Yiddish world. We made a big hit and a little money, and Yonkel decided we owed ourselves a vacation. So we went to Monte Carlo and watched tall, complacent Englishmen lose thousands of pounds in the gambling casinos. Yonkel told me to watch the lady gamblers, since I might someday have to play such a character.

We went to the Opera and afterward walked so much that we crossed the border from Monte Carlo into France again. Trying to get back into Monte Carlo, we were accosted by a sleepy French guide, who winked at me and said, "*Quel homme avez vous?*" (What kind of a man have you got?)— and by implication, To walk you on high heels from one country to another? He gave me one of those looks only a Frenchman can give and let us pass. Yonkel turned me around and around and shook his head solemnly as he said, "Molly, you are growing into a very attractive woman." A hug, a kiss, a laugh and we were back in Monte Carlo.

We stayed until our money ran out, during which time Yonkel had written a Mr. Zelmeister, who was running a Yiddish theater in Lodz, Poland. We received an offer from him, and we were off.

How we managed to drag all those trunks and my thrift shop evening gowns I'll never know. But on this trip, at least, we didn't have to carry Grandma's *challa* or Grandpa's Manischewitz wine—they were long gone.

On the train to Poland, however, we did have a very sumptuous meal in the dining car, with five different types of French wine and a long loaf of that wonderful French bread. We went to town, starting with one of the wines, just a little glassful, then another glass with the bread and butter, and so on, and when our main course came we were pretty full. And then the shock: we had to pay for the five nearly full bottles of wine besides the meal. So we took the wine with us to Poland, where the customs officer told us we had to pay duty on them. Luckily, Zelmeister was waiting for us. He took over, gave the customs officer a few zlotys and carted us, our bags, my evening gowns and five bottles of French wine to the hotel in Lodz. He had arranged for us to have a room and a bathtub, which was quite a luxury in Poland. The only drawback was that the bathtub had water only on Fridays. So we took a droshky to the public bathhouse. And another shock! We paid five zlotys for one bath for the two of us with our own soap. And after we finished and came out, there was a woman waiting with a little boy. They both used our tub and our water and paid only three zlotys. Yonkel gave the woman our soap.

The company in Lodz was not bad. Zelmeister, our impresario, did everything in a flamboyant way. He had us driven to the theater in a horse and carriage with banners flying. He was a bombastic press agent, but he always worked in legitimate theater. (Years later, when the Nazis came, we

tried to get him to come to America but he refused. He felt
he still had a good thing going, which he had, before Hitler.
He eventually was shipped to Russia, run over by a horse
and killed.)

Again, we did *Yonkele* first, and we were very successful.
Every evening there was a very distinguished man in the
audience. On my twenty-third birthday I received a bouquet
of twenty-three long-stemmed American Beauty roses from
the Belgian consul, the man who had been coming every
night. He came backstage to meet me, and in perfect English
he said our theater was his only diversion in Lodz. He was
very complimentary to both of us and said he especially enjoyed the audience singing along with me when I sang the
Hebrew national anthem. Actually, we were not singing "Hatikvah," the national anthem, but a song, "Meshiach Is Gekumen"—"The Messiah Has Come." We didn't disillusion
him, and for the rest of our stay in Lodz, whenever we played
Yonkele, the Belgian consul joined the audience in singing
"Meshiach Is Gekumen."

After Lodz, Yonkel took me to Chaboufka, a little village
in the mountains where his mother lived with her fourth or
fifth husband—we weren't quite sure. In Orthodox tradition,
a widow must marry again when her husband dies. So she
did—we used to call her "the Peggy Joyce of Poland." She
was a tiny, bright-eyed little lady with a *sheitel* (the traditional wig) and a wonderful approach to life, which certainly
wasn't easy in Chaboufka. Yonkel sent her money every
month, and she had a little grocery store which she managed
mostly herself, because her latest husband, *Foigel Gonif*
(freely translated as Conniving Thief), was busy praying in
the synagogue, where he and his cronies studied the Torah
and took a little nip of *schnapps* now and then. He only
turned up at the store in time for meals. Yonkel was her only
son, and it had been a great sacrifice for her to send him away
to study with the famous rabbis. She hadn't seen much of him
as a child—and their meeting now was the first one in nearly
twenty years. Her life had been hard, but she had a great
sense of humor and could even laugh about her life. She
called her husband Foigel Gonif (we never knew his real

name) because he wouldn't do an honest day's work. When
we asked her why she married him, she'd say, "He had a nice
beard, so I married him." Soon his children from other mar-
riages began moving in with them, and their poor household
grew poorer.

Yonkel tried to persuade his mother to move to Lodz, but
she said she couldn't leave the store because the *goyim* owed
her money. And she brought out her account book to prove
it. In the book she had noted, "Anna, the cross-eyed saloon
keeper with the *brodifka* (wart) on her nose, took three sacks
of grain. Maybe she paid and maybe she didn't. . . ." All the
other accounts were the same.

In her little room behind the store (somewhat like
Mama's store in Philadelphia) she had twin beds, a stove, a
table, a few chairs and a big cupboard. When Yonkel ex-
plored the cupboard he saw it was empty, so he scolded,
"Don't I send you enough money?" And she answered,
"More than enough. But I'm an old woman. How much
longer do I have to live? So I'm saving the money you send
me to leave you an inheritance."

Then she asked what kind of a profession we were in.
Orthodox Jews are not allowed to go to shows, and she had
never been in a theater. Yonkel's father had been a rabbi, and
his grandfather and great-grandfather were rabbis. Yonkel explained to his mother that we were in the theater and that a
theater is just like a synagogue—only instead of preaching to
the people, we sing for them.

Then she asked what kind of songs we sing. I dug down
into our old Yiddish theater repertoire and sang "God in His
Judgment Is Always Right," "Never Be Proud if You Have
Money," "Write a Letter to Your Mother" and more of the
same virtuous songs. She laughed and cried, clapped her
hands and stamped her feet in time with the music, and after
about an hour's concert, she turned to Yonkel and said, "It's
wonderful—but tell me, my son, the Jews in America are
such idiots that they pay money for that?"

Of course she wouldn't hear of our going to a hotel to
sleep. She gave me her bed, and in the middle of the night it
began to pour. Without any fuss she got up (she'd been sleep-

ing on a makeshift cot), took out a big tin pan, put it on the
perrina (quilt) between my legs, and all night long the rain
kept drip, drip, dripping into the pan, and, as you can imagine, there was no sleep for me.

Eventually we did prevail upon her to move to Lodz,
which she did, with Foigel Gonif and, by then, four of his
children who'd moved in with them. Our impresario, Zelmeister, found a little flat for them, for which Yonkel paid.
We were happy that she was in a big city with a synagogue
close by and a large Jewish population. We sent her posters
with our pictures on them, which she hung on the walls to
show off to her neighbors what a famous daughter-in-law she
had.

From Poland, we played Vienna for three months before
going on a concert tour of Czechoslovakia. While we were in
Vienna, in 1921, there was a terrible devaluation of the
money, the krone. To give you some idea of its worthless-
ness, when we first arrived in Vienna, kronen were valued at
seven for a dollar. The next day, they were seventy for a
dollar, then seven hundred for a dollar, and before we left,
seven million for a dollar. We had a valise stuffed full of
kronen, and it wasn't enough to pay our taxi fare. The money
was printed on shoddy paper only good for wallpaper. People
were wiped out, and there was chaos at the banks.

We had given a concert in the Grossen Concert Zaal for
which we had been paid the equivalent of one hundred and
fifty dollars, but after the devaluation it wasn't enough even
to tip a waiter.

We saved some of those kronen for souvenirs, and in
1969, at our golden wedding party in New York, we had occasion to make use of a ten-million-kronen note. Among the
guests at our party was Robert Merrill, whom we both loved
dearly. When we did our radio shows, around 1938, we used
to present a "find of the week"—a singer, a comedian, whatever—and Merrill had been one of them, for which we paid
him a snappy ten bucks. Now, in 1969, Merrill was one of the
leading baritones of the Metropolitan Opera, and we were
thrilled when he accepted our invitation and insisted on singing, "Oh, Promise Me." I still can feel the shivers going up
and down my spine. And the applause was thunderous.

When we came home, as a joke, we decided to dig up the ten-million-kronen note and send it to him, wishing only that we could have sent its former value.

In 1922 we seemed to be in and out of Austria, Czecho-slovakia, Poland and Romania. It was in Bahoosh, Romania, that I met my first wonder rabbi.

The *Bahoosher*, as he was known to his followers all over the world, was related to Yonkel, and when Yonkel took me to meet him, he welcomed me without looking directly at me, extending his hand to me, but first placing the bottom of his *kaftan* (long black coat) on top of it, so that he wouldn't be touching a woman's hand. The women sat in one room, the men in another. When the rabbi's daughter asked me to sing, and I did, I noticed that the door to the men's quarters opened ever so quietly. Yonkel told me later that the rabbi's little grandson had opened it so he could hear me sing, and that the rabbi didn't object to hearing a woman's voice (sur-reptitiously) either.

Nineteen twenty-three was an eventful year for us, most of it spent in Bucharest, Romania. We brought Mama and Helen over, rented a general's villa to live in, and dug in for a long season at the Eforie Theater (also called Teater Carl al Marre).

Yonkel had written another play for me inspired by *Kiki*, which Lenore Ulric had done with David Belasco. We weren't averse to borrowing or copying (or would you call it simply plagiarizing?) *goyish* plays, especially if there was a part in them that suited me. This one was called *Tzipke*, and Yonkel did a magnificent job of adapting the part of a poor, illiterate ragamuffin for me. In the second act, one of his lines that always got a big laugh was, "My father is a *shikker*" (drunk). And when the haughty lady repeated, "A *shikker*?" I answered, "A *groiser shikker*" (big drunk).

Many non-Jews came to see the show, among them army men, who invited us to cafés after the show. When we walked in with them, the orchestra would strike up the Romanian national anthem, "God Bless Our King." "Our King" was a famous imbiber. All the lieutenants would turn to me and in chorus say, "A *groiser shikker!*"

We were really flying high, in and out of the theater,

when out of nowhere, three hundred university students bought tickets in the gallery for a performance, and when I came on stage they started shouting, "Down with the Jews! Tzipke, go to Palestine!" They threw cabbages and eggs at me, and I kept right on singing my first song and dancing around to avoid being hit by a cabbage. Zelmeister, our Polish impresario, came running onstage and yelling, "Jews, save yourselves—they're out to kill us all!"

The conductor grabbed the music, the prompter grabbed the script, and they ran, while the stage manager brought the curtain down. I was still out there, mad as a hornet, singing and dancing, when the stage manager grabbed me and literally carried me up the stairs into the flies. He pushed me against a door, thinking he had me safely away from the rioters, not realizing we were on the gallery level and that door was the only thing between me and the crazy students.

The whole episode started because Zelmeister didn't allow the local impresario, Brownstein, to participate in our appearances. To get even with him, Brownstein informed the authorities that there were irregularities with what we took in at the box office.

The police were called in and somehow managed to clear the theater of the students. Yonkel went out in front of the asbestos curtain to see if anyone was left in the theater. Quite a few people had fled, but there were still a few hundred left, and when Yonkel asked, "Shall we go on with the play?" they all shouted, "Yes!" And we went on, without music, without some of the actors, and without Zelmeister, who had bolted with the cash. But, albeit nervously, we managed to finish the show.

The next morning a committee came to the theater and demanded we continue playing and not give in to the hooligans. So we continued. The audiences filled the theater, all the men (and some of the women) armed with clubs and umbrellas. Other ladies brought hatpins.

There were riots and bloodshed in the streets. We went to our American consul to ask for help, and he replied, in all sincerity, "Molly, dear, we can't start a war with Romania because of your playing here. I've been working all day and night to get hold of the instigators. But, my dear, you are putting the Romanian National Theater out of business."

We went home, talked to some prominent Jews, did two more shows to subdued, though angry audiences, and the consul called every day to say he was tired and wasn't I just a little tired, too? He even hinted we wouldn't be searched at the border for taking out of Romania anything we wanted, as well as being exempted from taxes—just so long as we left.

By this time, Yonkel, Mama and Helen and I were all worn out. We had toured Europe for two years from Paris to Latvia, so we rented a house in Bologne sur Mer, rested up, and started back home again.

We sailed on the *Ryndham,* bag and baggage, all four of us with little money among us. We arrived in New York to be greeted by Edwin A. Kelkin, a promoter, with an offer to appear in Baltimore, to which Yonkel replied, "I didn't *shlep* Molly all over Europe for two years to come back to America to play in Baltimore."

We took a look at all the shows on Second Avenue and saw the current performance (which wasn't doing too well) at the Second Avenue Theater, where Yonkel dreamed and hoped that I would make my debut in New York. Yonkel persuaded Joseph Rumshinsky, who was the top Yiddish theater composer, to talk old man Edelstein, the manager, into putting me on for a weekend. After a little bargaining we signed to appear for one weekend, in *Yonkele,* starting December 24th, 1923.

Rumshinsky immediately began rewriting the music, I worked on the lyrics and Yonkel started changing some of the characters in the play to suit the actors in the company. Many of them had refused to play with "the Picon's daughter," so we finished up with an inferior cast. But Yonkel did such a good job on the rewrite that every single bad actor became perfect for his or her part.

Curiously enough, when the first ads appeared in the Jewish press, lines started forming at the box office. Edelstein couldn't understand why, so he asked some of the people, "Do you know her? Why are you buying tickets?" And they answered, "My uncle from Warsaw wrote me when

Molly Picon appeared in *Yonkele* to go and see her." Another customer added, "My cousin from Bucharest wrote me not to miss Molly's *Yonkele*." It seems we had a subscription audience before I even started.

And this is the best heritage my Yonkel has given me: an adoring audience that dates back over half a century to Vienna, Kishinev, Lemberg, Jassy, Bucharest, London and Paris.

I often ask myself, Why this warm affection for me? And I think back to a story I read by Verlaine (I think), whose mistress had died. Naturally he found another, who was jealous of his first mistress. She asked, "Why did you love your first mistress more than you love me? Am I not as beautiful?" And he answered, "You are more beautiful." "Was she more intelligent?" And his answer: "You are more intelligent." "Then what did she have that I haven't got?" And he answered, "She had my youth."

I think that's what I have in my audiences—their youth, when they were healthy, had small children whom they *shlepped* to see me, and when, even in what we would consider now as poverty, they were rich in love and laughter and just the joy of being young. I think whenever they come to see me, even now, they see themselves as they were in 1923, and all their ailments and afflictions of old age leave them as they laugh and cry with me in 1979. No one could have asked for a greater gift, and Yonkel certainly created it for me.

From Christmas 1923 to 1925 we were working for Edelstein in a number of plays—*Yonkele, Tzipke, Shmendrick, Gypsy Girl, Molly Dolly* and *The Little Devil.* Then, in 1926, we took over the theater from Edelstein and went on to do our own plays to very good business—*Mamale, Raizele, Oy Is Dus a Madel (You're Some Girl!),* followed by *The Circus Girl,* for which, to please Yonkel, I learned to climb a rope way up to the flies and did a real Leitzel routine. I trained all summer with an ex-acrobat in New York to toughen and strengthen my arm muscles for that long climb to the top, where I fanned out to the audience, one foot in a noose and my arms spread like a bird's wings. I did a split and twirled around forty feet into the flies. Then I slowly climbed back down the rope, all to Rumshinsky's music.

We thought when I finally came down there would be a thunderous burst of applause, instead of which there was one big heavy sigh of relief, followed by remarks like "Kalich must be crazy to let her risk her life like that," etcetera, etcetera. But the play ran, I climbed, and we did very well.

We toured all the big cities—Philadelphia, Boston, Baltimore, Chicago, Cleveland and Detroit—all the way to Los Angeles. In those days there were audiences all over who understood Yiddish, and we played to crowded houses.

Ours was a very popular theater. Often Yonkel, when he was managing and not acting with me, would come rushing backstage to tell me Greta Garbo was out front, Einstein, Jimmy Walker. Sometimes they were and sometimes they weren't. But just hearing him say, "You know who's out there tonight?" would put us all on our toes, and we'd pep up the performance.

Jimmy Walker *did* come, and he took a bow from his box. And D. W. Griffith, in cape and high hat, was a steady customer who often made a speech from the box to us and to the audience. He always mentioned what a privilege it was for him to see our work.

One night after the show, Griffith took us to see Clayton, Jackson and Durante in a cabaret uptown, telling me to watch Durante ("He *is* the act"). Many, many years later, I was appearing at the Palladium in London on the bill with Durante. He had never played in England, and the audiences knew nothing about him or his special kind of comedy. My act followed his, and, after having played the British vaudeville circuit many times, I knew how to handle a Palladium audience. But this was all new for Jimmy. He went on, did his act—no laughs, no applause—and he came off shaken. "Wotsa matter, Molly? Why ain't dey laughin'?" I told him he had to slow down a little so they could understand his English. The next night he tried to slow down, but again no response. The third night he came off livid, foaming at the mouth. "Wotsa matter," he yelled, "don't dey understand English?" Of course, after Jimmy's films played there, they began to dig his style, and he became one of England's big headliners.

D. W. Griffith, after seeing one of our shows at the Second Avenue Theater, came to our apartment, where Mama served him herring and potatoes boiled in their skins, which he loved. He had come to tell us he had an idea to make a film with me. He wanted Yonkel to work on the script with him because he felt Yonkel had the tempo that he himself hadn't acquired. He tried to raise a million dollars, but he was on his way down—a has-been to backers—so nothing happened. We remained in the Yiddish theater, which was then thriving, and in which we were happy and productive.

There were four fancy Yiddish theaters on Second Avenue: the National, with Aaron Lebedeff; the Public, a new one, with a translation of *Bayadere* from the German; the Folks Theater, with Maurice Schwartz; and the Second Avenue, with us. There were also Yiddish theaters in Brooklyn (including Coney Island), Queens, the Bronx and Newark. All in all there were twelve, most of them supported by the newly arrived immigrants in New York, who organized in little groups, each named after its hometown in Poland, Russia, Romania, etcetera. They gathered in halls on the lower East Side to be with their relatives and friends from Minsk, Pinsk, or Berdichev, and they bought blocks of tickets for the Yiddish theater at a discount, then sold them at a profit to raise money to send to their impoverished relatives and friends in the old country. There were hundreds of such organizations, and our theater thrived on their patronage. Actually, with their backing, the nut of running a season was 80 percent covered.

At one performance, the money was to be used to help an orphanage in Lemberg (now Lvov). The Lvover-Americans brought along a few local orphans and presented them onstage, in front of the curtain, while the president of their society made an impassioned speech to wring out a few tears and a few more dollars from this supposedly affluent gathering. Tears flowed, coins rang in the tin containers (*pishkes* we called them) as they were passed up and down the aisles, and everyone had a good time, especially the managers of the theater, who were assured of a good, profitable season.

There were many other ethnic theaters in New York then

—German, Russian, Polish, French, Italian, Ukrainian—
even a Chinese theater on the Bowery.

Slowly, as immigration diminished, the ethnic theaters
petered out, but the Yiddish theater outlasted them all, in
spite of the fact that the younger, American-born generation
no longer could speak, or even understand, *mama-loshen,*
the mother tongue (so called, I suppose, because Mama did
all the talking). Since Mama was so anxious to see her children become Americans, not remain greenhorns, she urged
them on to learn English, to be able to go to college, to become a Somebody. Unfortunately, she didn't realize then
what a wonderful heritage and what a vivid, juicy language
they were losing and would never be able to recapture again.

What a colorful group we were. Our ushers, for instance,
were all well over sixty, and when people came rushing into
the theater late while I was onstage singing, they would
calmly say, "Don't rush! You wouldn't miss nothing!"

One evening, Dick Manning, who wrote *Two to Tango,*
was waiting in the back of the theater for the usher to show
him to his seat, when a little boy came up and asked the old
usher where the bathroom was. And the usher turned to Dick
Manning and said, "*Here* he comes to take a bath?"

When the theater was opened after the summer, we had
it freshened up. The ladies' room was painted, and new car-
pets were put on the floor. The very elegant lady attendant
delicately admonished the women during intermission,
"Please, ladies, *pisht nisht* on the carpet." (In other fancy
terms, "Don't urinate on the carpet.")

Early in my career I also played with third- and fourth-
rate actors in Newark. In one play I appeared with a star who
had had a nervous breakdown and had just been released
from the mental institution where she'd been for a year. In
the play, I was her daughter, and she was jealous of the man
who was her sweetheart. When she caught him joking with
me, she shot him. Police came, fire-engine sirens shrieked,
and as I picked up the gun, she was supposed to cry, "No, no,
I did it!" Then the curtain came down.

She went through the first act fine—that is until the shot,
the fire alarms and the sirens. I picked up the gun and she

froze, speechless. Desperately I ad-libbed, "Mama, mama, tell them I didn't do it. *Red,* Mama, *red*" (*red* in Yiddish is speak). She snapped out of her trance and said, "Red . . . white and blue."

Many an ad lib unexpectedly backfired! Henrietta Jacobson, one of our very talented Yiddish comediennes, told me how she, as a child, was in a play called *God, Man and the Devil,* the Jewish version of *Faust.* The Devil was the star part; he also was the producer and director and had no money.

When the play was done on Second Avenue, they hired a trumpet player to imitate the sound of the *shofar,* which is blown on the Day of Atonement. When the Devil defies God and boasts he will seduce man and bring him to Hell, the sound of the *shofar* is heard, and then God's voice answers as he takes on the challenge of the Devil. But the star in Henrietta's company couldn't afford to hire a trumpet player. While they were rehearsing, Henrietta, while playing backstage, discovered a player piano. She put a penny in it, and the music came forth—the "Traumerei." "That's fine, Henriettale," the star shouted, "the 'Traumerei,' the *shofar,* the audience wouldn't know the difference. At night I'll give you a signal, and you put in another penny in the piano, and I'll give it back to you in your wages."

Came the evening. The Devil in his cape and horns threw his challenge at God and then flourished his hands in a circle as a signal. Henrietta put the penny in the machine, and the music blared out: "Everybody's Doing It, Doing What, Turkey Trot!"

Fortunately we were rarely caught off guard in our theater. Ours was a kind of *commedia dell'arte* technique and we could always ad-lib. For example, in one scene a wife had to say to her husband, "I hate you! I hate you!" and make her exit, which she did by sort of slumping offstage. The director came running over to her, shouting, "Why don't you hate him until you get offstage?" To which she replied, "I don't have any words." "Then improvise!" he shouted. "Find words— you're an actress, no?" The next evening, fully equipped, she said, "I hate you! I hate you!" took a few steps, turned around and added, "You stink!" She spat and exited like a queen.

The theater was not the only thing on the East Side that had a special kind of flavor. So did the neighborhood, the streets, the pushcarts—and especially the people. The East Side of New York? It was like a turbulent little brook running alongside a huge river. The people there spoke their own jargon, a mixture of the language of their native lands and New Yorkese, which in itself is a mixture of many tongues. Neighbors there were still interested in the good or bad fortune of the *next-doorekeh* (*ekeh* makes anything feminine). There was only one class—no wealthy, no nouveaux riches —all were on the same level. And ofttimes I thought they were all the same age in spirit, both young and old. There, no one looked back. Everyone looked forward to a future, if not for themselves, then surely for their children.

Although our neighborhood then was only a few blocks from the East River, few of the people there had ever seen it. In fact, not many of them knew New York was surrounded by water. In our neighborhood they dreamed not of what was now, but of what will be some day. And every family lived only to see the day when their children would get somewhere. Mothers and fathers worked side by side to send a son through college, to see him graduate and become a doctor. And the daughter, too, must learn something—maybe to play the piano—but play it well.

One of the special attractions in my neighborhood was the *shvitzbud* (steam baths) on Ludlow Street. Since very few people had bathrooms in their tenements, we started early in life going to the *shvitz* once a week. And I was so hooked on these old-fashioned purges that even after I became a star on Second Avenue, I still went to the Ludlow Street Baths and had a ball with the little old ladies.

In case some people have never been in a *shvitzbud*, I must clarify. The steam room is made of a huge open oven, heated by huge stones (I don't know how). The attendant pours cold water on the hot stones, and the steam steams out, so you can't see where you are, and it becomes quite a feat to climb to the top bench, which is the hottest spot, because heat goes up, not down. The older the little *bubbes* (grandmas), the higher they climbed. They would all beat themselves with *baizems* (brooms) made of leaves.

One of the younger ladies I met every week on the top bench was a waitress in a Romanian restaurant. One day she told me she had married. She was a snappy sixty and presumably a virgin. Why, I asked, why all of a sudden had she gotten married? She raised her hand as if she were carrying a heavy tray and answered, "Why? Because my hand started hurting me!"

The huge Polish masseuse drank cans and cans of beer. We had her pour beer on the hot stones to give a little malt perfume to the steam, and for every can she poured on the stones, she poured two down her mouth. Of course, we paid for the lot. When I lay on the massage table and she beat me, standing over me with her huge naked breasts and beer breath (a proper beating, nonetheless), she'd boast, "I got daughter—beautiful. I got daughter—beautiful. I got husband—*fui!*"

One day I dared Bella Spevak (who with her husband, Sam, wrote *Boy Meets Girl* and many other Broadway smash hits) to go to the baths with me. She had so much fun with the old ladies and the Polish masseuse that after it was over she said, "You know, Molly, if they put us into a ghetto here, it wouldn't be too bad!"

And the restaurants in our neighborhood were equally super—the dairy ones, the delicatessens, and especially the Romanian ones.

One evening, Flo Ziegfeld and Billie Burke came to see one of our shows, and Yonkel asked me where we should take them afterward. So I said, "Why not take them across the street to Moskowitz and Lupowitz. It'll be something different and the food's delicious." So we did, and when we came into the restaurant, nobody knew them and everybody knew us. We got the big hellos and the best table, and immediately the waiter brought a big platter with sour pickles, sour tomatoes and sauerkraut. And naturally, a big bottle of seltzer. The menu was all steak, fried with lots of garlic, and *karnatzlach,* which are ham—God forgive me!—*beef*-burgers. There was also a side dish of grated black radishes covered with chicken fat.

Surprisingly, at 1:00 A.M. there were children there with

their parents, eating the *karnatzlach*, the black radishes and especially the sour pickles.

Billie Burke could never have digested such food even at the proper dinner hour, so she called the waiter and with her lovely smile said, "Excuse me, sir, but do you have any vegetables?" He gave her an indignant look along with a little push on her shoulder and disdainfully answered, "Wotsa matter, lady—pickles isn't vegetables? Sauerkraut isn't vegetables?"

Yonkel had a similar experience with Sal Maglie, the famous Dodgers pitcher. They were making a film together for television, *The Littlest Leaguer,* and rehearsing on Second Avenue in a hall over the famous Ratner's Dairy Restaurant (now extinct). Sal asked Yonkel to suggest a restaurant because he didn't know our neighborhood, so Yonkel took him to a typical Second Avenue deli across the street. When they came in together, Yonkel's favorite waiter greeted him. "Hello, Yonkel. Don't tell me. I know what *you* want, but what about the *goy?*"

Yonkel asked Maglie what he would like, and Maglie asked the waiter for a boiled egg. If a bomb had exploded in that deli, the waiter would have been less shocked. He actually stuttered, "Eh . . . eh . . . *eggs* he wants?" And Sal asked him, "Don't you have eggs?" And the waiter stuttered, "Uh . . . uh . . . of course we have eggs. But who eats eggs?" Result: Yonkel and Maglie had pastrami sandwiches on rye bread, with the usual sauerkraut, sour pickles and heartburn.

Those were the good old days for our Yiddish theater. Old man Edelstein, our first impresario in New York, did such good business with us in our first play, *Yonkele,* and later on with *Tzipke,* that he gave us an unheard-of bonus, one thousand dollars in cash, right from the box office. The next day Yonkel was busy writing a new play, so Helen and I put the money in a brown paper bag, and we went, not in a taxi, but on a trolley car, to the bank to deposit our fortune.

CHAPTER 4

I HAVE KEPT DIARIES for over fifty years, and as I write this book, I keep referring to them. Over and over again, I'm left wondering how we did all we did. For example, the following snippet from 1924–25:

> Open Second Avenue Theater in *Yonkele* . . . Out two days tonsillectomy . . . back to *Yonkele* . . . Open *Tzipke* . . . Tour Detroit, Philadelphia and on to Loch Sheldrake . . . Two weeks rest . . . Open Second Avenue with *Tzipke* . . . then new Easter Show, *Shmendrick.* . . .

While my memories catch a breath, let me explain the word *shmendrick*.

Shmendrick is the traditional fool in Yiddish literature, a sort of Simple Simon. Abraham Goldfaden, who was our Gilbert and Sullivan, coined the name for a musical he wrote in the early twenties. Later, that marvelous name grew into *shlemiel*, *schmo* and *shmuck*, a word a nice girl never uses, so excuse me.

I once asked Al Hirschfeld, the famous theatrical cartoonist, if he knew any *shmendrick* stories, and he told me this one:

A father brought his little son to the zoo. At the lion's cage, he said, "You see that ferocious lion, Sonny? If he broke out of his cage, he would jump on me and tear me apart. He would eat me up, and there would be nothing left of Papa." Well, the little boy was shocked indeed, but not quite in the way his father expected. Mulling over the sad scenario, the little boy answered, "If the lion does eat you up, Papa, and there's nothing left of you—what number bus do I take home?"

That's a *shmendrick* for you.

The diaries, the years, the back-to-back productions build like bricks in a wall. Between 1925 and 1929, within twenty-four weeks, we would open with eight new shows, then take one of them on the road for twenty weeks more. In the process, Yonkel and I took over the control of the Second Avenue Theater (along with Joseph Rumshinsky and the three cashiers), at the same time also doing Second Avenue Follies and American Vaudeville.

We were so busy on Second Avenue—and had done so well—that we had no desire to spread out to Broadway (or, as we called it, "uptown"). In the spring of 1929, however, Jennie Jacobs, an agent, came to me and offered me $2,500 a week to appear at the Palace. What she dangled before me meant both an enormous fee and enormous prestige. I said yes and Yonkel agreed.

Then came the question: What would Molly do at the Palace? All I had were the Yiddish songs I had written for our plays. I needed something everyone could understand.

I went to the big Broadway music publishers and asked them for songs, but they brushed me aside. Finally one of them told me quite frankly that any uptown chorus girl could sing those songs better than I. No doubt. What he suggested was that I translate some of my own numbers into English. And, he and everyone else added, don't use your hands too much.

The first suggestion wasn't too difficult to follow. My very first songs had been in English and I quickly retranslated. But, the second suggestion—oh, boy! So much of what I communicated involved hands (enough that I finally wrote one of my most famous songs just on that subject). So, rather than risk a slip, I decided not to use my hands at all. During my first performance at the Palace I stood with my hands locked firmly behind my back. I sang my own songs and told my own stories—and actually played to my own audience because all of Second Avenue came uptown with me to make sure their girl wouldn't flop!

I also had some unexpected help. Sophie Tucker, my costar for that first week, knew I would be drawing the downtowners, and so she did half her act in pure Yiddish (and she was great). *Variety,* our theatrical bible, wrote: "The Broadway actress did a Second Avenue show, and the Second Avenue actress did a Broadway show." I was held over for three more weeks and the barriers between me and the *goyim* were down for good.

Sophie Tucker was one Jewish woman who'd already made the leap, and that first week at the Palace gave me a chance to strengthen our bonds. By today's standards, she probably seems pretty tame; but in those days, her bawdy songs were hot stuff. Success, however, didn't provide her with everything she needed. Sophie was a solid, straightforward, unspoiled woman who was always with the wrong man. She was a big, robust, beautifully groomed woman, and she invariably fell for some shy, slovenly type who could never be her equal. Soon she was supporting him and he never gave her anything in return. His resentment would build up and he'd turn nasty and abusive to her. She had three lousy husbands and a no-goodnik brother who managed her career and robbed her blind. When she sang "A Good Man Is Hard to Find," she meant every word.

After my Broadway debut I moved immediately on to the Chicago Palace. I was aware now of different audiences and hence delighted when the manager came backstage to tell me my act was a hit. I asked if the Chicago critics were out front, and he roared, "Who needs the critics?" Al Capone had been there. He, and thirty of his henchmen, had bought three rows and they were all the favorable judges I needed. After the show, one of his "boys" came backstage and invited me and the entire cast to Capone's cabaret in Cicero.

In 1929, when Capone invited you, you went. Earlier, the Duncan Sisters had refused, and one of them was beaten up. So we didn't argue about it. We went. We sat at one table and Capone and his entourage sat at another. I always felt that each of them had a hand on his gun all the time. Capone, however, never spoke directly to me or approached us in any way. Instead, the same henchman messenger came over and asked me if I wouldn't repeat a song the Boss liked. He called it "The Immigrant Boy," and Yonkel quickly figured out he meant "The Rabbi's Melody," a poignant song about a little boy who comes to America from Poland and longs for his old hometown. My accompanist was with me, and I got up and sang. To my astonishment, the notorious gangster Al Capone sat and cried like a baby. Later he sent us a case of liquor, put a car at our disposal and even asked us to join him at the races. He obviously took good care of a lot of people. He was running a breadline for the poor at the time and it was pretty impossible to find anyone alive who'd utter a bad word about him. Whenever I do that song now, I introduce it as the one which made Al Capone cry.

Our stories keep going on and on, just as we do. A sequel to my Al Capone concert occurred when I first played the London Palladium in 1932. The management gave a press party for me at the Savoy and I began it by telling the newsmen about the famous people who had came to see me— Albert Einstein, Jimmy Walker, Greta Garbo, even the King and Queen of Romania. Nothing impressed them. Then Yonkel blurted out, "Molly also gave a command performance for Al Capone." Lo! All the pens started scribbling, and the next day the headlines in all the papers announced: MOLLY PICON, THE "MOLL" WHO SANG FOR AL CAPONE.

Back in 1929, however, a lot of laughter was muffled by the stock-market crashing. We, too, had bought heavily on margin, whatever that means. All I know is that it translated into a $45,000 loss. In one shot. All the money we had.

Yonkel was on his way to Europe when the banks closed. He had read that a famous Viennese soubrette was doing a successful operetta, and he thought he could get the rights to do it in Yiddish. After my summer vaudeville season, I was back at our Second Avenue Theater. When I learned that all our money was in the market, I frantically tried to cover our losses. I went from bankers to brokers to pawnshops without much luck. Amid all this, I still did nine shows a week, singing, dancing, and blaming Yonkel for investing all the money I had worked so hard to acquire. Finally, I decided, *Que será*

será. The boys in the theater wanted to take me out and get me drunk, but I refused. My hangover then was from heartache. We were right back where we had started ten years before.

All through this disaster, Yonkel was still in Europe trying to find me a new play. I had wired him, lying that all was well, but it wasn't. Every theater uptown and down was hit, and ours along with them.

Desperate for an audience-grabber, my producers searched for a "touch," a play that would tug at the heartstrings. We settled on a promising tearjerker, *The Jolly Orphan.* It not only had a ragamuffin orphan for me to exploit but also a shabby little dog. We found a mutt we named Motel (mostly because we were suspicious about its sex life), then began hours of aimless rehearsal. Without Yonkel to direct us, however, we were falling apart. I grew more worried, tired and slightly hysterical.

Yonkel finally did arrive and turned a certain disaster into a great evening. But to little use. The audiences had vanished. We couldn't meet our lease and were thrown out. Somehow, we finagled the Folks Theater at Twelfth Street and Second Avenue to lease to us and on September 30, 1930, miraculously, we opened a new season. We grandly renamed our house the Molly Picon Theater. Strangely enough, amid such goings on, I never learned how Yonkel managed to extricate us from the crash. He seemed to take it all in his stride and we never, ever, spoke about it. Instead, we plunged into furthering my career in our new theater.

During the next two years we clung ferociously to the Depression's edge but luckily did not fall into the abyss. We introduced *Girl of Yesterday* and *The Love Thief,* often the only theater that paid salaries. Our bankbook was aided by my vaudeville stints, especially when the Fox Theater in Brooklyn upped my salary to the astronomical sum of $2,700 a week.

The "Picon's daughter" was catching on—despite America's sad state. Yet, Yonkel and I continued to break away from our growing success in order to return to Europe to perform. We needed repeatedly to touch base with Yiddish roots, and so we found ourselves back every few years to play Bucharest, Galatz, Jassy, Kishinev, Belz and Bakau.

We also played Paris and the London Palladium, but our most intriguing foreign success in 1932 had to be our six-month engagement in South America. It's some neat trick finding a packed Yiddish house in Buenos Aires.

Suddenly we had a benefactor, and all we knew was that he was willing and able to bring Yonkel, Abe Ellstein, our musical conductor, and me from Vienna to Buenos Aires, all expenses paid.

It seems our backer had come to South America from Warsaw. In Warsaw, as a boy of twelve or thirteen, he used to wait at the stage door of the Kaminska theater when we were playing because he had no money for a ticket. Yonkel spotted him and gave him a pass to see the show whenever he wanted to. That was in 1922!

He eventually migrated to Buenos Aires, looked around and decided Argentina sorely lacked good mattresses. He started a small mattress factory to fill the gap and eventually became the Millionaire Mattress King. When he heard that the Yiddish theater was trying to bring us to Buenos Aires but didn't have enough money, he offered to finance the whole venture. And from our first performance, he was there every night—not waiting at the stage door, but sitting in his own box seat. For six months he was our most appreciative audience.

He was not our only fan, however. Many Jews had come to South America in the late twenties after stringent quotas were set up in the United States. While many of them prospered in the same capitalistic fashion as our Mattress King, others were more unorthodox. One Jewish movie mogul in Buenos Aires had a grandmother who had once been South America's most popular prostitute. In those days, the Jewish audience divided themselves into sections, one for the clean (mostly male and virtuous) and one for the unclean (mostly fallen women). Despite her grandson's high position, the elderly *bubbe* insisted on sitting with the other ladies of the night. Even as she neared death, she refused her family's plea that she be laid to rest amid the sanctified and not in the cemetery set aside for sinners. Checking over the imposing gravestones, she chuckled, "I don't want to be buried here just so people can spit on me and say, '*Ptui!* She doesn't belong here!' "

After our Latin-American excursion, Yonkel and I returned to the warm American audiences who'd missed us in our absence. In quick succession we played Loew's Fox in Washington, the Century in Baltimore, the Palace in Chicago and the Albee and State on Broadway. My sister Helen, now married, presented us with a new baby, her son George, whom we enjoyed greatly.

Still, the wanderlust pulled at our feet. Soon we were on the *Rex,* sailing for Europe and, at long last, Palestine. We were to be guests of Chaim Nachman Bialik, the great Hebrew poet. He immediately took us to Ein Chared, a *kibbutz,* to give a concert.

At that time, the Palestinians were adamant about speaking only Hebrew. Yiddish was outlawed, and very often bloody fights occurred between those who spoke only Hebrew and those who spoke only Yiddish. But Bialik was revered as a great writer, and arranging the free concert at Ein Chared—one of the oldest *kibbutzim* in the Holy Land—he demanded that all listen to us, even though we performed in the forbidden language. As our master of ceremonies, he cautioned that we were artists first and should be heard.

The concert was outdoors, and all the *kibbutzniks* came and sat on makeshift benches. Farmers came on wagons and horseback. Some Arabs came on camels. They listened, they laughed and they applauded. Then the *kibbutz* staged a show for us in Hebrew, and we sang and danced the *horah* with them until the wee hours. It was a very special evening for us and we determined to do something special for those people someday. Our plans had to wait because engagements called us to Warsaw and Russia and American vaudeville first. We returned to the United States in September of 1933, when I made my first talkie, a three-reel film for Warner Brothers.

For those days, it was a spectacular—over sixty people, big dance numbers and routines on bicycles. I sang some of my vaudeville songs. The film was called *Money Talks* (I don't know why), a Mr. Hennebury directed it and my leading man was Jay Velie. It's probably a museum piece now!

On December 11, 1933, I opened in my first American musical, *Birdie*, written by Clairborne Foster, at the Majestic in Brooklyn. In the cast were Mae Vogts, a very funny character actress, Roscoe Ates, a hoofer, and Raymond Hackett, the leading man. Monty Woolley directed the show, but nevertheless it just didn't make it. Everything slipped twixt the reading and opening night, and we seemed to have slipped right into a full-sized flop. Our backer, one of our dearest friends, Jack Seidman, advised us to close the show, "take our knocks" and do better next time—advice that has come in very handy many times in my uptown shows.

The first week of rehearsal, our assistant stage manager asked us to release him. He had an offer from the Theatre Guild to do a small part, and he wanted to act, so Yonkel gave him his release. His name was Henry Fonda. I often wonder whether he remembers *Birdie*.

After that trying, tiring episode, Yonkel decided we needed a rest, so we took a cruise. We tried, like the rest of the passengers, to play shuffleboard, swim in the pool, relax, dress up for dinner, etcetera. But it seemed to me that we Americans were so busy trying to make money, we simply didn't know how to relax.

We stopped at many ports. In Havana, the Western Union messenger brought us a wire, and when he saw my name he rushed off and in half an hour was back with a committee to invite us to the graduation ceremony at the Jewish Community Center. We went, we sang, Yonkel spoke, and we were home again!

In Cristobal Colón we walked through the usual shops with their perfumes and fancy *tchotchkes* (knicknacks), but somehow ended up in the red light district. As we were walking, we heard one of the "girls" shouting, in Yiddish, *"Geb achtung vif'n beitel."* ("Be careful of your handbag"). When we talked to her, she told us the usual story: Her father was a rabbi in Poland, she was duped into going to Havana with a man, and he made her work for him as a prostitute. The other girls were jealous of her, she also added—she knew the business better than all of them.

Fancy ladies, as Mama used to call them, the gambling crowd and just plain shoddy characters all seem to feel a close kinship with our profession.

While I'm on the subject of fancy ladies—when we were in Paris in 1921, one of the actors asked us if we would like to visit The House of All Nations, a notorious brothel in which each room was decorated in the style of another country. The nationality of each girl who plied her trade there corresponded with a room. There were rooms with special beds built for corpulent shahs, sheiks and other royal dignitaries; the reception room was done in French antique, very subdued and proper. Yonkel was writing a column for *The Jewish Daily Forward,* and he jumped at the idea of visiting this world-known brothel.

Since Ladies were welcome, I went, too. All we had to do was buy a bottle of champagne (for which they charged twenty-five dollars), half of which the actor who was our guide got as his share for our visit. The girls mingled freely with the guests and coaxed them to buy champagne. Quite casually they captured customers and vanished with them up the stairs.

Yonkel then asked our guide if we could meet the madam who ran the house, because he wanted to write an article for the *Forward* about her. Our guide sent up a note, and the madam came walking slowly down the stairs. Her appearance staggered us. Usually, in the theater, a madam was rouged and elaborately coiffed and walked like Mae West, with a cigarette in a long holder, and wearing tons of jewelry. This madam wore a very simple black velvet evening gown, one string of pearls on her neck, and hair tightly drawn back into a simple little bun.

She walked over to us and in perfect English greeted us and said she would be delighted to give Yonkel an interview for his paper. We started by asking her how she got into the business, and she gave us her whole background. Her father ran a house out West and was shot by a gangster. Then two of her brothers were in the Gold Rush doing a thriving business with another house . . . and on and on, until Yonkel turned to me and whispered in Yiddish, "*A shayner meshpocheh!*" ("A lovely family!"). She stopped talking and asked, "Are you Jewish?" to which of course we replied, Yes. Then she added, "You know, I'm Jewish, too, and I'm not ashamed of it."

One more brothel story before the police break in on us. When we played in Paris, one of the actors had a wife who openly plied her trade. The French-Yiddish actors all accepted it as the norm. The couple lived in a one-room apartment where she entertained clients when he was out. One day he came rushing to rehearsal, livid with rage. "I caught her!" he yelled. "I caught her in my bed with a man!" We didn't know whether to laugh or cry, it had all been so obvious; but Yonkel, always ready for disasters, quietly asked, "So what did you do?" "What did I do?" he yelled. "I told her to change the bed linens!"

The French have their own rationalizations about sex and their own linguistic approach. One of the oldest actresses of the Comédie Française was to receive the Legion of Honor on her eightieth birthday. In her acceptance speech she thanked them and then said, "But why did you have to wait until my breasts hung down to my knees before giving me the token of your esteem?"

Despite my global travels, I have little hope for the world at times, especially when I see how much anti-Semitism still prevails. One painful experience with that ugly thing occurred in May of 1935. The year before Yonkel and I had started our first radio shows for Jell-O (and later on for Maxwell House coffee). We did five programs a week in Yiddish, while also performing in and out of the Yiddish theater, working all winter and summer. I was also doing my vaudeville act and was very tired. Since Yonkel was going to Palestine for new material, I decided to take a short vacation by myself. I asked some actors that were in vaudeville with me where I could go to rest up—somewhere no one would know me. They suggested Ogunquit, Maine.

So off I went by train, arriving in Ogunquit at 10:00 P.M. I hailed a taxi and told the driver I knew nothing about Ogunquit and to drive me around—when I saw a hotel I liked, I'd tell him to stop. I saw a lovely old hotel and said, "I think I'll check in here." He turned around to me and said, "Lady, are you Jewish?" Jokingly, I answered, "I've been Jewish for years." To which he replied, "They won't take you in here, lady—no Jews and no dogs."

I sat there stunned! I had just appeared at the Palace on Broadway, doing "Working Girl"; my name was up in lights on the marquee, and I was earning $3,500 a week. But they wouldn't take me into this hotel? I asked him where they would take me, and he answered, "Dunno." We started going from one hotel to another, yelling, "Hey, do you take in Jews?" And the answer: "Never did—ain't gonna start now." It was near midnight, with no trains going back to New York, when the driver graciously offered to put me up in his house overnight. As he put it, "I don't care who I take in, as long as they pay me."

I slept there overnight and got up mad as a hornet. I asked the driver to take me around the farming area, where I finally found a Norwegian farmer lady who gave me a warm welcome and a nice room. I boarded with her.

I wanted to find out, Why the antagonism toward Jews? I rented a broken-down car and started driving around and talking to people on the beaches. One man gave me a rather sensible, if not sensitive, answer. "We have nothing against you people, only we don't want to be too progressive. Take a look at Old Orchard Beach and see what your people have done there. You've turned it into another Coney Island. We don't want that to happen to our town. We like it quiet and old-fashioned. We just don't want the prosperity you bring and the ulcers that accompany it."

Ogunquit was my first overt encounter with anti-Semitism, although as a child I remember being turned down for parts in the Chestnut Street stock company because I looked too Jewish.

Nevertheless, Ogunquit had a wonderful summer theater season which I planned to enjoy. I met a part of it head-on. While driving in my jalopy, which I called the "Wreck of the Hesperus," I bumped into the car ahead of me. When I got out to see what damage I had done, I found that Ethel Barrymore was in the car I had hit. We both sat on the fenders and talked about theater. We had supper together, and I forgot all about the unpleasantness.

In the theater, it seems to me, we are color blind and religion blind. If a performer is talented, it's Open, Sesame!

Nineteen thirty-six was one of our busiest years. I made a one-reel short, again for Warner Brothers, in which I sang my "East Side Symphony." And I played the Palace again, where Hank Greenberg, the famous baseball player, came backstage to meet me—six feet, four inches, and every inch Jewish. Boris Thomashefsky appeared at Sadie Banks's Allen Street Cabaret, and when he heard we were in the audience, he put on a special costume from *Ben HaDor,* complete with tights and high-laced gold boots. When we went to his shabby dressing room to compliment him, he told us he was going to build a dozen such clubs all over the States and appear in them all.

Roosevelt was our President, and there were Fireside Chats on the radio. Fanny Brice was a terrific hit in the Ziegfeld *Follies,* as was Belle Baker at the Palace. Fanny, Belle and I were at lunch together at Lindy's one day, and Belle asked me to write some good songs for her. Fanny laughed and said, "Dope, if Molly writes a good song, she'll keep it for herself." Poor Fanny. She was not pretty, but she knew comedy and was a great performer—after she had her nose fixed, however, she just wasn't funny anymore.

Katharine Cornell was doing *Joan of Arc* on Broadway. Helen Hayes was in *Victoria Regina,* and Lucienne Boyer was doing a French review. We went to see it immediately because Yonkel had signed for me to appear at the Alhambra in Paris for two weeks in April.

I was on Broadway again with Sophie Tucker. I told her I was engaged to do my act in Paris. She asked me if I spoke French, and I told her I didn't. "Then you'd better start learning," she said ominously. "The French are very chauvinistic, and since your material is geared to comedy, if they don't understand a word they'll boo you off the stage. I went through the experience one night in a café."

Our producer, Kurt Robitcheck, had cabled me I would
only have to do one chorus in French. He had just taken over
the Alhambra, after having come from Berlin's famous Cabaret de Komiker. Some Jews in Germany saw trouble ahead
for them. Robitcheck was one of them who had fled to Paris.
Unfortunately, he knew little about French audiences, so I
heeded Sophie's warning and began taking a French *leçon*
every day in the Village.

On March 27, 1936, we sailed on the *Champlain* for
Paris. I had my costumes and repertoire all ready, so when
the captain asked me to give a concert on the boat, I accepted
and tried to make friends with all the passengers and win
them over. I very much wanted them to root for me when I
went on to do my French act. It's a sneaky way of trying to
avoid a flop—but I wasn't a flop; it worked. I made a little
speech before my act, dived in, and it went fairly well.

Robitcheck was waiting for us in Le Havre. We took the
boat train to Paris, then on to the Hotel Moderne on the rue
de Rivoli near the Alhambra. We began rehearsing for him,
but his French wasn't too good, either. He chose five songs,
and took us to see the theater. For us, the program was peculiar—mostly acrobats, magicians and animal acts, plus a
poet reading his poetry. Pils and Tabet were the stars and did
a wonderful act, Tabet at the piano and Pils singing lovely
French songs. I shriveled, listening to them. I'd had three
months of French lessons and didn't understand a word. How
would the typical French middle-class audience understand
me? Well, I liked a challenge and this was it!

On April 10th I made my debut, *tout en français,* at the
Alhambra. Since the theater was in the Jewish section and it
was Passover, 50 percent of the audience were the same people I had played for at the Lancry in 1921. It was the Palace
debut all over again: a captive audience come to see that
their girl was a *triomphe.*

I came on to a nice round of applause and did my first
number, which had always gotten a lot of laughs in the States.
Here, there was not a snicker. I'm in trouble, I thought. They
don't understand my French. What shall I do? Very calmly,
I stepped over the footlights and asked, in French, *"Vous*

me comprenez? Si non, je vais chanter en anglais." And the whole audience shouted, *"Non, non, chantez en français."* From then on we were friends, and I stopped the show.

After my act, "Roby" (as we called him) came back all excited and asked whether the speech I made after my first song was part of my act. When I told him it wasn't, he said, "Keep it in," which I did for the rest of my two-week engagement.

There was, however, an occurrence for which we hadn't bargained. The French actors' union allowed vaudeville theaters to engage only 50 percent foreign acts, the other half having to be French. Roby, perhaps unaware of this law, had engaged 80 percent foreigners; so the French actors staged a protest against the theater in a typical French manner.

When the first act went on (an accordion player from Italy) there suddenly appeared a Frenchman walking up and down the theater aisles, playing the accordion and shouting, *"Regardez mois—je suis français et je fais la même chose"* ("Look at me, I'm French and I do the same thing"). He played and shouted, and the audience applauded and booed, until the Italian actor had to bow off. After that act, eight Polish acrobats came on, to the same response—eight French acrobats doing the same stunts. The Poles, too, were booed off. The demonstration even included a trapeze act, with a girl on a rope that hung from the gallery, shouting, *"Je suis française—je fais la même chose,"* etcetera.

By this time there was pandemonium in the theater, and Roby came running backstage to tell me to go on fourth instead of tenth. It was the starring spot, and he assured me there would be no demonstration, since no French actors had my kind of repertoire. I went on. They listened attentively to me, applauded and shouted, *"Bravo, Mali, formidable!"* Obviously the French demonstrators didn't have time to recruit a ninety-five-pound French chanteuse who did somersaults. Somehow we got through that two-week engagement.

Best of all, for Yonkel and me, were the notices in the French papers, especially *Paris Soir,* where one critic wrote, "Even Hitler would applaud our petite Mali Picon."

Paris was gay and cheerful then, even though there was

a little tension floating in from Germany. We went to all the plays and cabarets, of which one was run by Harry Pilcer. Harry was an East Side boy, who did a dance act with Gaby Deslys, the former mistress of a Spanish nobleman. When she left the nobility and fell in love with Harry, she brought all her furniture and pictures from Spain to Paris. They had a lovely home, which we visited after Gaby died.

Among the treasures she left was a huge painting of the Last Supper, with Christ and all his disciples at a table together. Harry told us when his father, who was a small merchant on the East Side of New York, came to visit, the first thing Harry did before his father arrived was to cover the picture of Christ with gauze. Later on, Harry went out on some business, and his father, curious to see what was under the gauze, took a peek. When Harry came back and caught his father peeking under the gauze, the old man chuckled and said, "It's a good thing you don't have to feed them all."

While in Paris, we also went to the famous Jewish restaurant, Flambaum's, near the Folies Bergère. When I asked Madam Flambaum what they had to eat, she answered, "We have *toujours kreplach.*" (*Kreplach* are like the Russian *pirogen,* or the Chinese *won ton,* but not like *knishes* or *knaydlach.* If you've ever been in Miami, all these delicacies would be familiar to you, for big blimps fly over the beaches advertising the three K's: *kreplach, knishes* and *knaydlach.*)

We left Paris to appear in London and Glasgow and Leeds, and then back to London, where I found a new combination of vaudeville and movies. That partnership had originated in America and was the beginning of the end for vaudeville.

Yonkel had left earlier for Warsaw to work on a script for our first Yiddish musical film, *Yiddel Mit'n Fiddle.* Abe Ellstein, our composer, was with me and he had started writing music to the lyrics of Manger, a gifted Yiddish poet. He and I then left for Poland by train. Riding through Germany was painful, and I hated to look out the windows. I could feel the waves of hatred as we went through the towns, and we arrived in Warsaw heavy-hearted.

Fortunately, once again being with actors, musicians,

stagehands, and the Polish director, Pshebilski, shook off the depression we were in, and we began to work on the film. Our producer, Joseph Green, and his wife, Annette, gave parties for us, and we worked twelve hours a day on the script and the songs until we were ready to shoot outdoors in Kazimierz, a shabby, broken-down village, where King Kazimierz (Casimir III) had once reigned with his Jewish queen.

I had never seen such poverty—outdoor plumbing, rickety wooden houses bent into fantastic shapes, and the people unbelievably threadbare. The skeletal children, with their long *payess* (sideburns) and little *yarmulkes* (skullcaps), wore trousers that were in shreds and shoes tied on their feet with rope. My heart went out to every one of them. We gave them coins (they wouldn't accept food—it wasn't kosher), and with the coins they bought grapes and came back to share them with me.

The story of *Yiddel* concerned a girl who had to wear boys' clothes so she could perform on the fiddle with her father, who played a bass. Together they played in all the backyards of Poland.

The whole town was on our heels while we filmed their story. We ordered them around, and they followed us like lambs. When the stagehands and camera men yelled *"Psha krev"* (a Polish cuss word), every time the sun went down, the whole town yelled with them. The filming went on from 6:00 A.M. to 6:00 P.M. every day, and with a *slontze nyeman* (no sun) and a *psha krev*, we made *Yiddel*.

The wedding scene in *Yiddel* took over thirty consecutive hours to film. The food had to be truly kosher, because we hired the Orthodox Jewish men, women and children of Kazimierz to be the guests. As we filmed, they ate, and for the successive shots of the table, the food had to be replenished, over and over again. Our poverty-striken guests couldn't figure out what was happening. They thought they had been invited to a real wedding, and when one woman asked why so much food, we explained to her it wasn't a real wedding, we were just making a film. I don't think she had ever seen a film, but she said, "Why didn't you tell me that before? With so much food, I could have brought my daughter to get married for real. She has a *chassen* (bridegroom), but we have no money for a dowry to make a proper wedding." I have a slight suspicion that Yonkel gave her the money, because later in the day she smiled at me and said, "Are you lucky to have such a rich husband."

Years later, when Norman Jewison asked me to play the part of Yente in *Fiddler on the Roof*, he told me that when he visited Israel he had gone to see *Yiddel* in a museum there to absorb the atmosphere and character of the *shtetl* in which *Fiddler* was to be filmed. He also said *Yiddel* was fifty years ahead of its time.

Having finished filming in Kazimierz, we returned to Warsaw and found that Yonkel's mother had arrived and was staying with cousins who lived on the Nyalefkes, the predominantly Jewish street where I had played in 1921–22 at the Kaminska Theater. It was still all hustle and bustle, and when we went to see my mother-in-law and took her for a walk, she accosted several men on the street and came back to us without explaining her actions. Finally Yonkel asked her if she knew these men, and she answered, "No, but you can see they are good Jews, and wealthy ones, so I only asked them if they knew someone who was going to America and would sell me his *shtreimel* (a hat trimmed with sable or mink, worn by Orthodox Jews), because I want to bring back a present, a hat for Foigel Gonif."

We gave a concert in Warsaw so mother could have some idea of our profession, which she still suspected wasn't entirely kosher. We gave her a seat down front near the stage. Young people were sitting, older ones standing, so she began rearranging the whole orchestra, and if so many people couldn't get in, why didn't they make more tickets? By the time we came to the end of the first act, she had settled down to listen to us singing "Meshiach Is Gekumen," and as she applauded with the rest of the audience, she shouted, "From my children's mouth into God's ears!" I think she was a bigger hit than we were that day.

CHAPTER ✺5

EVERYTHING LOOKED THE SAME to me in New York after our hectic year abroad. The only thing we missed were the trolley cars, which the city had removed in our absence. Even my old Ludlow Street steam bath was just as I left it. The same ladies welcomed me back with their same old aches and same old-age pains. My life, too, went back to an old routine: concerts and benefits.

One concert in Brooklyn featured Benny Fields as master of ceremonies. Moyshe Oysher, the famous cantor, and I were the entertainers. Benny sat between us on the dais and started to introduce Moyshe with great fanfare.

"The next performer I want to pay special tribute to. Not only is he a great cantor, but also one of the best tenors in the whole world today and a very dear friend of mine, Mister . . . Mister . . ." He stopped and whispered to me, "What's his name?" and I whispered back, "Moyshe Oysher." And he whispered back, "No double-talk! What's the guy's name?"

I moved on to Baltimore and did five shows a day at the Hippodrome. I was so exhausted that Yonkel sent me to Miami to rest while he went back to New York to negotiate for a theater to open our film, *Yiddel Mit'n Fiddle.*

I traveled by train and was shocked to see the poverty in the Southern countryside. It looked just as bad and sad as Kazimierz. It looked even worse when I considered that in the cities, at least, the poor for the most part had running water and indoor plumbing. Here black people were living in broken-down shacks without any sanitary facilities. At the railroad station a line divided the blacks and whites. Each had separate booths, restrooms and compartments. It was my first real exposure to the Southern attitude toward blacks in our country, and it made me very sad. All my life, especially while growing up in Philadelphia, black and white had always mingled.

Only the Miami sunshine and ocean cheered me up. I registered at a hotel and went out immediately to hire a bike and mail home baskets of fruit. Then, suddenly, I realized I was there to rest. I tried, but it was difficult for me to relax. I was just too wound up. I knew I had only a certain amount of time to rest, and rest quickly, before going back to work.

All the guests in the hotel had the same problem. The garment trade from Seventh Avenue, doctors, lawyers—all looked desperate for a good time. Everyone wanted to take me out to dinner. (Look out, Yonkel, your little *shmendrick* is a popular lady!) Many of them were those moneyed men looking for romance and full of bicarbonate. I was happy when Yonkel wired that it was time for me to come home, and happier still to see him again.

He wasted no time getting my trunks from the train, piled me into the car and drove straight to the Ambassador Theater. There was my name up in lights for *Yiddel Mit'n Fiddle*.

Yiddel opened in December and I first saw it as part of the midnight show on New Year's Eve. The film was the beginning of a whirlwind evening of people and restaurants that ended up at Reuben's at 7:00 A.M. with a "Happy New Year"; then a morning train to Hartford, where I was winding up a vaudeville act!

Nineteen thirty-seven continued the pace—concerts, radio, plugs for *Yiddel*—but we were merely marking time until we took to the seas again. This time we were heading for Africa—one of the few places left on the globe we hadn't played in.

We were sailing, this time on the *S.S. Paris*. I had to stay in my cabin to fight a bad cold I'd caught, but most of all I wanted to stay close to Yonkel. We had been away from each other so much, and we both felt we had to renew our love for each other. This trip was a kind of second honeymoon.

We landed at Plymouth and went on to rainy London,

where I opened at the Trocadero, in the Elephant & Castle neighborhood. What a peculiar audience! They all looked like characters out of a Dickens novel, and after the show, the aisles were covered with orange peels and peanut shells. I had doubted they would understand my act—but we managed to communicate very well.

How the English live is a miracle to me. The stage was so cold I could hardly breathe, and of course the theater was, too. In an evening gown, décolletée front and back, and nothing else, I felt plenty drafty. I just hoped to survive.

On this trip, I did my first television show in London. The technicians put purple makeup on me and told me to be careful how I held my hands—not to hold them in front of my face because they would come out enormous on the screen. I never saw the film, but it has to be a relic.

We sailed on the *Winchester Castle* for South Africa. Twenty days lay ahead of us on an English ship. God help us. No excitement, no movies, nothing. The English demand little and are resigned and terribly efficient, at least outwardly. We slowly began getting acquainted, not quite at the smiling stage, just a sort of indefinite nod. We called at Madeira—warm, sunny, palms, and kids begging for pennies. Women sold flowers and young boys would dive for sixpence (which we threw overboard). We also discovered Madeira wine. We bought two bottles so we could take a nip and lift our spirits.

The trip had been rough, but the sea suddenly gave up struggling and calmed down. The sun was hot and welcome. Off went our British long johns. I got into culottes, all the men put on their whites; it was summer in February!

We met one lady, a teacher, who spoke Afrikaans. Since I was going to Africa with a group of vaudeville actors to appear there in a vaudeville show, I thought it would be a nice gesture to do one of my songs in Afrikaans. I asked the lady if she would translate one of them for me, and it turned out to be one of the audiences' favorite numbers, especially in the smaller cities.

We also discovered some *real* millionaires on board, not like the kind we used to call in the Yiddish theater *reiche millionaren.* To us, anyone with ten thousand dollars was a millionaire; anything more than that and he was a *reiche millionaren* (a *rich* millionaire). Two of these real millionaires were big gold-mine owners, a Sir John Maxwell and a Mr. Murphy, a Scotsman. We met them during a fancy-dress ball where Yonkel won first prize. He wore a Dutch costume, which I had brought along, and everyone loosened up and it was fun, especially for me, four feet eleven, dancing with the tall English lords. We found out they're human, *les anglais.*

We landed at Capetown, and the silhouette of the hills —Table Mountain, Lion's Head and the Twelve Apostles— was an extraordinary sight. We took on new passengers here, including our tour manager. We were now on salary until we left the country.

Our African impresario was a man named Schlesinger who ran all the theaters in the area. He had come to South Africa originally to sell insurance, but the major companies wouldn't hire him because he was Jewish. (Their anti-Semitism was as deep then as their racism still is.) Schlesinger was extremely angered and vowed, "Boys, some day you'll be working for me!" He bought up all the theaters in South Africa and made them into one chain. With such a monopoly, he could afford to hire the big-name talent that individual theater owners could never afford, and he sent them touring from one theater to the next. He made a lot more money than he would have selling policies!

We landed at Port Elizabeth, and our opening was riotous. I headed the bill with Rose Perfect, a well-known singer and socializer. Rose was a gay old gal. She already had six or seven husbands under her belt and was a fourteen-carat gold digger. She instinctively went for the richest mine owners, and was more practical about feathering her nest than she was about performing. She abused her voice with all her antics and ended up croaking on every note.

Joining us were Tex McLeod, a London comedian, Ted Ray and Jimmy Hunter, two English vaudevillians; our musical backup was the BBC Balalaika Band. This was variety with a capital *V!* And the audiences loved us. I did six numbers and closed the first half amid shouts and sweat. It was February, and it was hot.

On our Sundays off we saw the town's big attraction—about a dozen sorry-looking penguins—then went with the local manager to see Sea View, the Jewish seaside development. We also saw monkeys in the trees—the veldt, the bush, Africa.

Our posters had announced a "Big Variety Season." That big season was four days, and we were finished and on to Johannesburg. We traveled by train first-class in a roomy compartment with two big beds. Not bad for darkest Africa. We traveled hundreds of miles past veldt and blacks and mud huts. Wherever there was a tree, there was a house. The train stopped at every hitching post, and we'd get out to see Africa—Dutch, English, Kaffir—Africa!

Johannesburg topped everything I'd ever experienced.

First, of course, we performed, opening at the Empire Theater to an ecstatic audience. They laughed and bravoed and I encored and encored and they had trouble getting me off the stage. Later, we were taken to the Rand Leases mines and went three thousand feet down into the bowels of the earth with the miners. In the mine compound we saw the Kaffirs and Zulu dancers.

The natives were exciting and exotic. None of the blacks were allowed into the city proper—blacks and whites were completely separated—but on Sundays the Zulus were permitted to walk the streets to church. The Zulu women would pile their hair several feet high and pack it with mud. Then they would decorate this mound with amazing things: feathers, can openers, buttonhooks, knives. Somehow, on them, such headdresses looked elegant.

I sang some Negro spirituals for them and they grunted their approval in a language with sounds that were unique to me, but I understood it was their way of applauding. I would have liked very much for them to have seen me perform onstage, but they were not allowed in any theaters.

To wrap up our stay there was a rainstorm such as can be seen only there: full of thunder, lightning and hail big as baseballs. As we stood petrified, several beams fell, killing four people. A small earthquake followed as a sort of encore. I was trembling in my boots but, to them, it was just another day in Africa and business in the theater was grand.

We sailed to England on my birthday, June first. Yonkel, who had gone ahead to see his mother, wired me, "To the girl who gets older every year and younger every day." I, at thirty-nine, just kept going: to Leeds, back to London, and to Glasgow.

Mostly, now, I wanted to go home. I sailed for New York on the *Île de France,* while Yonkel, who'd gone ahead to New York, waited there. He came aboard (via boat) with the gentlemen of the press or, as we called them, gentlemen of the *fress* (gluttons for free food). Our pictures were taken and sent off to city desks by pigeon. The birds flew off ship to land in their individual roosts in city rooms throughout New York. So much for modern times!

We drove to our brand-new apartment, a duplex at One University Place. In 1937, New York in summer looked just as dirty and hot as it does now; the people, however, looked prosperous. It was hard for me to adjust to the noise and city rhythms after Africa, but I dug in. I did a broadcast with Rudy Vallee, opened at the Steel Pier in Atlantic City and began rehearsals for *My Malkale* (My Little Molly). My co-star was the famous Aaron Lebedeff, our George M. Cohan. He had a fabulous voice, terrific charisma, and dressed like a dandy.

I met Maurice Schwartz, the producer, walking on Second Avenue. He said, in his elegant British-accented English, "Molly, I don't want to belittle Yonkel—he certainly did a lot for you. But I see a Molly that he doesn't see, and I have a play for you and me in which you would reach untold heights as an actress." But when I answered that I would be delighted to work with him had Yonkel not booked me on the Loew's circuit after *My Malkale* for $3,500 a week, he gasped, dropped his British accent, and in real New Yorkese said, "So who's your agent?"

Everybody came to our theater, especially on Sundays, when there were no shows on Broadway. Paul Muni and his wife, Bella, who was a Thomashefsky, came, and we talked about our childhood. Bella and her mother, Emme Finkel, and her brother, Abe, and sister, Lucy, had all practically lived in the dressing rooms of the Columbia Theater in Philadelphia, together with Mama, Helen and me.

David Sarnoff, the radio and television pioneer, was one of our fans. He told us a very amusing story about his mother while we were chatting after a show. Somehow, he could never convince her that he was an important man—to her he was just Duvidel (little David). One Friday, in the days when he was involved with plans for the construction of Radio City, he came to her, as he always did, for supper, and he told her, "You see, Mom, no matter what I'm doing, I come to you for supper on Fridays—even today, when I'm busy with plans for Radio City. I had lunch with Morgan, and he gave me ten million dollars; I had cocktails with Vanderbilt and he gave me twenty million dollars; but for fish on Friday, I still come to you." His mother looked at him and quietly answered, "Duvidel, why do you *shlep* around with those *goyim?*"

Although our plays did well enough, we began sensing that our audiences were forgetting Yiddish. As immigration slowed almost to a halt, there were fewer greenhorns who didn't understand English and who needed the Yiddish theater. Now, even the older people spoke English, and it wasn't unusual to hear an old lady ask her grandchild, "How do you say *matches* in English?"

Of course, this had a disastrous effect on the Yiddish theater, and we had to produce three, sometimes four new shows a season to attract the same limited audience. Consequently, we put on another play, *Bublichki,* to bolster the sagging season. I played a ragamuffin Russian boy and had to learn to play the harmonica, so I took lessons, at five dollars a half-hour. Yonkel commented, "That's more than Larry Adler paid for his whole career."

Nineteen thirty-eight started with *Malkale,* rehearsing *Bublichki,* and *Yiddel* running on Broadway. Also, we began our first radio contract on WMCA for Maxwell House coffee. In between, I did a benefit show in Casa Mañana. I sang "East Side Symphony" and "The Working Girl"; it went nicely, but no riot. Some little kid singer stole the show—her name was Judy Garland.

For the first six months, I toured in all the big cities while Yonkel, who had sailed on a Polish boat, the *Batory,* for Warsaw, started preparing the script for another Yiddish

film. I joined him in June with Gertie Bulman, a gifted young
ingenue. We sailed on the *M.S. Pilsudski* from Hoboken. Another birthday arrived and with it another wire from Yonkel:
"*Mamale* is getting older." Yet I had no feelings then about
my age. I had no fear of the years. I felt young physically, and
no audience found fault with my youthful roles. Unlike film,
which often is a lie detector of your years, theater provides a
distance that allows you to be younger than you are. So I
celebrated my fortieth.

Most of the passengers on the *Pilsudski* were Danes,
going home after thirty or forty years in the States—old,
weather-beaten, salt-of-the-earth folks. I sang for them, and
they were so appreciative. It felt good to reach people of
another background, another world.

When we reached Copenhagen, thousands of people
were on the pier to greet their brother Danes in their quiet,
dignified fashion. Even the dogs didn't bark. I said good-bye
to Denmark, sailed to Gdynia, and there wasn't one person
to meet us. Dignified or otherwise. I boarded a Polish train
to Warsaw—no sleepers, a dirty compartment, and the contrast to Denmark so pathetic. However, we made it, arrived
in Warsaw, and seeing Yonkel's smiling face made me forget
the train, the discomfort and everything.

Immediately work began on *Mamale*—I forty years old,
having to play a twelve-year-old girl. The makeup man
looked skeptical, and I didn't blame him. But the first rushes
were encouraging—not too many close-ups. I almost looked
like *Mamale,* and with Abe Ellstein's music and my lyrics,
the score sounded promising, too. The plot involved a little
girl whose mother dies and leaves her to be Mama to the rest
of the family. Outdoor scenes were shot in Chechochinek, a
Polish watering spa with gardens, parks, bathhouses, but no
indoor plumbing. Not too many guests, either, because Jews
didn't go there. But we needed the parks for the film, so we
went, and got out okay.

We returned to Warsaw, where we saw the film starting
to take form. On July Fourth we celebrated at American Ambassador Biddle's palace. Beyond that little diversion, we
committed ourselves to nothing but work. There were no

unusual obstacles to our filming. We worked hard and kept within the budget until all was finished, *koniec, finis,* done. And we were thankful. Poland had begun to feel like Germany, hatred of Jews was everywhere, and we wanted out as quickly as possible.

After the filming, we sailed on an English yacht to the North Atlantic and Spitsbergen. Our lively vessel, formerly an 18,000-ton cruiser, was now fitted out for fun: outdoor pool, games, and a nice English crew, all smiling, thank God. We saw the little islands and the birds called Mother Carey's chickens and stopped at Reykjavik, Iceland, enjoying its ice-capped mountains, hot geyser waterfalls and miles of lava-covered fields. There was not a tree in sight—but there were fields filled with small ponies. The tall Nordic people enjoyed a modernistic theater and their country of ice and fire and abundant fishing.

We began to sight ice floes as we rounded North Cape to Spitsbergen. This was real glacier land. We drank aquavit (Nordic gin), did some business at the last post office we would find (we were only five hundred miles from the "Nord Pol"). The glaciers were fifty miles large.

Our ship sailed right into the ice. The sun shone at night, and all we saw were snow and ice over us, under us and around us.

We journeyed to Green Harbor, which was full of Russian miners and pictures of Stalin and Lenin. Then on to Bear Island, another rock in the ocean.

At Bird Rock, millions of birds gathered; the ship shot off a cannon and they flew around like snowflakes. We sailed through the beautiful fjords, and the captain asked me if I would sing with the Seaman's choir on Sunday at church services—he knew I had played the Palladium—and I accepted. I told him, however, that the only hymn I knew was "Onward Christian Soldiers." He said everyone would sing it with me, and they did. Unfortunately they sang very slowly, like a dirge. I felt this was a militant hymn, so I started tapping my foot to quicken the tempo and even took a high note on the end (excuse the ham in me). Afterward the captain came over to thank me. I told him I felt the choir didn't have the right spirit and that I had tried to give them the right tempo. To which he replied, "Give them the tempo, Miss Picon? I thought you were going into a tap dance." The British have a wry sense of humor.

The yacht returned us to England and I was in London at the Holborn Empire with Long Tack Sam and his Chinese Acrobats. Edward Everett Horton was also there. A hundred years before, I had played with him and Blanche Yurka in George M. Cohan's play *Broadway Jones*. He was always an elegant man and devoted to his mother. I went through the British vaudeville circuit again—the Palladium, with Tom Mix and his horse, the Diamond Brothers, played Manchester again, Leeds, with the famous Duncan Sisters—but there was an uneasiness all over Great Britain. Premier Chamberlain flew to see Hitler; despite his assurances, Londoners began to dig ditches in Hyde Park.

Yonkel had to go back to New York, and I still played on, growing edgier every day. Old friends from Vienna came to me to help them get their relatives out of Austria before it was too late. I ran around and got nowhere. I did a few more vaudeville shows and even played the Trocadero, where I began learning to sing in saloons. A wire from Yonkel, however, told me to cancel all engagements and come home.

I sailed on the S.S. *Washington,* my first American ship. I was relaxed, but there were many tense and bewildered people on board. It was a relief to see Yonkel on the tender to meet me. But he didn't take me home, he took me straight to the Paramount in Newark! Crazy. How could I adjust, after the swank British Trocadero, to the Newark Paramount, four shows a day! Jitterbugs, bands, kids—they almost booed me off the stage. I was still talking with a British accent and they thought I was putting on the Ritz. I hadn't even unpacked my clothes. There was an Italian puppet show on the bill, the Salici Puppets, and the Jews boycotted the theater because of Mussolini, and the Italians boycotted the theater because of me.

Meanwhile, America recalled our ambassador from Berlin, and I whipped into the tempo of New York—the Strand in Brooklyn, no more British accent but New Yorkese, four and five shows a day. Jitterbug contests, and what vitality our kids had—as they say, Wow! During my engagement at the Oceana, in Brighton Beach, a trailer preceded me and announced over a loudspeaker, "Tuesday: twenty turkeys to be given away by the Brighton Laundry; Wednesday: a skunk coat; and Friday, Molly Picon!"

Kurt Robitcheck turned up again, not in Paris, but on Broadway, with a new project, *Vaudeville Marches On*, at the Majestic Theater. In the cast were Al Trahan, Eddie Garr, Fats Waller and acrobats. I headlined the bill; I was to do my act, sketches and stunts, including the acrobatics that the Arabs had taught me. We opened December 30th and made quite an impression. In *The New York Times*, Brooks Atkinson wrote I was an honor to the profession, and Yonkel agreed with him.

Following the Majestic there was more vaudeville, a coast-to-coast radio broadcast on WABC with Frank Fay, Gertrude Neisen, Deems Taylor and Archie Gardner; I even gave a concert at Sing Sing! The banker Richard Whitney, then an inmate, sat out front, along with 2,200 other convicts. The atmosphere was very friendly. One prisoner who worked onstage with us complained to Yonkel that he had never stolen any money, all he did was work out the plans for others to do the job.

La Guardia was our mayor and very capable. There was trouble in Czechoslovakia, five thousand Italian Jews were wandering around in the Alps, driven out by Mussolini and not admitted anywhere, while Hitler took Prague and more Jews were sacrificed. But I kept giving benefits—Madison Square Garden for Gustav Hartman's Orphanage, the Astor for a moving-picture charity.

I kept going and going—then suddenly felt there was something wrong between Yonkel and me. I had been so wrapped up in my work I had forgotten how much he had contributed to my success, and I now wondered if all the praise hadn't gone to my head. I told Yonkel not to book me anywhere if he couldn't come and be with me, and he immediately brightened up. He needed pampering, as we all do.

At this time, a Federal theater board was created to weed out nonprofessionals from the W.P.A. theater project. I sat in on the board with Mitzi Hajos, Joe Laurie, Jack Norworth and others, on the saddest job of our lives. We had over 1,300 actors on W.P.A., young and old, all worried Congress would cut off appropriations and they'd be out of work. Some brought programs dating from 1893, in which their names had appeared. But Congress did throw them out, pleading no money, which meant they would all be on relief. Yonkel, meanwhile, signed us for another twenty-six weeks for Maxwell House, and I was happy only because we were working together. Otherwise, I was plagued by blues.

As Mama used to say, "People are dying who never died before." Bertha Kalish passed on and Boris Thomashefsky. And no other performers of their stature were around to keep the Yiddish theater alive.

My blues deepened and Yonkel sent me off for a little vacation. I was run-down and weary. My therapy was the Cutaloosa Inn in New Hope, a regular honest-to-goodness farm. I loved it. I milked the cows, gathered berries in the rain and met the neighbors—Rollins, the strawberry man, who lived alone, and Mr. and Mrs. Siel, he eighty-four and she eighty-two, Quakers, with a cat named Obadiah and a dog named Zachariah.

I came back to Yonkel a regular *farmerkeh* (feminine for "farmer"), and he seemed very happy to have me back again, smelling of hay.

Still, the new year (1940) was not without plenty of trouble. Europe was at war, earthquakes had devastated Turkey, Jews were being driven madly about, and the Yiddish theater had hit a new low. The world was in shambles and my career along with it. I needed something to spark it. Something different. Something not dependent on Yiddish and not dependent on travel. I wanted to stay put and make good, in my work and in my life with Yonkel. When Sylvia Regan brought me her play, *Morning Star,* I grabbed it.

The part involved something new for me, a sophisticated New York Jewish woman trying to raise several children alone. No more Shmendricks and Yonkeles. Yonkel agreed that the role might put me in a new category. Its range also excited me, as the play opens when she's thirty-eight, chronicles her life for the next twenty years, and manages to include World War One and the Triangle fire. Becky Felderman was not a complex character, but she had been written with some depth and was just the acting challenge I craved.

I readied myself with a *shvitzbud* on Ludlow Street and contemplated my first dramatic role on Broadway. On the surface, I'm sure I very much wanted a big success. Underneath, however, I was also hoping for something stable to secure my strung-about life.

CHAPTER 6

I WENT INTO REHEARSALS for *Morning Star* eager to succeed in this new phase of my career—but I was a little uneasy as to just how to go about it. My anchor was the Yiddish stage. I had performed in its comedy and melodrama, had helped write many of its songs; and I knew thoroughly how to entertain its audiences. Uptown, however, I felt a bit adrift. It wasn't that I feared tackling my first English-speaking dramatic role. I relished that chance. But I knew I was now part of a theater world completely foreign to my own. I would have no cute songs or dances to fall back on.

My director, Charlie Freeman, didn't help either. Freeman insisted on a Stanislavsky method of rehearsing (all emotions being internalized—you act with your head) and the going was brutally slow. Too slow to get a show together in three weeks' time.

Freeman was dismissed and Stella Adler brought in. Stella was a godsend; brisk and professional, she knew what she wanted and what we needed and she whipped us into shape in no time. I, however, continually struggled with my part and Stella was not too happy with my performance. My moods rose and fell with her appraisals and for once I couldn't look to Yonkel for help. It wasn't ethical to infringe on another director's direction.

Finally, on April 16, 1940, we opened in New York at the Longacre. Joining me in the cast were Joseph Buloff, a great actor, Jeanne Green, Ruth York, Celia Evans, Georgette Harvey and B. Schacht. The role of young Hymie Tashman was played by thirteen-year-old Sidney Lumet—now a world-famous director. (Today, when we meet, Sidney will often drop to his knees in mimicry of his part in *Morning Star.*) We had a swank first-night audience and the show went nicely. That night, Bide Dudley, the radio critic, gave us a very good review, being especially kind to me.

The newspapers were also favorable toward me the following day, but not toward the play (a pattern to follow in many of my Broadway plays). It was an old story—an audience show, not for the critics. People loved the play. Enthusiastic letters poured in and very supportive pieces appeared in John Mason Brown's and the Sobel column. The *Daily News* gave us a big spread, we cut prices to two bucks and so managed to stay open for two more weeks.

A group of survivors of the tragic Triangle fire came to see it and I brought them onstage. I just kept plugging the show, even doing free benefits to keep us going, but we barely limped through the sixth week. It's not easy, McGee. One day we were in, the next day we were out, and nobody knew anything for sure.

The weather helped, briefly. A heat wave hit the city and business went boom. Everyone said our show was doing much better than most, but the end was near. And not just for us. Hitler was marching, Paris had been bombed, and the world was, as we say in good Yiddish, *oif gehoketh tsuris* (literally translated, on chopped troubles).

On June 8th, after eight weeks on Broadway, *Morning Star* closed. Not too bad a run for Broadway those days, but, let's face it, not too good either. Yonkel and I signed for another year with Maxwell House on the radio, so we knew we'd have enough to eat on, but there was little joy in it.

We were desperate to be happy. We moved into another, larger apartment at One University Place, the first we had ever really furnished well. Yonkel was thrilled, especially as there was room for his thousands of books. We were now on the twenty-first floor and celebrating our twenty-first anniversary with all of New York at our feet.

But our lofty nest was only a stopover. We needed to keep working and with the collapse of my Broadway debut, we were back on the road. We did the Borsht Circuit in the Catskills, Swan Lake, New Concord, Lake Kiamesha, Ambas-

sador Fallsburg, and did well in all of them. We even took
Morning Star out to the Brighton Theater, the Garden Pier
and to our first arena theater in Long Beach.

The theater was actually a boxing arena. The producer,
who was a fight promoter, didn't know quite what to expect.
I have a feeling he thought he had hired some kind of burlesque show, however, because all through the first act he
kept saying, "When do the broads come on?" He finally got
involved with the story, thankfully, and then started shushing
the crickets, which chirped all night. Many people came to
see the play and seemed to like it better in the round than on
the Longacre stage.

I also began doing nightclubs, singing and dancing. I
played Detroit, and, in New York, the Bowery and Maxim's,
where I had a rather unusual experience.

Maxim's bosses were in some kind of racket—the milk
business, I think. Yet, at my first show, every table was taken
by senior citizens—men with skullcaps and white-haired
grandmas. Not the usual rowdy bunch I'd been facing. Only
one tough guy was sitting amid all these old folks and later I
learned that he was in the racket, too, but trying to convince
his kosher folks that what he did was legit. Obviously they
had engaged me as proof positive!

After that opening night, however, the usual club crowd
came and I did three shows a night to very receptive audiences. One night Harry Richman and Joe E. Lewis were in
and I asked Joe for advice on how to handle nightclub audiences.

"Molly," he said, "at the first show they're all eating
steak, and Jesus, Mary and the Holy Ghost couldn't get them
to stop eating and listen to an act. At the second show the
boys are a bit woozy, having had a drink or two, and star or
no star, they're all waiting for the broads to come on. And by
the third show, they're all so plastered nobody can see or
hear. If you approach nightclubs with that in mind, you'll be
able to take the punishment!"

But Maxim's was very good for me, held me over for four
weeks, and I kept on writing material for our Maxwell House
shows. I wrapped up the year singing on WOR in a Daniel

Frohman Memorial program. George M. Cohan, Bill Robinson and Fannie Hurst joined me for an impressive send-off for the old year.

Nineteen forty-one began with contrast. I sang at St. Mark's Church in Harlem—the only white person among the congregation. Then I dug back into my own roots with a performance at Yeshiva College. It was during January of 1941 that we also received word that Yonkel's mother had died at eighty-three. She had been living in the ghetto in Lodz. We had no details and feared the worst.

Yonkel buried his own personal woes by trying to prepare his play *Shmendrick* for Broadway. I had translated his Yiddish version into English and wondered what would come of nearly two years' work.

In the meantime, I substituted for Belle Baker in a pinch and added another performance to my growing string of all-American song-and-dance acts. It was on the heels of this stand-in that the growing split between Yonkel and me broke wide open.

Yonkel had been working one way and I another, and we had slowly been drifting apart. I was also getting work that no longer required his presence in my career. He was no longer the mentor of my future, and it obviously rankled. One evening I forgot to introduce him to some actors who had come backstage to see me—not the first time I had slighted him that way—and he walked out of my dressing room and checked into a hotel. After twenty-two years together, we were under separate roofs.

I was shocked at his drastic move, but I made up my mind to clear up the problems between us. If I didn't—or he wouldn't—the split would be a permanent one.

Yonkel had always babied me and never realized I was a grown-up woman. He told me when to go to sleep, what to eat, how to dress and handle myself. He also did the talking for me—I was always doing the listening. As I began to go on concerts alone, I built up a resentment toward such "behind-the-scenes" mothering on Yonkel's part, especially when I felt I was carrying the heavier load. One night I returned from a vaudeville stint which closed at 2:00 A.M. We didn't have a car then, and I was forced to lug a huge valise while searching for a taxi. None could be found and I had to take the elevated train, kicking that lousy valise up every stair. By the time I got home, it was nearing dawn and I had my angry speech all ready to deliver to Yonkel's face: how I needed more help, more expense money, and so forth. Naturally, I found Yonkel fast asleep and so I kept yet another bit of pique bound up inside me. I guess one way I retaliated was by ignoring him when I made introductions.

Our biggest problem, however, was sexual. In an attempt to be considerate of me, Yonkel never forced himself on me. He especially avoided making any advances if he thought I had had an exhausting show. Unfortunately, his attempt to be sensitive just backfired. I wanted more sex with him and began to feel that he no longer desired me. First I was frustrated and then angry because Yonkel was often responsible for creating my most exhausting roles. Here was a man who was asking me to climb ropes and spin on roller skates but then denied me sex because he thought I was worn out!

That was too much. I needed Yonkel as a man and as an advisor. It was just wrong for us to break up over problems which simply needed to be talked out. Despite everything, I knew we were meant for each other.

I went to his hotel and for the first time in all our years together, I told him how I felt, and he listened. We talked openly and honestly at long last. I wanted him to realize that I was more than his working puppet, that I was my own person; but I also wanted him to know that despite my career, I needed him as a human being, that emotionally and sensually he was still deeply important to me.

We agreed to try to get together again as man and wife. He took me to a show and a cabaret and we came home together to a new life. We were a couple again, completely but as equals, and we realized we still had a terrific attraction for each other. We were in love and it was thrilling. The wall between us was broken and we talked and loved and lived again.

I sang at the Hunts Point Palace and felt the whole world was as full of joy as I was. I was no longer inhibited with

Yonkel nor he with me. It was the beginning of a new way of life, and we were delighted with it.

I threw myself back into my work with a benefit at Madison Square Garden, then vaudeville at the City Theater on Fourteenth Street. There were five acts, two feature films, and a line of girls, all for twenty cents. What, no Bingo?

Yonkel ordered us a dreamy Chrysler convertible, fluid drive, cost, twelve hundred dollars. We got the notion to drive together all over the world—or, at least, to our concerts and back. We called the car the *Tsatske*, quickly got the urge to travel in it, and decided on Mexico for our destination.

We wanted to leave every care behind. President Roosevelt had declared a state of emergency. We were convoying ships and supplies to Britain. And everyone started to form civil defense groups. It was all a prelude to war, and scary. We had seen *Citizen Kane* and were stunned. The movie had not one cliché, and it underscored the media's drumbeating for war. With a new contract with Colgate for a daily morning program, plus our Maxwell show, we were no longer forced to tour for a buck. It seemed like the best time to enjoy ourselves before everything exploded.

We started out one night after a concert. It seems I was weaving in and out and we both were singing "Don't Fence Me In," when we heard a siren and a cop drove up. I stopped and asked, "Have I done something wrong, Officer?" And he answered, "No, only tell me where are you going? You're driving in both lanes. Your license, please." I gave him my license, he took one look and gasped, "Molly Picon? *The* Molly Picon? I saw you when I was a little boy on Second Avenue. Will my mother be surprised when I tell her I saw her favorite in person." We almost kissed good-bye—and hit the road again.

We continued driving straight through the Blue Ridge Mountains of Virginia, the Smokies, and south until we got to San Antonio. For four days we'd been driving and not one deli on the whole trip! In San Antonio we felt sure there must be a Jewish restaurant where we could get a piece of herring. We stopped in midtown where a policeman was directing traffic. Yonkel stepped out of the car and the traffic stopped dead while he asked the cop where we could find a Jewish restaurant. The poor cop looked puzzled. He muttered, "Jewish? Jewish? You mean Hebrew?" Then he added, "You know, mister, someone asked me that before and I didn't know what to answer him!" He blew his whistle, the traffic started whizzing by and I grabbed the wheel as Yonkel jumped into the *Tsatske,* and we drove to a drugstore where there was a telephone book listing a kosher delicatessen.

Yonkel was then writing a column for the *Daily Forward* called *Molly's Vinkel* (Molly's Corner) and it had a picture of me on top.

We found the restaurant. The owner, sitting in a corner, wore a beard and a skullcap, and he was reading Yonkel's column. Never one to miss a chance to make friends, Yonkel walked over to him and said, "I see you're reading *Molly's Vinkel.*" Mr. Herring (as we thought of him) looked up and answered "So what?" at which Yonkel pointed to me and said, "This is Molly Picon!!" Again Mr. Herring took a look at me and answered, "Of course, and you're a New Yorker wise guy!"

Getting nowhere, we called a waitress, sat down at a table, and ordered our herring. Meanwhile Mr. Herring scrutinized us more closely, went into the kitchen, conferred with his wife, who peeked out and almost fainted, nodded her head, Yes, and rushed back into the kitchen. Our host then walked slowly over to our table just as the waitress brought the herring. He joined us, uninvited, shook his head and said, "Molly Picon, Molly Picon in mine restaurant. You know what? The herring is on me." Big sport!

Years later, when I was filming *Come Blow Your Horn* with Frank Sinatra, we had another such experience. Walking on Sunset Boulevard, I spotted a deli and we went in and were greeted by a young girl with a Brooklyn accent. "Oh my Gawd," she yelled, "I have to call my fatha, he'll never forgive me if he misses seeing you." She called the old man and he came down (wearing his *yarmulke*) and said, "Oy, such a surprise. Such a surprise. Molly Picon in mine restaurant! You know, my wife died six months ago. If she was here now and saw you, she would die all over again."

We left the *Tsatske* in San Antonio and took the *Sunshine Limited* for Mexico. We had an air-conditioned Pullman and a dinner Mexican style, and we reached Laredo, Mexico. Squalor, dirt and cactus! The shock of the Indians living in hovels, crowded like cattle, beggars, peddlers—and the most ornate fountains—and we began to understand Diego Rivera's paintings.

Finally we reached Mexico City and the Hotel Reforma, where the radio announced our arrival. Immediately, a committee of Yiddish actors with flowers appeared, and we might as well have stood in bed! They accompanied us to Xochimilco, the "Venice of Mexico," then gave us a banquet, for which Yonkel paid. They took us to the Pyramids of Teotihuacán and to dinner in La Gruta, a restaurant in a natural cave, and again Yonkel picked up the check and no one stopped him. Next day we felt like we were doing one-night stands, and our company kept getting bigger—I visited Cholula (from where I sent Tallulah [Cholula] Bankhead a card), and this time at dinner a group of Mexican actors joined us, ate and sang, and I reciprocated and sang—and Yonkel paid. We saw a Mexican dance on glass and visited some hotels with a mixture of Jewish and other refugees, and I sang for them, and Yonkel paid for this dinner, and the next day, despite sad farewells, we told them we had to get back to work —our bankroll was dwindling.

Our way back home through Mexico was a nightmare. We were delayed in San Luis Potosí—a bridge had been washed away—and it was thirty-eight hours, sitting and trying to sleep in a hot train and eating bad food, before we finally got moving and were back in San Antonio, where we picked up the *Tsatske* and hit the road and sang, "America" and "My Country, 'Tis of Thee." We felt like singing its praises to the sky.

We stopped in New Orleans, the most exciting city ever, ate at Antoine's and celebrated our twenty-second anniversary in the *Tsatske,* singing our way through Alabama, Tennessee, Georgia and Virginia. And, just the way we left, we arrived home driving through the night, in the wrong lane, and into a terrific heat wave. Home never looked better.

Immediately the summer season caught up with us . . .
the Catskills . . . hotels . . . food . . . people; back and forth in
the *Tsatske*. New York was the quietest place in the whole
country, deserted, not a sound.

We kept working and writing, and were very upset to
hear Lindbergh openly accuse the Jews of being warmongers
(this, and a German killed his child!).

Children who were victims of the war were very much
on our minds, and we wrote to the Foster Care agency offering to help. They wrote us about a young Belgian boy, a Jew,
whose parents had been killed and who was now orphaned
in London. His name was George Weinstein. We adopted
him on the spot. He was the first of our four foster children.
The others would come to us in more unorthodox ways.

Yonkel was a father, and fifty years old. At his birthday
party, I had planned for four Western Union boys to sing
"Happy Birthday, Dear Yonkele," wearing black beards.
Over fifty guests waited downstairs in our fancy duplex while
my sister Helen got the beards and we outfitted the Western
Union boys with them. Then lights out, lights on, and there
they were: four blond Irish boys with black beards stuck on
helter-skelter. They began to sing, "Happy birthday to you,
happy birthday—" Suddenly they stopped, huddled, and
then came out with *"Dear John Kelly,* happy birthday to
you!" The party lasted two days.

Winter crept up on us and, suddenly, Pearl Harbor and
we're at war! Air-raid warnings in San Francisco; La Guardia
warns New York; air wardens stand by for duty; and I go to
my Ludlow Street Baths and discuss war with little old ladies
on the top benches. We're taking a terrific beating in the
Philippines while my Polish masseuse gives me a terrific
beating in the steam room.

Yonkel was an air warden, the only one in our house of
two hundred and ninety tenants to enlist. I traveled to Washington for a concert and the train was loaded with sailors and
soldiers, all young kids. Ammunition factories were working
night and day—war.

With all the concerts, success and applause, something
had gone out of me. I just couldn't pull myself together.

There seemed to be too little time between performances for me to get myself into shape. I'd skip rope, do dance routines, and generally I would stay in training like a fighter preparing for a bout. Suddenly I was listless and unable to get myself up.

Part of my problem was that I was doing a lot of things I shouldn't have been doing. I wrote my own music, my own lyrics, even typed my own programs. We never had a secretary, never had an assistant, and it all caught up with me. As we ushered 1941 out, I wondered what 1942 would bring to the world and me.

I began urging Yonkel to buy a house in the country. But when we went to see houses in wooded areas and I asked him if he'd like living there, he answered, "Sure, if Carnegie Hall was under one tree and the Palace under another"—and we ended up back in New York and saw Eddie Cantor in *Banjo Eyes*. He ended with a slogan for 1942: "Liberty, Equality and the Pursuit of Japanese."

Papa died—a heart attack—and as he lived so he died, alone. Few people were at Mt. Hebron Cemetery. It was a simple funeral and very pathetic. Even I couldn't mourn for I never knew him.

To bring a little excitement into our lives, Yonkel started writing a new Yiddish play for a road tour, and he worked like a demon. While I *shlepped* around doing benefits, he and Joseph Rumshinsky, our old conductor and composer, prepared the play. I felt Yonkel had a great, exciting show. But, as rehearsals began (I was doing dance routines with the daughters of the old chorus girls in our plays!) all the usual heartaches and frustrations of putting on a play returned. Still, Yonkel's writing was way ahead of that of our colleagues and I was confident. Despite a blackout in lower Manhattan, a mediocre cast, a small chorus, no scenery and bad costumes, I still felt we'd do well because we had a *play!*

We previewed in Philadelphia, at the Academy of Music. Our new musical, called *Oy, Is Dus a Leben* (Oh, What a Life), and written in both Yiddish and English, was, as I expected, an instantaneous success. All we needed was a little tightening--that's all. The next night was SRO, and a unanimous reaction: the best play we ever had! And just like my first play, *Yonkele*, Yonkel did this one all by himself.

The story was all about Yonkel and me, handled seriously but full of humor. The play begins with me playing myself as a child. It then proceeds to our meeting in Boston (where Yonkel is seen onstage, directing), our love affair and marriage, ending with a visit to his mother in Poland. Yonkel played himself, and I did a number with two little boys, all dressed in prayer shawls, singing in Hebrew, which stopped the show. It was our biggest success in the Yiddish theater.

Before we plunged with it into the New York season, Yonkel and I previewed it in Montreal, Ottawa, Toronto, Detroit, St. Louis, Milwaukee, Chicago, Rochester, Hartford, Providence and Boston. In every one of these cities, there were Jews in the audience who still understood the Yiddish, and we were delighted.

I also managed to squeeze in some vaudeville, and we both sold War Bonds ($12,000 at one clip) for our daily *mitzvah* (good deed).

We had signed to open *Oy, Is Dus a Leben* at the Al Jolson Theater in New York. We returned to find our agent had renamed it the Molly Picon.

Despite the fact that the Second Avenue El was coming down, New York in the summer of 1942 was dark. It was filled with men in uniform, and the war was felt everywhere. We took our first Hudson River boat ride—our manager, Edward Relken, warned us to look out for enemy submarines. To escape the oppressive heat in the city, we rented a house upstate. Yonkel kept rewriting *Oh, What a Life*, looking for more laughs.

We approached our venture with some trepidation. A Yiddish play on Broadway in a theater where Al Jolson had played? We set out to engage the best actors our union had, including three of the really great character actors, Isidore Cashier, Hannah Appel and Dora Weisman, who played Mama.

Rehearsals started with everything wrong, beginning with a dirty, neglected theater. Yonkel kept polishing the script, changing lines that the actors had to relearn, while I had to have new costumes made and still write four radio scripts a week for Maxwell House. Yom Kippur, the Day of Atonement, was upon us, the world was on fire, yet Broadway was crowded, bars were full and the burlesque shows were selling out. The whole atmosphere was a bit hysterical.

Then, lo and behold! the new costumes arrived, new scenery, and at dress rehearsal, the miracle—a cast and crew of over one hundred and fifty people and they're all enthused, not one complaint, and *we've got it.*

On Sunday, October 12th, we previewed *Oy Is Dus a Leben* at the Molly Picon Theater to a full house and a good reaction. On Monday the critics came, all the first-string boys, including Bide Dudley from the radio networks and Brooks Atkinson and Arthur Brisbane from the press. There was unanimous praise. One writer said he had not realized he was watching a show in a language he didn't understand! Bide Dudley called it "Another Triumph for Molly." David Sarnoff took us to Reuben's and everyone stood up and applauded as we walked in. Yonkel beamed.

Every night was celebrity night. Danny Kaye, Fred Allen, Kenny Baker and Sholem Asch all came to see us. Even the taxi drivers were excited. One of them said, "Molly, you're gonna cost me four dollas and forty cents. I'm takin' the wife ta see ya for our fourteenth annaversry."

Joseph Schildkraut, the actor, and Broadway Sam, the agent, came and laughed so loud it was a joy to hear them. Louis Nizer, visiting us backstage, said, "I sat spellbound. It was tremendous theater and a privilege to be in the audience. I must come again."

Relkin, our manager, took us to the Belmont Victory Week races, where a horse, Hopewell, had been renamed after me, and it won. We had Yiddish handbills passed out in the grandstands and joined Jolson for some pictures.

Our proudest reactions, however, were from fans. One letter went: "The last Yiddish show I saw when I was a kid —but *Oy Is Dus a Leben* makes me glad to be a Yid."

One letter from a Corporal Grossinger, from somewhere in the Middle East, included a $5.50 check for "two tickets for my mother." The corporal wished us success and ended,

"Our success is near." When his parents came to the show, Yonkel announced their presence to the audience and read his letter. His mother stood up and said, "My boy!" and everyone cried.

My own Mama was then very ill with pneumonia and we had night and day nurses to tend her. I had faith she'd get well. Knowing Mama, she'd have a funny story to tell soon. I prayed and she recovered. Naturally, she saw the play again and again and never liked Dora Weisman's version of Mama Picon. Mama probably wanted to play it herself.

We rang in the New Year, 1943, with *Oy Is Dus a Leben* going strong even after we'd exhausted our Jewish audience. The celebs kept coming—Leo Cherne, Irving Stone, Boris Aronson, Al Hirschfeld, Dolly Haas; but our managers were afraid of losing money and decided to close while they were still ahead.

So, to two jammed houses, we said finis to *Leben* on Broadway, its first Yiddish play, and our biggest moral and financial success.

CHAPTER 7

WE STARTED 1943 with a visit to Heatherdell Farms, a diet farm where most of the clients weighed in at two hundred and fifty pounds and up. Yonkel said the only ones who looked "human" were the dogs. That sort of life wasn't for us, and we were soon back in New York, opening a bottle of champagne and drinking to Russia, where we hoped to be playing soon.

War fever had everyone a little crazy and fired up to pitch in and win. As my way of helping the war effort, I began touring the various Army camps. I sang to 1,400 boys at Camp Ritchie in Maryland, and it was thrilling. I played the Portsmouth Navy Base, the seamen's canteens and the USOs. In between, I did vaudeville at the Greenwich Village Inn, with shows at 9:00, 12:00 and 2:00 A.M. I'd crawl into bed at four in the morning, then wake with a headache that lasted all day. I also opened at Loew's State and tried house-hunting at the same time. How did I stay sane?

Soon, I just had to flee, and when a last-minute offer came in time to play Hollywood, I accepted.

Yonkel and I left hastily, *hekel pekel* (bag and baggage), but we managed to celebrate our anniversary by dancing together for the first time in twenty-four years. We were close as never before, and the trip was a honeymoon.

We traveled leisurely by train, with stops for me to do some American vaudeville along the way. My railside stages varied from the seedy Glen Rendezvous in Kentucky to the swank 5100 Club in Chicago, Illinois, where I followed Danny Thomas, who'd made his fame there.

After Chicago, we rolled straight on to Hollywood. We

had a gorgeous roomette with lots of privacy, but no food. Because of the war, all the soldiers on the train were being served first. That would leave very little for the rest of us, so we had prepared ourselves with big bags of fruit and hunks of cheese, and thus dined, while America's wide-open spaces and fat, yellow cornfields passed by.

We arrived in California to find Mary Bran, our agent, waiting with more war-conditioned news. There wasn't a hotel room to be had in the entire city of Los Angeles, so we became her house guests. Luckily we had secured reservations for Lake Arrowhead while we were in New York, and soon were off to see Sophie Tucker there.

Sophie's voice was going, but she was still a dynamic act, bawdy and a big hit. As usual, she was still trying to keep a few bucks. Sophie had written her autobiography and was selling copies of it between sets. She described the proceeds as going to charity, but informed me privately that "charity" began at home.

Hollywood functioned at a lazy pace. We took in the sulphur baths at San Bernardino, I learned to swim, and we discovered Lew Wertheimer's Casino. The outside of the place looked just like a barn, but inside it was a gilded palace with free drinks, a buffet lunch and especially, gambling. We big spenders jumped right in, played blackjack because Jimmy Ritz was dealing, and won all of twenty-eight dollars.

We did everything but perform. Mary Bran had arranged only one concert, and financially my Hollywood debut was a failure.

The West Coast was not for Jewish Jews. Jews there had lost their language and their heritage and didn't seem to have room for me. All stayed in their tight little professional circles (directors with directors, actors with actors, cameramen with cameramen). If you went to a party, you were expected to do one discreet number, then melt into the crowd. (I did manage to impress John Barrymore once. Granted he was drunk, and being made drunker by some not-so-well-meaning friends. However, I did a medley of my songs, and he jumped up and yelled, "You S.O.B.! Where have you been all my life? That's talent.")

Molly at nine months

Below left, Molly plays in *Fagan's Decision* and, below right, sings "Don't You Want a Little Doggie?" These vaudeville acts played in the nickelodeons, and Molly Picon became the more "theatrical" Baby Margaret.

Molly (the oldest) and her sister Helen in Philadelphia in 1908. Mama made "everything except the shoes and socks."

Grandma and Grandpa Ostrovsky

The Picon family, Mama, Molly, Papa and Helen

Yonkel's mother and stepfather (Foigel Gonif) in Chaboufka, Galicia, 1920

Right, Molly and Yonkel's adopted children, Mariana and Dov, in Tel Aviv

A family gathering on Yonkel's birthday: sister Helen, her husband Bill, Molly, Yonkel and Mama

Molly and Helen in 1978

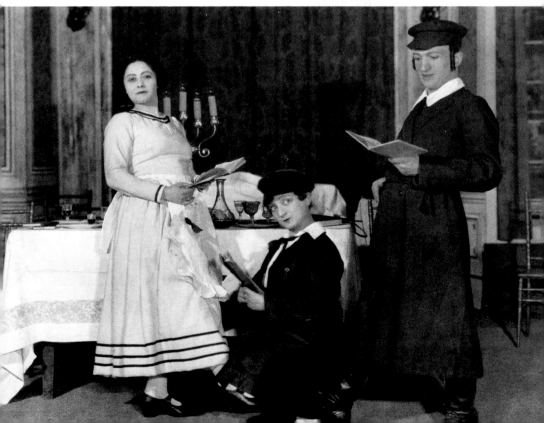

Opposite far left, a vaudeville act in England, 1912

Opposite left, young Molly in Vienna, 1921

Opposite bottom, the famous *Yonkele* on Second Avenue in 1923 with Lucy Finkle, Molly and Jacob Kalich

Right, in *Raizele,* 1928, a rags-to-riches romance

Below, *The Circus Girl,* 1928, for which Molly had to learn some Lillian Leitzel-type rope tricks. The audience would "sigh with relief" when she came down safely.

MUSEUM OF THE CITY OF NEW YORK

MUSEUM OF THE CITY OF NEW YORK

Above left, Molly in her famous characterization of Shmendrick, in *Oy Is Dus a Leben,* with Hannah Appel

Above right, 1928, a more glamorous Molly in *Mazel Bruch (Good Luck)*

Below left, Molly Picon with Muni Serebroff in *Jolly Orphan*

Below right, 1927, as Czarevitch Feodor, who didn't want to grow up to be a Czar

Opposite top, *Yiddel Mit'n Fiddle* was filmed in Poland in 1936. It had an authentic background of *shtetl* life and is a valued item in film archives in Israel.

Opposite, two scenes from the Polish-made film *Mamale,* in which Molly had to play a twelve-year-old

MUSEUM OF THE CITY OF NEW YORK

MOVIE STAR NEWS

MOVIE STAR NEWS

THE PLAYBILL

LONGACRE THEATRE

Left, Molly in the early 1930s

Above, the program for *Morning Star,* her first Broadway show, with Joseph Buloff and Sidney Lumet

Below, the prayer from *Oy Is Dus a Leben,* 1942

"ABI GEZUNT"

Comedy-Operetta in 2 Acts and 7 Scenes by JACOB KALICH and SHOLOM PERLMUTTER. Music by JOSEPH RUMSHINSKY. Lyrics by MOLLY PICON. Directed by JACOB KALICH. Choreography by LILLION SHAPERO. Settings by MICHAEL SALTZMAN. Assistant Stage Director, IZIDORE GOLDSTEIN.

— o —

· CHARACTERS ·

REZNICK	Two partners of a	MUNI SEREBROFF
PEMPICK	Hotel in Mountains	IRVING JACOBSON
TZIRELE, Reznick's wife		MOLLY PICON
MIRELE, her sister		
FETER PINYE, Tzirele's uncle		MAX BOZHYK
COOKIE, the Hotel cook		HENRIETTA JACOBSON
SALLY, her daughter		MIRIAM FEDER
LUCKY, her other daughter		SYLVIA FEDER
HAPPY, the Social Director		JULIUS ADLER
JANET, his wife		MAE SCHOENFELD
MRS. VIERNICK, a guest		REIZL BOZHYK
BENNIE, another guest		CHARLES COHAN
JENNIE, still another guest		ROSE GREENFIELD
ALTER, original Hotel owner		BEN ZION SCHOENFELD
The real husband		JACOB KALICH

Place of Action:
The Catskills in the good old summertime. Ballet of Cards,
Mosquitos, Dancers, Guests, Men and Women, etc.
Time - - - - From the Present to Once Upon a Time.

Credits:
Miss Picon's Gowns by Wilma
Hot Dogs, courtesy of Shmulke Bernstein Kosher Products.
Baloons, courtesy of Maxwell House Coffee

MUSEUM OF THE CITY OF NEW YORK

Above, *Abi Gezunt*, Second Avenue, 1949

Right, *Sadie Is a Lady*, 1950, with "new flaming-red hair"

Below, on a U.S.O. tour in 1945

Yonkel and Molly in
Carlsbad in 1920

In the dressing room of
Sarah Bernhardt in Paris,
1946

Together at Chez Schmendrick, Mahopac

In London, 1960

The golden wedding, 1969

ARCHER ASSOCIATES

With Sam at Chez Schmendrick, 1975

DAVID MCLANE

ANGUS MCBEAN

MUSEUM OF THE CITY OF NEW YORK

MOLLY PICON · ROBERT MORLEY

"A MAJORITY OF ONE"

PHOENIX

MOVIE STAR NEWS

WERNER J. KUHN

Top, starring in London with Robert Morley in *A Majority of One,* 1960

Above, filming *Come Blow Your Horn,* with Frank Sinatra and Lee J. Cobb

Left, *Milk and Honey,* a musical on Broadway, 1962

MUSEUM OF THE CITY OF NEW YORK

FRIEDMAN-ABELES

BERT ANDREWS

MOVIE STAR NEWS

Top, *How to Be a Jewish Mother,* a comedy on Broadway with Godfrey Cambridge

Above, *Hello, Dolly* in Massachusetts, 1971

Right, a 1974 film, *For Pete's Sake,* with Barbra Streisand

BERT MORGAN

1940, with Al Jolson

With Governor Al Smith while playing in *Morning Star* on Broadway

Working on *The Jazz Singer* with Jerry Lewis on TV

Molly and Yonkel with Golda Meir in Jerusalem, 1955

Backstage at *Milk and Honey* with Mary Martin, Ethel Merman and Mimi Benzell

Backstage with Helen Hayes

Robert Merrill sang "O Promise Me" at Molly and Yonkel's golden wedding.

Maurice Chevalier wanted to do a show with Molly in France but other commitments always interfered.

ARCHER ASSOCIATES

Molly and Yonkel in the film *Fiddler on the Roof*

Otherwise the few concerts I gave were badly received, and going to California clearly had been a big mistake. You can't win them all.

Our only accomplishment was seeing the other coast of America at war. We visited the Kaiser shipyards and saw 150,000 people working under one roof. Men and women in overalls scurried around the bony bowels of skeleton warships, and it was all a surrealistic, mechanical world. Spooky.

Many years later, we were in Israel when the Kaiser people began assembling cars there. A big to-do was arranged celebrating the first car to come off the assembly line. The car was to be presented very ceremoniously to David Ben-Gurion, the Israeli prime minister. However, since no government official was permitted to accept free gifts, Ben-Gurion was to give the Kaiser officials a token one-pound note. The car came off the line, was driven over to Ben-Gurion, who stood waiting with his wife, Paula, and someone gave him the keys. Ben-Gurion put his hand in his pocket and discovered that all he had was a two-pound note. Turning to his wife, he said, "What shall I do?" And Paula answered, "At this price, take two."

Our Kaiser tour aside, we were glad to say good-bye to California and hello to New York. I did my first club date at the Waldorf and was gratified that its audience still understood Yiddish.

Outside New York, however, Yonkel and I knew we would have to Anglicize our Jewish repertoire. Audiences just didn't understand the language anymore. All ethnic groups have gone through the same problem: How do you keep your own heritage while absorbing a new language and culture? Most of us fail, and thus we lose an entire world: the world of Sholem Aleichem, of the *shtetl*, of the wonder rabbis. In our profession there was no compromise, we would have to give up Yiddish, especially since Orthodox Jews avoided the theater. Yonkel and I managed to survive only because we started translating our act into what Sholem Asch had told me was the language of our people: English!

Later, while on a train trip upstate, I wrote a homage to a part of that language for our radio show. I called my song

"A Day in the Life of a New York Woiking Goil." It's been part of my show ever since.

Another memorable appearance I had at this time was a benefit for the Harlem Christmas Fund at the Apollo Theater. Bill Robinson introduced me and, although I was the only whitey in the hall, I felt accepted and appreciated—something not many of those great black entertainers could say about their treatment by others. A classic example occurred some years later when Yonkel and I were visiting Conrad Bercovici, the Romanian gypsy writer, then living on Central Park West. As we entered the lobby and stepped into an elevator, we heard the elevator operator say to someone behind us, "You'll have to take the servants' elevator." We turned around just as he shut the door on Paul Robeson and his wife. And the elevator man was black.

Racism, Jew bastard, war. When would we learn to follow the Bible and love thy neighbor?

We celebrated the welcome demise of 1943 with Yonkel dressed as Father Time and I, in a diaper, as the New Year. And lo, because I was now appearing in so many *goyisher* clubs, I finally broke through into the Jewish hotels where they had shied away from Jewish acts. It was okay for non-Jews to sing Yiddish songs, but, as Yonkel used to say, "If a Jew wanted to sing 'Eli Eli' he had to blacken his face." That year, I played Grossinger's, Breezelawn, Fallsview, Brickman's, even Saratoga, which was full of Hasidim—all those Orthodox Jews who weren't supposed to go to theater.

Mostly, however, Yonkel and I joined our colleagues on the "Soldier Circuit." We went first to Camp Patrick, where I did two shows for the service clubs and one Oneg Shabbat for the Jewish boys. The elderly Jews from nearby towns brought in chopped chicken livers and strudel and the boys loved it. At the next camp, the Norfolk U.S.O., after I had sung ten songs, one of the boys yelled, "Molly, you don't have to sing anymore. Just let us look at you."

In Dayton, the Jewish Welfare Board gave our servicemen a bagel-and-lox Sunday breakfast, and me for morale. In Indianapolis and Chicago, the Jewish boys all asked me to sign autographs written in Yiddish for their mothers. At home, many of them had never been to a Jewish show. It took a war to remind them of their roots.

Yonkel was wonderful at all these concerts. He knew just what to say, and the boys loved him. He always took down the names and addresses of their families back home; later we'd call the families, and so many mothers would ask, "Is my boy eating all right?"

In the midst of all this, we did manage to squeeze in a party at the home of Mrs. Gershwin and her "Georgie." We arrived late and I told George how sorry I was we had missed hearing him play. It was after midnight, but Gershwin immediately sat down at the piano and played his "Rhapsody in Blue." He played brilliantly; then he sang for us. As he said, "I don't sing good—but I do sing loud." Gershwin told us his dream was to go to Poland, live there for a year and absorb its Jewish life, especially the rabbinate. Eventually he wanted to write an opera based on *The Dybbuk*. Instead, he died too young to realize his dream.

Fortunately, another youngster we heard around that same time did survive. A few months earlier, at Carnegie Hall, we had seen a twenty-six-year-old Jewish conductor named Leonard Bernstein conduct his own symphony, *Jeremiah*. Were we proud!

The war news also swelled our chests. Germany seemed weakened, and, in a burst of crazy optimism, I began to study Russian grammar for our next European tour. Soon afterward, the radio stations all carried reports that Rome had fallen to the Allies. The enormity of the invasion was beyond our comprehension. President Roosevelt broadcast a prayer and predicted Russia would also start an offensive soon. My travel plans seemed less fantastic.

In the interim, however, what could we do? Tour, tour, and tour some more! We were off to Chattanooga to Camp Oglethorpe and a (small) all-girl audience of Army WACS.

What followed was a khaki blur: Camp Wheeler in Georgia, where the spangles on my gown melted in the hundred-degree heat; Anniston and Fort McClellan; Keesler Field in Biloxi, and someplace in Augusta. That summer, every show was done in seething weather, my bare midriff glistened, and

I kept on singing. At the end of that tour, the Jewish Welfare Board presented me with a bracelet of silver charms representing each branch of the Army. But I had already collected my laurels from those young faces in the sweltering crowds.

On August 23, 1944, we were all rewarded with great news. Paris was free! The French patriots effected the final liberation. We took Marseilles, and Bucharest announced it had accepted the Russian peace offer. I celebrated in song at Father Duffy's Canteen and the Marine Base Hospital on Staten Island. Every victory meant I was closer to getting back to Europe and performing for my beloved people—whatever was left of them.

When I played Fort Ontario in Oswego, New York, I got a sad inkling of their fate. It was September 14, 1944. I remember the day clearly.

Throughout the war, practically no Jewish refugees were allowed to migrate freely to America. Instead, at Oswego, nine hundred Jews from Poland, Vienna, Paris, Greece and Africa were being held on the Canadian border behind barbed wire and guard towers—exactly like the prisoners of war they were.

All of them had seen me or my films, and their faces were wonderful to behold. We ate with them, listened to their heartbreaking stories, and tried to give them something joyful. One poor man had a magazine he had managed to hang onto all through the Holocaust. It had a picture of me from 1923.

With so many people wanting to see and hear us, I insisted that we do two shows instead of the single one that had been scheduled. The show's organizer, a German Jew, refused, insisting that only one show had been planned. I, however, was equally adamant.

"We didn't come all this way," I fumed, "to perform for only half these people!" The organizer relented and we played two shows to packed houses. In gratitude, those poor, homeless Jews gave us the only treat they had: fresh orange juice.

There were many non-Jews, of course, soldiers who also needed cheering up. Once, after performing some *vodvil* at the National Theater, we picked up four Scottish soldiers to give them some kind of treat. These Scots had ferried a boatload of German prisoners to New York City and they looked so bewildered on the lower East Side. Trying to put them at ease, Yonkel and I took them to a bar on Second Avenue. We insisted that they enjoy a round of Scotch whiskey on us. They gulped down one drink, then another. By the third round, we interrupted to ask them if they liked the drinks, and they said they didn't know what they were drinking! When we told them it was Scotch whiskey, they said they never drank it in Scotland because they preferred beer. We could have saved ourselves a bit of money had we asked them what they wanted to start with.

Our vaudeville at the National was a new venture, with songs and scenes from *Shmendrick*. Robert Garland of the *Journal-American* saw the show and wrote that he didn't know why I didn't come uptown unless it was that I didn't like Gentiles. Then he added, "But some of Molly's best friends are *goyim* like me." He was hospitalized soon after and I sent him flowers and some of Mama's cookies. He was so touched he nearly kissed me over the phone.

In a schedule already stuffed with vaudeville and bond rallies, I squeezed in some nightclubs and was shocked at the changes. The comics were waving the flag and toilet paper interchangeably and everyone seemed happy with the jokes but me. I never liked a level of humor which made me shrivel inside. Following a dirty comic is like stepping into a dirty latrine—something to be avoided at all cost. I was glad to get back to playing benefits.

Nineteen forty-five was a tumultuous year. F.D.R. died, and the shock was so great that people still hadn't absorbed it. Mrs. Roosevelt sensed this when she said she was sorrier for America than she was for herself. We felt terribly lost. Then Germany surrendered; yet we worked as if it was just another day. (Yonkel had called to remind me it was my birthday, and he joked that he loved me even in my old age.) But not a mention of the Nazis' fall.

I continued touring, and the visits with wounded servicemen—young boys who'd never walk again—depressed me more and more. I had little joy in the sensational new atomic bomb that was dropped on Hiroshima. We didn't discuss, nor did we know, its future effects. But at the war's end, we just screamed "Hurrah, it's over," along with everyone else.

Yonkel and I immediately applied to the Jewish Labor Committee for the chance to go to Europe. We had already been fingerprinted, had filled out all the forms, and just prayed we'd be eligible. We offered to pay all our expenses, and they accepted *if* we got our passports and visas. Our plan was to leave in the early spring and do free concerts wherever we found survivors.

Yonkel announced our plans during his radio show and his sponsor immediately offered us a shipload of free food for the survivors. Others began donating odds and ends, and our anxiety to fulfill our plans mounted with each gift.

A friend returned from overseas and told us gruesome stories about the destruction. When the New Year arrived, our passports came with it, complete with discouraging literature about the hardship and disease that awaited. All the news from Europe was bad—but we were going just the same.

CHAPTER 8

As WE AWAITED the proper visas from Belgium, Poland, Sweden and other countries, Yonkel and I had the whole family making packages to take overseas. In them were needles, thread, buttons and some of life's little pleasures: makeup and some costume jewelry. Everyone laughed at the idea, saying that all the D.P.s needed was food and medicine. But I felt that if I were a woman deprived for seven years of a lipstick or a nice piece of glitter, those would be the things I longed for—and so we packed them. All were new, no leftovers, and we wrapped them in gay, colorful paper. Many people sent beautiful little gifts for us to include, and I knew the women in the camps would appreciate such luxuries.

Our mail was also full of special pleas, both small and large. In one batch were requests from women asking for nylon stockings (and perhaps some Max Factor rouge), along with a letter from Harry Herbert in Shanghai telling about the hopeless lot of the twenty thousand Jews there, all D.P.s. Patients in a hospital collected fifty dollars among themselves and asked us to buy presents for the refugees, while the wife of Rabbi Stephen Wise urged us to write to her about whatever bad things we uncovered at the camps that she might help to correct.

We, in the meantime, bit our nails over our missing visas. We spent an entire day at the French Consulate but without luck. They were understaffed and inefficient and late, late, late. Ditto the English, who had not even answered our cables, and the Swedish—who didn't come through until the week we were supposed to sail.

It was all hurry up and wait as we tried to pack. We

bought two U.S.O. fiber bags, light but sturdy, and had quite a mixture of things to put into them. Medicines were the first items on our list, then sanitary pads, Kleenex, toilet paper, towels, pens and pencils and—due to the rumors that Europe's cupboards were bare—concentrated food tablets. All absolute necessities.

All the visas arrived and our friends and colleagues sent us off with a round of farewell luncheons. Everyone's emotions were high. The Daughters of Israel presented me with a citation and Stella Adler gave a most sensitive, elegant speech. She cried, I cried, the women cried. Finally, in gratitude, I sang, made all the crying women laugh and came home emotionally exhausted. Yonkel and I would be the first entertainers to tour the D.P. camps since the war's end and we wanted so much for our mission to be a success.

Strangers, too, wished us well. People would stop us on the street and give us a dollar bill to "buy something for the children." One man slipped us fifty dollars for the young boys in the hospitals. One woman brought an old fur coat to take to a sister in Brussels and another woman brought a package of infant's clothes to take to her sister's baby in Lodz. Our janitor gave us a box of chocolate bars for any little one, while our friend Dora Weisman, a fine Yiddish actress, brought Yiddish plays and music for surviving Yiddish actors, wherever we might find them. We could have collected even more. Everybody wanted to give something, especially to us, because they felt we would have direct contact with people there.

A seamen's strike postponed our sailing briefly, but on May 9, 1946, we were off. And did we have luggage! A trunkful of cosmetics, a duffel bag full of food, the U.S.O. bags and the four valises and the package of plays and music.

We sailed on the U.S. warship *Santa Paula,* a gray, drab vessel. We shared a drab room that contained two bunks, one on top of the other, and two chairs. Our only luxury was a shower and a toilet, which we had to ourselves. Other passengers were jammed five and six to a room, families were separated, crying children put in with feeble old people.

Half the cabins were reserved as hospitals for the wounded who'd be returning. The dining room consisted of long army tables; there was no bar, no lounge, nothing but bare necessities. Food would be plentiful, but absolutely Army Ordinary. Standards were definitely down. There was no service of any kind so we just fell into the ship's routine. We were up at eight for breakfast, where we'd gossip about the rich cruise food, then stuff ourselves full of greasy fried eggs. We'd walk on deck, then return for lunch at one, always meat and soup, and again we'd all eat too much and too nervously. Eating was the only activity on board, and most passengers devoured the whole works.

Our shipmates were varied. There were French, English and Scandinavians, all going home to visit. There were some war brides anxious to join their husbands, one English vocalist who had heard me sing "Woiking Goil" on the B.B.C., and an appropriately proper Bostonian who had two hounds in France, and the family jewels. When we weren't eating, our other major pastime was trading rumors on what we were allowed and not allowed to take into France. As I remember, cigarettes, matches and soap seemed to be on the forbidden list, but I still haven't the faintest idea why.

Yonkel and I used the voyage as a chance to recapture the pure Yiddish we had anglicized. We began talking only in Yiddish to each other. We'd start each day with language lessons and bicarbonate pills.

We arrived in Plymouth on the 16th. From afar, all I could see was a cool green countryside with no visible signs of the havoc of war. Then some ruddy-faced inspectors came on board and interviewed passengers landing in England. I hid my store of nylons and got ready for France.

We reached Le Havre the next day. Its harbor was less tranquil than Plymouth's. A Liberty Ship lay half submerged and another was almost completely sunk. On board, there was a quick inspection of passports, then we were off to customs. We declared our six cartons of cigarettes, gave the inspector a packet, and he let us quickly through.

Le Havre was in ruins, its port completely destroyed. Only an American lend-lease movable pier of steel still functioned. As we landed, a troop ship of American boys on their way home greeted us with "Hello, suckers! You'll be sorry!"

Their words echoed in my head as Yonkel and I walked

around. People were in rags, with wooden shoes, no stockings, and their legs chapped and sore. Children were spindle-legged from malnutrition and vacant-looking. In the midst of such sorrow, we had a drink in a local café and were joined by two eternal Russian refugees, once-affluent Jews who had been on the run since the fall of the Czar. Here they were, still sitting on their suitcases, wondering what country in the world would take them.

We traveled by train to Paris—a clean, comfortable ride but without food. We bought a sandwich with a food coupon and observed the countryside. All the bridges we passed had been destroyed—a temporary one had been set up for our train. Everyone we saw was on bicycles and every inch of ground was cultivated, just like our victory gardens. Here, of course, these fields represented more than patriotism. They meant avoiding starvation.

We arrived in Paris, where the Jewish actors and the Labor Committee awaited us with flowers. Our taxi looked like a jalopy out of the 1890s.

Our quarters were at the Hotel Moderne, rue de Rivoli, where we had once stayed in 1921. Then, we had seen a Paris without scars, although it had lacked extras—sugar, milk, white bread. In 1946, we found a city full of bread, butter, milk and jam, but with its soul gone. Everyone told his story with a kind of braggadocio: "See, I'm still alive!" Now and then there was a tear, but no hysterics. There was quiet sadness everywhere.

We sought out old places and, hopefully, old friends. Dining at Joseph's, our old Jewish restaurant, we learned that Joseph's wife had been a deportee, which meant killed. Meeting old friends, Dr. Louis and Chaikele Schwartz, we heard how they had once headed the American Hospital in Paris, fled to England, then returned to a demolished apartment. The Nazis didn't even leave a nail. Chaikele's parents, Yiddish actors who'd played with us when we did *Yonkele* at the Lancry in 1921, had been murdered in Auschwitz. All we could do was listen to their nightmares and offer scant balm: a medical book for Louis, some nylon stockings for Chaikele, and bars of chocolates for their children, one of whom had contracted polio.

In the evening, we attended a Circle Amical meeting full of Socialist red-hot radicals. Among the Jews who remained, it was all politics as before. They denounced all groups, especially Zionists and Americans who financed Zionism. During a break in their mad debate, a boy and girl from the Vilna ghetto got up and sang, and the entire thing was macabre.

Throughout our stay, Jewish actors came to our hotel to sit, talk about each other, and blame everyone for their situation. They all kept saying that American Jews had not done enough, that money never reached the right people. All of Paris seemed to be outdoors: street performers sang, acrobats did their stunts, orchestras played and queues were lined up everywhere.

Our first performance was a return to the Lancry, and the house was full, since everyone knew we would be there. Yonkel began with a touching speech about brotherhood when he was suddenly interrupted by a fistfight in the balcony. Apparently a refugee from a concentration camp had recognized a Jew who had been in charge there and who beat the inmates. The audience took the fracas quite calmly; someone said, "See what Hitler taught us." Later, a sister of one of our actresses came to our hotel. She was dirty and bedraggled. We gave her some things that had been sent to her, and she told us woefully, "You are our pride and joy. We are none of us normal any more."

The next day we began seeing people in the American Embassy who might help us get into Germany. We also met a Polish government official who promised to help us get into Poland. We gave him a stack of food and candy and asked that it be distributed in his country. He accepted, then added he'd like some for himself and his family. We just prayed he wouldn't help himself too generously.

Edith Piaf, one of France's legendary entertainers, was singing at the Club Cinq that evening and we walked over to catch her show. She was the most amazing, glorious chanteuse I'd ever heard.

Piaf was about fifty then, small, frail and disheveled. Her features were not pretty. She looked like an ugly little girl in a short black dress with her petticoat showing. But—how she could sing! She didn't belt out a song, but she had tremendous presence, a good register, and a full, honest voice laced with tears. She would just stand up and sing out. We sat on the floor and were spellbound for over an hour. We were especially thrilled that, knowing we'd be in the audience, she directed her songs to us and sang right in front of us. Her biggest anger, she told us that night, was that the Nazis took her youth away. We were moved and horrified. The next day I sent her three pairs of nylons and a fan letter.

The gesture was the most wildly extravagant one I could make, considering France's shortages at that time. Prices were just crazy then, but few protested against the black market and lawlessness was rampant. All the Jews we met (each with a number branded on his arm) complained that the French didn't want to work but preferred to live day to day by whatever means were the easiest. They said there were French who had helped Jews, but also others who sold them out for a few francs. What a sorry state!

The disintegration of the French depressed me, and we arranged to spend a day out in the country at La Verenne, where the Jewish Labor Committee ran an orphans' home. The children, ranging in age from four to sixteen, were well-behaved and well-fed, but still very frightened after their concentration camp experiences. All had lost one or both of their parents; other family and friends had been lost as well. I sang for them in French and Yiddish and they laughed and applauded and sneezed with me when I sang "I have a cold in my nose—*ketchu!*" We had brought along a bar of chocolate for each one, and they smelled them rapturously and were loath to open and eat them. Although they were being well cared for, it was clear what they wanted was to be fondled and loved.

The laughter of these damaged children prepared us for our first big concert in front of an entirely Jewish audience. We appeared in Salle Gaveau, Paris, on the 28th of May and there was an air of expectancy throughout the hall when we walked onstage. Everyone came knowing a crucial barrier was about to fall, and it did. Although it took us twenty minutes to do it, we made these tragic Jews laugh and our hearts expanded with joy at the sound. Yonkel almost fainted with emotion. Once the dam of pain and terror and fear was burst, their warmth and appreciation just flew up to us. We did five hundred years of Yiddish theater in song and dance in appreciation. It was a memorable evening for the audience and for us.

Our second concert for the local Jewish Actors Group, provided a similar response. We were the first actors to come to them simply as performers—not for charity or inspection. We gave a good concert, in full gear, and were thrilled to the core.

On June 1st, I also celebrated my second birthday of the year. (Various records list me as having been born either February 28th or June 1st. Naturally, I celebrate both dates.) I was forty-eight, suddenly becoming a legendary figure to the Jews, but I didn't feel it. The Allied French Kultur Verband gave a reception full of praise and gratitude for my mission. Unfortunately, we were having a great deal of trouble getting to the camps. Even England refused us permission. So I accepted everyone's thanks with a great deal of anxiety, hoping to get on with the work I had come to do.

Not that there weren't concerts to give right in France. We improvised stages and did hastily arranged shows (always for free) at homes and orphanages, at shabby halls and grand theaters, but Eastern Europe—Warsaw, Lodz and Rybach— was always at the back of our minds.

Our little traveling show did get out of Paris in June, when we arranged to perform in Belgium and Holland. Slowly we were branching out to reach more survivors, and spending a day with them proved more of a strain than the concerts.

All the deportees had horror stories. How the Nazis killed the children first, forcing the parents to give them up knowing they would be gassed and burned. If the parents didn't surrender their children, they took the parents too. Inmates dreamed of eating just a chunk of fresh bread or potatoes in their skins. A shoestring was a cherished item, because they wore heavy wooden shoes and needed the strings to tie them on. If they came untied and inmates stumbled and fell, they were beaten or shot for falling.

But the worst stories were about the degradation among themselves. How such suffering weakened morale so that they often fought among themselves for that shoestring. Jews were ordered to beat other Jews, and some became so sadistic that they were more brutal than the Germans. These survivors said the most intelligent died first because they didn't have the resistance (and cunning) to last. And imagine the horror of having survived and then living with such memories.

In Bruxelles, we sang for the Jewish Brigade. They were leaving for Palestine (and, hopefully, a future) but for that night, they just laughed and applauded. Brigadier General Benjamin, an English Jew with a monocle, sat in front, and he had no British reserve—he laughed until tears were in his eyes.

Another moving concert was given at the Children's Summer Colony near the Ardennes Forest. Seventy-six homeless children were being cared for by only four women. There were no toys, no organized games, just food and sleep. The tots took care of themselves and each other. They were dirty and unkempt but seemed healthy; I guess they were used to dirt and self-reliance. We came away feeling the relief work to be done was a gargantuan task.

Not only did physical wounds need healing, but so many philosophical splits remained—despite even the Holocaust. A banquet was given for us in Bruxelles, and there we quickly sensed how divided, politically, the Jews were. An undercurrent of discord ran through all their speeches, and it was so sad that they hadn't grown a bit by their shared trauma. To us, it felt like this was where we came in, twenty-five years ago, after World War I. Not just in Jewish life, but in European thinking, it was the same chauvinism, the same nationalism, the same class differences. They had learned nothing.

Back in Paris, we continued our rounds, trying to get into Poland. Finally a Madame Rosinoff, a Jew who hid her Jewishness, pulled some strings. M. Rosinoff was head of the Transportation Department at the Polish Embassy. For eighteen hundred francs each, she promised us plane reservations straight to Warsaw. However, her machinations would take a week, which meant hanging on in Paris.

So we waited, discouraged. All officialdom proved pompous and dishonest. They didn't say no and they didn't say yes. But they always took your money. As Mayor La Guardia used to say, "Patience and fortitude," to which we added, "And *mezuma*—money!"

At last the red tape broke, and our Polish visas were arranged within half an hour (no bribes). Our contact man, a Mr. Zayden, said he had plane reservations for the following day. I didn't believe it. But we were packed and ready, just in case.

Zayden's reservations did, in fact, come through; but nothing that followed had been planned on.

Eager to begin our trip, Yonkel and I were up by 7:00 A.M., and we quickly taxied to the airport. Madame Rosinoff, puffed up with her position, briefly floated in and out while her assistant casually relieved us of 36,000 francs, filled out forms, then piled us onto a bus along with ten others. We were abruptly deposited on (not near) the airfield, where we caught a glimpse of our plane, way out yonder on a grassy plot.

Groaning at the distance, we started lugging our bags out to the Polish military aircraft. We hoisted everything on board, then entered to find no seats, no belts, and nothing but parachute gadgets overhead. This was no luxury flight. We jammed ourselves onto long wooden benches, the pilot banged the door shut, and we awaited takeoff by gazing at a large picture of Stalin that glared down upon us.

The pilot started the motor, then stopped and announced, *"Magnet myema."* Yonkel, our Polish expert, gloomily translated the problem: a broken magnet. We were all made to pile out—nine of us and one Polish official. We were told to wait, and I rushed back to the station to buy something to eat because food was also *myema.* Several hours later, the magnet was fixed, we piled back in, the door closed, Stalin resumed his glaring at us and we were off!

We flew very high and everyone froze, I, too, despite a blanket of newspapers Yonkel had hastily arranged. Since we were late, the pilot decided to gamble on a shortcut, and he flew over forbidden territory. We held our breaths, waiting for gunfire. When we at last touched down safely, Yonkel opened a bottle of vodka we had sneaked aboard, passed out paper cups, and we toasted the ground. They cheered *Nazdrouga* and we, *L'chayim.*

Our passports were checked and we were unceremoniously packed onto a truck for the drive to Warsaw. The destruction that greeted us is impossible to fully describe.

The Germans had strafed and shelled this city unremittingly throughout 1944, and whatever buildings had still been left standing collapsed from the bombs and fires. Every public square, every park and other open space became a mass graveyard. A ghost town was all that remained of this once lively city, and everyone we saw looked haunted.

Somehow, and we don't know how, the Jewish Committee was there with flowers to meet us. Immediately they arranged for us to appear in barracks, in children's orphanages, on radio. They also provided a pianist, a lovely young girl, to accompany me. I explained my songs to her and she took the music home to study. Mainly, however, we gossiped about clothes and prices. I learned you could get everything in Poland—for money.

We wanted to get to Lodz, where Yonkel's mother had died, and knew the people there were still brutal. There had always been great anti-Semitism among the Poles, and it remained. A goodly number of Polish Jews had been extremely cultured and financially successful, and jealousy, combined with the old anti-Semitic feelings, had combined to make the Poles embrace the Nazi persecutions and join in. Now we had arrived, and many people clearly didn't want us around. I was hardened to their attitudes, but I was still not prepared for the tragedy of the Warsaw Ghetto.

Yonkel and I had sought out the old Nyalefkes, where we had appeared in the Kaminski Theater in 1921, but all was a heap of stones. There was not a sign of a house, or store, or synagogue, or theater. In 1940, 400,000 Jews had been herded here in an area two and a half miles long and only a mile wide. By 1943, 340,000 had perished, victims of starvation or worse—the death camps. Yet, the pitiful few thousands who remained staged the most dramatic Jewish counteroffensive of the war: the Warsaw Ghetto Uprising. For three weeks in April of 1943, they attacked both German and Polish Nazi forces until finally subdued by tanks, artillery fire, flames and dynamite. Fifty-six thousand Jews were exterminated. Only the ghetto streets—Mila, Lesno, Nalewki —remained. All else was rubble, totally wiped out, right down to the Orthodox cemetery, where graves were overturned and their contents desecrated. Not even Jews already dead were spared.

We also viewed the prison camps and the gas chambers. Out of the stones and the ashes of human bodies, Yonkel and I picked up the scraps from a prayer book and the sole of a baby's shoe. We then went to see the cornerstone erected in memory of the Jewish heroes who died in the Ghetto Uprising. It was a poor little stone, still unfinished, but beautiful to our eyes, which were filled with the horrors committed by the Nazi hordes. May they never be forgiven for their crimes —never!

But enough. We had expected the worst and we had seen it, but we had no time to cry. Yonkel and I put our emotions aside and gave thanks for the sweet balm of music. We had concerts to provide and plenty of problems about how to provide them.

We needed lights and seating and music. We remembered these audiences and wanted to show them the laughter and song they once knew. We especially wanted to be elegant for the highly cultivated Warsaw Jews. Years before, during a visit in 1936, they had presented me with an exquisite cut-crystal vase, then and now worth a small fortune (I treasure it still). Yonkel and I wanted to pay them homage, and so I had carted a long white gown through the wreckage and Yonkel his white tie and tails. Dressed to the hilt, on whatever makeshift stage was provided, we prepared to meet the survivors.

Our concerts began in the barracks for repatriates—in this case, Jews who had returned from Russia only to find nothing. They were four or five hundred miserable creatures, in rags, sick, dirty, living with only the barest necessities. Yet these unfortunates had built a hall, improvised a stage, found benches, rigged up three lights overhead, and even made a poster by hand (all Jewish print had been destroyed by the Nazis). We gratefully appeared in their fantastic creation.

They jammed into the hall, leaving no room to breathe. Yonkel and I had planned for comedy, comedy, comedy—you don't cry in front of a dying patient. We knew there would be that stunned silence at first, as in Paris, but we were determined to reach past the war's barriers. We sang for over two hours, without a pause, and for the first time in six or seven years, these Jews were laughing, clapping their hands and yelling *Bis*—More! A little girl brought us flowers onstage, daisies and buttercups, and she curtsied as she handed them to us. Everyone tried so hard to make the evening *yontifdig* (full of holiday spirit). Afterward, they all crowded around us, each with letters to take to relatives elsewhere in Europe. It was all so hopeless, there was so little we could do, and I cried, "God help them."

In Prague the following morning, we gave another concert with a piano this time, and we began to feel at home on the improvised stages. Then, still dressed in our evening clothes from the night before, we boarded an open truck and were driven to a children's summer colony. Waiting were over five hundred little ones sitting on the grass.

I sang and danced, recited and did somersaults in my elegant gown while Yonkel, in his tuxedo, told funny stories. Most of the children had returned from Russia seeking parents who were no longer there. Others had been hidden during the war on nearby farms. They were intelligent, talented, beautiful children and—despite what they had endured—responsive.

Let me share an example. It started raining while I sang, and, since the children were sitting on the wet grass, I said, "We better stop. It's raining." And a little boy, four or five, stood up and said, "There is no rain. Sing!" So I sang with the rain pouring down my fancy dress, and they sat there and laughed and shouted for more. They went back to their children's home jammed into trucks, standing up, singing and waving good-bye. We cried and laughed and waved back, soaking wet, but who cared?

Everywhere we went, we shared something pure and joyful after all the pain. Once, at a concert for grownups, a woman brought a small, undernourished child and it started to cry. Yonkel went over to her and asked her why she had brought such a young child to the concert. She answered, "My baby is three years old and she has never heard the sound of laughter. I don't want her to grow up without hearing people laugh!"

Every story was poignant. People began visiting us and soon theirs would tumble out, such as the dancers who spent seven years in Russia living on trains, cooking on stones, without a permanent address, always on the move. And everyone wants to go to America except the actors from Lodz.

There, in the place once the source from which all Yiddish theater drew its players, only about fifty actors remained. They eagerly accepted the plays Dora Weisman had sent, and they spoke excitedly of filling their small hall with acting again. Today, of course, nothing is left of Yiddish life there. What those poor, forsaken actors didn't realize was that Hitler had already exterminated their audience—nobody was left for whom to perform.

There was no way we could impart those sad realities to them when we shared a humble banquet Artisten Verein and the rest had prepared for us. We had reached Lodz by train courtesy of a Mr. Ornstein, an impresario who insisted he could arrange to ferry us all over to give our free concerts. We reached Lodz after three and a half hours, and what was left of the Jewish theater in Lodz immediately began fussing over us. They looked to us as a harbinger of a new lease on life. We were the first to come to them out of any kind of goodness. The women received our gift packages and each one recalled how for six years she had never had a powder compact, or a puff, or a lipstick. In their poverty, our little pieces of jewelry were deeply welcomed. How I wish we could have also preserved their former, now doomed, way of life.

Our next concert was in the Baltic *kino* (cinema) and

thank God, our performance went without mishap. To appear in Poland in 1946 in Yiddish and in public was a risk. But to appear in a Polish *kino* at 11:00 P.M. was foolhardy. The Poles emptied out when their film was finished (they hardly wanted to mingle) and the Jews came in and jammed the theater. No one believed we'd have more than half a house. Jews just didn't congregate like that anymore. They especially avoided being seen at night, even after the war. Yet there was standing room only by 11:00 P.M. and nobody left. We played to an audience of heroes and heroines and they stayed to enjoy it. People who were on the run, here, there, anywhere, to get out of Poland took their lives in their hands in order to see and hear us. It was more than a performance. It was an outpouring of love, for us and for anything Yiddish.

One last journey still remained for us in Lodz. We knew Yonkel's mother had died during the war but we lacked details. Yonkel set out to find answers and he began at the apartment he had bought for his mother long ago. There he found two Polish girls living, with crucifixes on the walls but still sleeping on his mother's bedding. They had taken over everything but knew nothing about how she died—or so they said.

Yonkel returned sad and confused. His mother had been in her eighties when she died so her life had been a long one. All Yonkel worried about was that it might have ended brutally like so many others. Then a neighbor of Yonkel's mother came to see us. He was a tailor who had lived near her during the last months of her life. From him, Yonkel learned that his mother had been forced to move out of Lodz and into the ghetto. She grew a garden and the whole ghetto loved her. She always carried our pictures and sang our songs for her neighbors. The tailor said that when she sang "Yiddel with His Fiddle," she had her own version. Instead of the verse, "A bird flies high, good morning," she sang, "A bird flies high and says good morning to the Jews." When he asked her why the Jews, she answered: "What then? To the *goyim*, let him say something else!"

The neighbor told us that she had died of dysentery, and was properly buried. A few months later, her husband, Foigel Gonif, also died a natural death, and our hearts were overjoyed that they were spared most of the Nazi horrors. But not all. Since here, too, the cemeteries were all desecrated or destroyed. There would be no stone, no plants for her grave, or for any of Yonkel's small family, all of whom had perished.

From Lodz, we went to Helenowka and yet another children's home. Here we were startled to find a young boy standing guard with a bayonet. The children were shabby, as expected, but well-fed and treated like children, with a few toys, decorations on the walls and a big picture of Yanushe Kerozak, the teacher who had led his children singing into the gas chambers at Treblinka and died with them.

We gave a big concert for the children, and as they laughed and applauded, we kept thinking, How soon will they, too, have to run away?

We ended our Warsaw tour shortly afterward, wrapping up our visit in a dirty hotel room we had wangled after the usual exchange of zlotys. The bed had more humps than a camel and its linen was filthy, but our discomfort was mild after what we had seen and heard.

We continued on to Rybach and Walbzych and the rest of that emotion-filled tour. There are memories of a drunken Polish soldier greeting us before one concert in the former German Staadt Theater by chanting, "I kill you, I kill you," mingled with touching scenes of survivors in our audiences finding relatives they thought were dead. I remember orphaned Jewish children marching in the streets of Rybach singing "We will build Palestine," while other repatriates just sat resignedly waiting—for what?

Our bones hurt from bad beds and bad buses, we felt grimy from no baths, but we were ashamed to complain after one look at our audiences. Our tour ended with a telegram from another impresario, Leonidoff, who wanted us back in Paris to play the Sarah Bernhardt Theater in September.

We wrapped things up with a farewell performance in the Polish Theater in Prague. The Poles actually called off their own performance in order to allow us to give a concert for the Jews.

And we played to a joyful full house. Cries of "Go in good health" and "Come back to us!" rang out. There was the ritual banquet and all political parties—left, right, center

—united to sing Hallelujah to us. They called us heroes to have braved the Polish-Yiddish front. Yonkel thanked them with a beautiful, stirring speech in which he pleaded for harmony. We left Poland at midnight and came away with the feeling that if we had done nothing but this tour, we had earned our *Olom Habah V'olom Hazeh*—our place in Heaven and Earth.

On August 22nd, at 6:00 A.M., we were at the airfield and eager, after four weeks of D.P. camps, to return to *jolie* Paris. We were still digesting all we had seen and heard in Poland and hoped Paris might soothe our unsettled stomachs.

But first, inspection. At that time, it was illegal to take any printed or written matter out of the country; yet Yonkel and I were carrying over fifty letters to be delivered to family and friends in America. We held our breath as we waited to see just how thoroughly the Polish officials would search. Strangely, they chose to be not too thorough. They didn't even open our baggage. Instead, they removed one letter I was carrying, then let us pass.

We laughed about having our load lightened in such a small way when we boarded our aircraft. It was piled high with packages and mail. The plane got off the ground, but not for long. Overloaded and out of gas, we were forced to land at Schönfeld Airport in Berlin. This was a Russian zone at the time, full of red flags and Russian soldiers. There the now not-very-supermanish Germans did the fetching and carrying. They reshuffled our cargo, refueled our plane and sent us aloft. During the brief hop between Berlin and Paris, we chatted with a Polish newspaperman, a Jew, who had recognized us. He had nothing but praise for Poland's "new democratic regime" and nothing but criticism for America, especially its treatment of Negroes. We listened, but that was all. We'd seen too much war to pick a fight.

One hour later we landed at Le Bourget, taxied to Les Invalides, arranged for a room, and let the revived charm of Paris seep into our bones. Our manager, Leonidoff, could scarcely believe our encounters in Poland. Even Yonkel and I couldn't fully grasp all that had happened only a few hours away. The change was too fast.

The next morning we walked to the American Express office and gathered up the threads of our American existence: letters, cables, offers of work and—best of all—a lovely new picture of Mama. Such bounty seemed like gifts from the moon after these past few weeks. Was there still a normal world somewhere?

We placed a request with the authorities for a September flight back home, then began to savor our surroundings.

Life was easier in Paris now. People dressed better, there was even more life in the streets and restaurants, cafés were full, and prices no longer exorbitant. Yonkel surmised that the sudden improvement over the Paris we had visited only a few months before was due to lots of fresh money from America—including ours. Here we had a triple bed, a wonderful mattress, a bath, towels and toilet paper. In Poland, I had carried an old telephone book with me—and used it.

Johannes Steel, a friend from New York who was in Paris for a conference, said post-war Paris was Lindy's without the herring. I told him Poland was not as black as was thought—which he liked hearing—but I should have added, "It's still blacker for our people."

We were just killing time, waiting for a plane home. Such leisure grew wearisome, however, especially for us. We were anxious to give our one concert at the Sarah Bernhardt and leave Paris. Thankfully, the evening proved worthy of the wait. Ben-Gurion was in our audience, along with many other international guests. We had worked hard preparing for that night and it paid off. The house was filled to the rafters and responded to every line. It was simply sky-high all the way. Afterward our dressing rooms were filled with well-wishers who said that what we had given them was more than a performance—that it had been an uplifting experience. Twenty violinists at Monseigneur Cabaret agreed. They saluted us with "Hatikvah," "Chusen," "Kaleh Mazel Tov" and "My Yiddishe Mama." Very French!

The next day offers poured in to tour around the world, but we had a radio contract to fulfill back home. Suddenly, however, we had to face some rather precarious travel plans. Three thousand Americans were stranded in Paris—but there was nothing to go home on. The best we could do was put ourselves on the "Show-Go" list—if, incredibly, someone with a ticket doesn't show, we go. But that was risky booking, especially with our Maxwell program ten days away.

Everyone knew we were desperate. Some suggested we go to Brazil and wait there for a connection; others cooked up equally farfetched schemes, but the reality was we had no way of getting home. Meanwhile, every wire from the United States brought added pressure, including the news that the Commodore Hotel had been reserved for a gala welcome home party only a week away. Yet, here we were, sitting at the Café de la Paix, along with other anxious people, listening to empty rumors and feeling hopeless.

Then, out of nowhere, a jeweler from Brussels suggested a plan. He introduced us to a man who had a ticket on the *Ernie Pyle* sailing the next day from Le Havre. The jeweler insisted that if we joined him, even without tickets, we still might get on board. We argued that this was impossible. He retorted, "You took a chance going to Poland where you might have been killed. So take a chance and go to Le Havre."

It was a crazy scheme—but nothing sane had worked so far. So we packed, then paid the hotel for the following week including money for the *petits déjeuners*. We were sure all was futile, yet we ventured forth. Optimists of the first order, we not only lugged bag and baggage, but also a bottle of champagne to uncork on departure!

The *Ernie Pyle* was an American troop ship that had been pressed into taking German-Americans back to the U.S. Many of these people had gone to Germany when Hitler took over and settled there. Now, with his fiasco over, they were having second thoughts. And, because their American citizenship was soon to expire—especially for those who'd been gone a while—many of them had to beat deadlines. Sailing on the *Ernie Pyle* was their last chance to get home. The ship was bulging with them—there was not an extra inch, let alone a berth.

We sat on an improvised pier at Le Havre, surrounded

by our bags, and stared at the teeming ship. Even the head man of the U.S. Lines told us there wasn't a ghost of a chance. We even tried our show biz "influence."

Yonkel noticed that one of the ship's officials looked Jewish. "Molly," he pleaded, "go over and tell him who you are. Please God, maybe he'll know you."

Well, I went, and he did. He beamed and asked for an autograph for his mother. Beyond that little exchange, however, he offered nothing. Six hours later, we were still standing on the pier. All the ships knew of our plight, and now and then someone would venture down and inform us, "Sorry," "Impossible" and all the words that meant No.

The bloom on our optimism wilted fast. Signaling to a purser, we gave him our *bon voyage* bottle of champagne, picked up our bags and prepared to leave.

Suddenly, the ship's captain came running down the gangplank shouting, "Wait! The dogs! The dogs!"

It seems two elderly German-Americans had smuggled their two dogs on board, which was against the law. One of our friendly pursers had ferreted them out. The captain told them they had two choices: Leave the dogs in Le Havre and sail home, or keep them and stay behind.

Without hesitating, they decided the dogs were more important than U.S. citizenship. They got off with their dogs and we got on. Until the gangplank was lowered, we still couldn't believe they had done it. Dogs have rated higher with us ever since.

CHAPTER 9

As for our trip on the *Ernie Pyle*—as we say on the East Side, "You shouldn't know from it." I had a berth in a cabin with twenty-four women, and Yonkel bunked with two hundred and forty men. All the passengers had to stand in line with their trays for meals. We ate with children and sick people, all of whom, thankfully, sat without making a noise. We needed at least some moments of quiet because sleep was impossible. My bed was the top berth in a triple-bunk bed, each berth set on top of another. I kept pads in my ears and a scarf over my eyes because the lights were on all night. We had been used to traveling with the privileged set; now we were traveling with the privy set. And the communal privies were anything but private—ditto the washroom. But —we were sailing!

Other than that glorious fact, however, our crossing proved to be a long, dull journey. There was absolutely nothing to do and absolutely nowhere to do it. The one indoor lounge, which ordinarily sat a hundred people, was now jammed with nine hundred and sixty souls—most of them sick. Only nine deck chairs were in sight, and the beleaguered Italian steward had already sold each one six times over. The purser called for war with the Russians, insisting we ought to drop the atom bomb on them immediately. Meanwhile, the German passengers talked about where the Jews should be dropped—preferably somewhere on the Equator! In such a mix we managed to pass the time with the UNRRA men, who played penny poker in their cabins.

UNRRA (United Nations Relief and Rehabilitation Administration) had a group of children on board, orphans whom they were taking back under U.S. Committee sponsorship to be placed in homes or adopted. Among them were eight Jews, seven Protestants, four Catholics and three "unknowns." One six-year-old Romanian-Jewish child, Clarissa Schwartz—who did not even have stockings—told us she had no parents, just one uncle in Baku, and that she spoke four languages. We fell in love with her and asked UNRRA for details about adoption. They said we must go through regular channels and wait.

Until then, we just sat with these damaged children and listened. One eight-year-old asked me, "If I lose my pencil in school, will they beat me?" Others just asked sadly with their eyes: Would people in America adopt us? They were both frightened and very friendly at the same time—desperately wounded by their pasts but equally desperate to please their way into some kind of future. Among them, only little Clarissa could speak a few words of English.

An old woman died on ship and was buried at sea. Another told how they took her sixty-two-year-old husband away and she never saw him again. And the Jewish youth spoke of the graft and thievery in the camps. We celebrated a very shabby Rosh Hashanah service on D deck with twenty deportees in rags. Yonkel and Mr. Storm, the man from HIAS, the Hebrew Immigrant Aid Society, performed the ceremony. Meanwhile, the head steward worried about the Orthodox women who wouldn't eat anything but hard-boiled eggs and baked potatoes. He asked me, "If Yonkel blessed a piece of pork bologna, would they eat it?" We were coming home once again with the same kind of tragic people who had emigrated in fear forty years before.

We did four hundred sixty miles a day, but the trip never got comfortable. In letters to our European friends explaining our getaway, I wrote, "What should have happened to the dogs happened to us." Poor Yonkel slept among two hundred and forty ill-assorted passengers, one of whom kept awakening at four in the morning. He hadn't set his watch back. When Yonkel would tell him it was 4:00 A.M., he'd say, "Impossible. I'm hungry now and I'm going to eat!" He told time by his stomach.

As our voyage was coming to an end the rumors began about when we'd dock: 6:00 P.M., 2:00 P.M., 8:00 P.M. All we hoped was that it'd be in time for our first Maxwell House program.

September 30, 1946. The fantastic finale to our fantastic tour. We docked at 9:30 A.M. and our radio producer, Mr. Kielson, was waiting on the pier. We were to do our radio spot at noon! But six hundred immigrants had to be cleared before us. No matter. We pushed our way to the head inspector, an Irishman who had seen me at the Palace, got him to shove us up front against every regulation, then turned to another inspector who'd seen me perform at the Albee in Brooklyn. He gave our passports a quick look and out we went.

Kielson had also done a little finagling on his own. On the dock, he'd mobilized a Jewish officer at Customs who knew us from the National. In five minutes we were through. Mama was waiting with Helen and Helen's son George. We kissed them all, handed them our luggage, then taxied to WEVD. In the cab, Yonkel outlined our program, which would involve some ad-libbing. We arrived at the radio station at 11:15, talked briefly with our pianist, and at noontime we were on. Our new Maxwell House program was called *Du und Dort* (Here and There). We told stories of our *Ernie Pyle* trip and sang *"Zug Nit Kein Mul Az du Gehst Dem Letzten Tog"* (Come What May, You Mustn't Say This Is the End). So began our show together. Three hours later, Yonkel was on his own Baker's Cocoa radio show—and where he got his material, I don't know.

Home. Hearth. Then the Invasion! People, phone calls, reporters, free benefits and "Auntie, do my hair," supper, family and—we're back. Yonkel started writing new scripts while I translated songs from the French and German. Everyone called for regards from their surviving relatives. Even *The New York Times* took note, reprinting an article about our journey that had run in the *Jewish Forward*.

We stepped right back into routine. Up early, we immediately resumed our forty-five-minute walk to the radio station. A quick browse through the shops along the way showed us that in spite of cries of scarcity, all looked to us like Lady Bountiful. There was plenty to buy, although the prices were high—but still not as steep as Paris.

Lots of work was waiting for Yonkel and me as soon as we got "systematized," which wasn't difficult.

Our first project was to raise money for toys for the Children's Fund, and Adolph Held, of the Amalgamated Bank, gave us our first five-hundred-dollar donation. After that, the requests kept coming in. The Jewish Welfare Board wanted us to do Texas in April; the William Morris Agency scheduled Chicago, Detroit, Cincinnati; and Judge Jonah Goldstein corraled us for the Grand Street Boys Beefsteak Dinner for Sir Louis Sterling and his lovely wife, Tessie.

In the midst of all this, we also managed to lunch with the Maxwell House biggies and quickly eased their apprehensions about our going "political" in our programs. We'd abide by the Radio Rule: "When in doubt, cut it out!"

And we wrote and wrote and wrote like mad. Yonkel scripted twelve radio shows a week (for Maxwell and for Baker's) plus one ongoing series about our trip for the *Forward*. I wrote several Maxwell shows but mainly I created new songs at a crazy pace: Write 'em, learn 'em, sing 'em and forget 'em!

We also began looking for new talent, and I especially remember one girl who auditioned for us. She had a lovely voice and accompanied herself beautifully. When I asked her to sing in Yiddish, however, she revealed she was a Negro and hence didn't know a word. Her plight was a sad one. She was too white for colored shows but didn't last long in white shows when they found out she was black. That's our Democracy?

We, on the other hand, were favored with some royal treatment. Broadway Sam gave us tickets to the hit musical *Annie Get Your Gun* without even charging his usual fee. A woman complained and he yelled, "These people come first. They did a great job and they gotta be entertained." And we were. Ethel Merman was *great*, the house strictly SRO and deservedly so. I also had the good fortune of seeing Helen Hayes in *Happy Birthday*. I have seen her perform through the years and have always felt a kinship with her. She is somebody you can look at and learn from. She is superb. God bless her.

Despite such occasional luxuries, however, life was skimpy then. Just try and buy shoes. Prices were sky high and strikes were further holding production up. There were shortages of meat, rice, clothing, linens, cars—and people in long lines for what was left. This was politics running amuck, and boy, it was mucky!

Our life? It was quickly filled with radio shows and vaudeville at the National, where the audiences asked questions about our trip and we answered them just as if we were sitting in our own home. Yonkel spoke before our Jewish Union members in the Actors' Club and you could hear a pin drop. They even forgot to smoke! It was around this time that the U.S. Committee called to tell us that all the children who had come over with us on the *Ernie Pyle* had been placed. There would be no little Clarissa for us, though I'm sure she had stockings now.

On November 18th, we celebrated Yonkel's fifty-fifth birthday on the air with our entire radio audience singing "Happy Birthday." Meanwhile, a man walked over to me and handed me a summons—the first one I ever got. And from a ghost. Seems my father had left a debt of one hundred and sixty-nine dollars, incurred some fourteen years before, for some sort of Morris Plan (whatever that was). Now they wanted me to pay it. And I did. Then I went back to running myself ragged sending *peklach* (packages) to Poland, concertizing in New Britain's Temple B'nai Israel, and chalking up a hit in New England.

All our concerts seemed more thrilling. I don't know just what it was, but we were doing better than ever. Had we matured? Most likely so. One thing I do remember was one old woman who said to me, "Regards to Yonkel and use him in good health." Sage advice, I thought.

As 1947 stormed in, full of sleet and snow, our life was its own whirling blizzard of work and happiness. We had radio programs, concerts, vaudeville, plus talk of plays, tours of Europe, South America, Africa. Much of it was tentative so we continued on our icy treadmill. The city was snowed under, but I did my concerts and even wrote something new, "We Shall Live to See the Day." It's a stirring, vivid song, and it became an instant hit. That was an up.

But the downs, too, were always lurking on the other side of the crest. After a beautiful radio show, I had a shocking concert at a Garment Club show at the Plaza. Nothing went over but toilet jokes. I laid an atomic egg and felt terrible. The audience was up to their ears in filthy material by the time I got on, and nothing I said was what they wanted to hear.

I don't think I'm a prude. But I do feel there's a difference between material which is risqué and fun and that which is just plain vulgar. A case in point occurred a few nights later when Freddie Renault, a female impersonator, gave a concert and we went to see him. His show was hilarious. He called on me and I did my song about hands, a perfectly clean, moral little song, but his audience interpreted every line in their own image. And I enjoyed the fun they were having with my lyrics. I killed 'em, laid 'em in the aisles! And didn't have to soil myself in the process.

The Hartman Orphan Asylum Show was next on our agenda, with Lucienne Boyer, Fannie Hurst, *tout le monde* and me all appearing at Madison Square Garden. All was *très bien*. Except for the rest of the world.

Walter Winchell was predicting another World War. Here it was six months since we returned on the *Ernie Pyle*, and suddenly our President spoke openly of war with Russia, and the city was full of the jitters, which threw a damper on all of show biz. But, I was off on tour, trying to leave such dreadful cares behind. We did Florida, Tennessee, Arkansas, Texas, California. The memories of 1917 and my grand tour with the Four Seasons all came back to me. Once again, seven shows a day. But now, in Tulsa and San Antonio and Houston, we were meeting Jews who owned cattle, whose grandfathers had been born there on the ranch. A rare continuity in the lives of Jews.

After such a far-flung tour (accomplished in all of a week!) I was back in New York, and in spite of again following dirty comics and scared I'd lay another egg, I managed to overcome the stench left before me. Everyone said I'd improved with age.

Despite such an uplifting success, I crawled home to my Yonkel, sweet and tender and a blessing for my tired body and weary noives! I spent the whole next lazy day going over my wardrobe, but not knowing for what or where. Hawaii? Mount Clemens? Africa? Who knew? But hems came down, collars went up, everything was ready to go wherever our fate and agents willed us. That February, I celebrated my forty-ninth birthday with concerts in Detroit and Cleveland. After a visit to my only little Aunt Nan, I wired back: Accept Africa. I was in Los Angeles at the Beverly Wilshire, I had been cautioned to arrange for yellow fever shots, and our friend, Sam Jaffe, a top Hollywood agent, set everything up. He, too, yearned to get away from what they call "Tinsel Town." "In spite of the affluence," he cried, "there must be something more to life than Sonny Tufts!" I ruefully agreed, took my shots, and promptly ended up in bed with a wicked, fevered reaction to the so-called preventive medicine. Thankfully I was up and around for my last performance in the States. I gave a concert at the Embassy Auditorium with "We Shall Live to See the Day" sung in English really carrying the show. Paul Muni and his wife, Bella, Melvyn Douglas, Stella Adler were all in the audience and it was bedlam backstage afterward. Somehow, I broke away to the airport, flew back to New York in the night and in about nine hours was home for breakfast!

Yonkel was off to get our visas and tickets, but our passports for Africa had already arrived. Suddenly, all was excitement, a house on wheels, as I packed, shopped, occasionally got a little hysterical, and—just not to lose touch—did a benefit concert.

We left for South Africa on June 23, 1947, our second visit there in ten years. Travel had changed a bit from the nineteen thirties, of course. Instead of a three-week trip by boat, we would be flying over at the then speedy pace of about thirty hours. In fact, with stopovers forced by fog, visa problems and faulty landing gear, the trip took almost three days. When we finally reached Johannesburg, South Africa,

John Schlesinger, Jr., the son of old man Schlesinger, our first African producer, was out at the airfield to meet us. We were escorted to the Carlton Hotel and a room full of flowers. There were the obligatory cocktails, the press, photographers. Then, thankfully, everyone left and Yonkel and I collapsed into bed, exhausted after nearly two days in the air.

Once we were rested and acclimated to Joburg's, as they call it, locally high altitude, rehearsals began with Herman Herz, a fine musician from Germany. We also began visiting the friends we'd made on our previous tour when I was just one part of a big English vaudeville troupe. This time, however, I was the sole act when I took the stage on June 30th at His Majesty's Theater in Johannesburg. For over an hour, every story, every song I presented was beautifully received. The next day's press was unanimous in its praise, even better than the last time.

After a week's performing, we were flushed with success and lucre. My first check was for seven hundred and fifty pounds, then worth more than double that in American dollars. We decided to take a day of rest and went out to the mines to see about thirteen tribes do their fantastic war dances. In the evening, we went to the Coliseum to hear Benno Moiseiwitsch, the concert pianist, and rather different from the war dancers' native instruments. Still later on, we somehow got roped into dinner at a Jewish wrestler's home. There were pictures of lions and tigers and Stein, the wrestler, in his costume, along with his daughter, also man-hungry. What a country!

The next day we traveled to Durban in a bitter cold. (Luckily, I thought to pack my mink coat.) We had good food and a bottle of wine to keep us warm, but had to pay extra for bedding on the train. The natives were colder, however. Amid a barren countryside, they lived in dirt hovels with only a fire outside to keep them warm.

After freezing all night, we arrived at Durban, the Miami of South Africa. We had a cheerful room with a balcony at the Edward Hotel overlooking the beach, and the area was as full of Jews as Grossinger's. They came in droves to see me at the Playhouse, where I opened.

Durban then was a colorful city but a bit scary, too. The

Indians, the natives, and every other color, including the whites, were fighting for power. The weather was also uncertain: hot in the sun, chilly in the shade. My shows, however, went well—even the old Boers thought me a hit.

Strangely, it was the Jews whom I found a bit stiff and money-conscious—and veddy British, you know. There was much anti-Semitism, and the Jews were tolerated only because they were important for business. And, as always, because Jews were considered outsiders, they insisted on trying to be just like everyone else, only more so. Sadly, I've seen it happen over and over again.

We moved on to Capetown, the Mt. Nelson Hotel, and the Alhambra, then to the top of Table Mountain by cable car and the most beautiful sight in all the world: the mountains, the ocean, the evergreens and the city nestled in the embrace of the sun. I found it inspiring and somehow cleansing to mind and body. The weather (subtropical) and the landscape (palm and cactus and exotic flowers) were equally delightful. It was here, after one of my shows, that Adele Astaire came back to see me. We remembered her from the Palace when she had danced years ago with her brother Fred. She said she just didn't know how I did it at my age.

Back at Joburg, we learned we were sold out for a week at the Standard, which was music to our ears. Hearing such news, Yonkel told Schlesinger we didn't want to leave Joburg without doing a show in Yiddish. When the old man said there weren't enough Jews who still understood the language, Yonkel made a deal with him—no salary. We'd play for a percentage of the receipts, however small. Well, they advertised in only one paper and every seat was sold the very next day. Instead of one concert, we were held over for two weeks and made more money than from our entire tour! Farmers from Bethel, one hundred and fifty miles away, came to see us, hungry for a Jewish word and song. We evidently had touched some deep, warm recess in their hearts; some came three and four times to hear the same program. As one lady put it, "The city shivers over you" (it sounds better in Yiddish).

After that great three-week run, Yonkel and I decided

we'd earned a small vacation so we arranged to visit a game reserve. Awaiting us were wild pigs, zebras, giraffes and wildebeests. We might even see lions.

We went to Springbok, an enclosed camp, and met General Smuts, who was our guide. Amazingly, Yonkel, who was scared of dogs, talked to the wild animals as if they were his buddies.

The next morning, after tea in our room, we set out by car to look for lions. *Niente.* Yonkel said they must have sensed we were coming and were afeared of us lion hunters. We saw zebras, hyenas, leopards, buffalo, giraffes, but no lions. Back at camp, we supped on steaks, which we had brought with us and which the natives barbecued over huge fires. And so to bed.

Our jungle camps had all the amenities—baths and restaurants, grocery stores and good native cooks. All day we drove in cars at fifteen miles an hour so as not to cause a stampede. Completely absorbed in our desire to see lions, we forgot the outside world, the eternal Jewish Question, *Weltschmerz.* Instead, we ate, slept and talked lions, impalas and wildebeests. All we got were monkeys, chimpanzees and dust. We did dare to leave our cars once when we saw a hovel with a native family. We went over to take pictures with them, but the squalor was overwhelming. We took one quick shot while they showed us their scars (where they had been bitten by the lions which we never saw). We gave them our food and ran.

From the game preserves we went to Lourenço Marques in Portuguese East Africa on the Indian Ocean. The city was very Portuguese and a good spot to rest up, clean up and perfume up before visiting its Havana-like casinos with their floor shows, gambling and shady characters. There were also very attractive shops, and I bought a French bag from an Englishman who'd seen me at the Palladium. But no lions.

Back to Joburg, we got ready to return to the States. The first step was to transfer our money from Barclay's Bank to Chase, and it was then that we discovered just how much we'd made in only seven weeks (over twenty thousand dollars as I remember). So, feeling extravagant, we threw a huge cocktail party for all our friends, about a hundred of whom insisted on taking us to our plane. But sorry, no flight. Engine trouble. The next night we were back with fifty friends ready to see us off. Again, no flight. By the third night, Yonkel and I arrived at the airport alone, and this time we did take off for Léopoldville, Belgian Congo, and, hopefully, home.

We almost made it. However, once in the air, Yonkel looked out the window and noticed one of the propellers wasn't moving at all. The captain told us not to worry, that we'd be landing in the Congo for a "minor adjustment." So down we went, right into the midday heat. Yonkel said, "Molly, when will we have a chance to look around the Belgian Congo? Let's get out and walk around." Which we did, until a young man spotted us and yelled, "Hey, don't walk in the sun; the tsetse flies are out." Then he took another look at me and said, "Oh my God, Molly Picon! Wait'll I tell my mother." That was too much, and we had to talk to him some more. He told us he was Ted Koton, an ex-actor who had once played in the Group Theater with Stella Adler, had been in the war, and couldn't get readjusted to life in New York, so he had come here. As we talked, I kept noticing the colorful printed costumes worn by the natives. I asked Ted, by now our buddy, where we could buy some for gifts. "Why buy them here?" he said. "I'll give you a card for my store in New York and you can get them wholesale. I import them and I'm doing fine."

By this time, the captain had told us we'd be spending the night and the airline would arrange for our hotel. Ted said, "Fine. Then I'll call for you at five to meet the American consul." Yonkel protested that we didn't want to impose but Ted insisted. Sure enough, at five, there he was. He drove us to the consulate, where the consul threw open the door with "Hello, Yonkel and Molly!" His name was Wolf, he was from the Bronx, and on his first diplomatic job. His wife had just received a letter from her mother, who had seen me at Grossinger's. The two of them had a very Brooklyn household out there in the Congo, right down to the dishes, silverware and Grand Rapids furniture. We joined them for a real Sabbath meal of gefilte fish, chicken soup, the works, all served by barefoot natives in those colorful robes. We finished the evening driving along the Congo River singing Jewish folk songs to the music of rhinoceri doing their thing in the water. Is this a life!

At 5:00 A.M. we started off again, flying to Accra, Dakar, Lisbon, and then home to Mama, Helen, Helen's husband, Bill, George, their son, everything just as we left it except for all that extra dough we were burning to spend.

We lavished some to celebrate Mama's seventieth birthday. God, keep her well and happy, I prayed, along with dozens of friends and relatives. Yonkel also bought a new typewriter and a new Chrysler Imperial. But I wanted something more.

Yonkel and I were both embracing our fifties and I thought it was time we had a home. All the stars seemed to have one, a special place to flee to during layovers and holidays. They always talked about "our house in the country" and I felt we, too, deserved one—especially for the luxury of begging off some unwanted affair by saying, "Sorry, we'll be off in the woods."

Of course, it had to be the right house, and we saw plenty of the other kind. Among them was Al Jolson's house which he'd built for Ruby Keeler when she was his wife. It was very Spanish, very ornate and entirely too Hollywood for our tastes. We also turned down the manse of David Belasco, the legendary theatrical producer, built for his exotic Broadway star, Lenore Ulric. Frankly, it was full of crap: old stage scenery, broken-down furniture, bars and bottles in every room, and her belongings strewn all over. Belasco was long dead and Ulric had become quite ill. I believe she ended up in some kind of home, and her disheveled house looked just like she must have left it when they took her away. We said "No" to that one.

We wanted something small, homey and surrounded by greenery. We found it in Mahopac, New York, in Putnam County. It was a lovely, warm, inviting house, hidden by hills but not too far from the city. Colonial in style, it had seven rooms and two baths and was owned by a sculptor. For years this had been the only residence in the area. Deer still came up to its fences.

Our only problem with the house was that it reflected

the artist's mercurial fortunes: when he had money, things in his house were built well; when he lacked money, things were built badly. We knew there would be lots of renovation, so we offered twenty-five thousand dollars and returned to our scripts and songs.

C'est fait or fate. But we got the house at our figure, and a good thing, too. Yonkel immediately christened it Chez Shmendrick, for it was going to cost us a small fortune to fix the house and grounds, and only a *shmendrick* (our traditional fool) would get into such a thing.

Pittsburgh wanted me, so off I went to help pay off the mortgage. I kept thinking, Every show means a new piece of furniture for our house. Meanwhile we had a painter in for an estimate, and he hit us with what sounded like the national debt. We began spending money like it grew on trees, and actually we began buying trees, too. But we were having a ball.

Finally, our predecessor evacuated, and we could really see what we bought. It should look like a little dollhouse when we finish furnishing it, I thought. So we spent our days buying. Went to Vim's for electric "equipment" as Mama called it. I also took up antique shopping with friends, looking for lovely old pieces with "character." I just hoped the pieces with character didn't cave in under us.

We were all wrapped up in the house, although we still lacked the title to it.

But Yonkel was set to love the country life. After years of his saying no to it, I sensed it would be a good thing for him, for both of us. We took title to Chez Shmendrick on November 21st, in, as they say, a lucky hour. I wrote a tiny prayer then: "May we have joy and peace and good health here." And we would, for nearly thirty years, so someone must have heard me.

But we were so full of country, we didn't even realize we were living through momentous times. The UN voted the partition of Palestine and people really thought the end of bloodshed had come. That hope vanished as the Arabs were in arms all over. We went to a Zionist mass meeting in Boston, full of fiery speakers, and we wondered, Who listens? Who really cares?

Everyone had his own life's focus and we, also. Despite all the sword-rattling in the Middle East, we were worrying about how to chop enough ice out of our road so we could reach the rest of Mahopac. We city folks had to learn about winter in the country. Our first Christmas there we had the worst snowfall in history. Yonkel and I looked out on a fairyland and, from inside, felt very cozy and snug. The fireplace was burning and we smiled at our good luck. We had twenty-six inches of snow, and people were marooned in theaters and trains; the city was crippled. But soon we were running out of food and it dawned on us that we couldn't get out either. Snowed in. And we'd never thought to buy a shovel. *Shmendrick* was the name for us, all right!

Somehow, Yonkel managed to scrape out a little path and we set out for the center of town on foot. After about half an hour, we managed to get there and were exhilarated. At the grocery we met our neighbor, Mr. Lorini, and after we loaded up on food, he drove us back and helped us up the road.

The holidays were refreshing in the country, but that winter in the city was brutal. Blizzards paralyzed New York, theaters lost a fortune and vaudeville exited, just in time. December 31st was the most disastrous New Year on record, and the Mayor broadcast that no private cars would be allowed in town. So for the first time in a long time, we became subway riders, although it was raining and snowing so, it wasn't worth your life to go out. We had two shows to do at the National, however, and although we found the place nearly empty, it wasn't *completely* empty, so we did our act for a gathering of fools: us who insisted on doing a show, and our tiny audience who insisted on being there.

CHAPTER ✤ 10

NINETEEN FORTY-EIGHT, and New York started the new year on the wrong foot. The weather made the city a ghost town, yet we began *Tzipke* at the National, joined friends for dinner between shows, even went off to the Copa (traveling I don't know how) to hear Peter Lind Hayes, who was very good. Broadway, however, was way off, the snow way on, and for us to have ventured forth in such weather equally off. But neither snow nor sleet etcetera keeps troupers from their appointed jobs. And National's vaudeville (Jewish vaudeville) was still alive. Maybe a little damp in that weather, but still alive.

So, too, our Maxwell show, at least for a while. In fact, their people decided to extend us for another five weeks, the first time in fourteen years that had ever happened.

My main activity, however, was bringing *Yonkele* back to the National, twenty-five years after we had first opened it on the Avenue. I was nearly fifty and playing a boy of thirteen, and when I somersaulted, the audience shouted, "Hurrah for Yonkele!" One lady brought her son because she had first seen *Yonkele* at his age. Our audiences were now comprised of three generations: grandparents, parents, children. Not too many American stars could boast of such a following! And I was delighted to do it. I had no trauma about approaching such an age, I never felt age, and the stage always provided that magical distance which makes years evaporate. I would go on tomorrow and still do *Yonkele*—but maybe without the somersaults!

Theater, radio, my Ludlow Street Baths, and scripts. Work was always ahead of us like weeds (that's country talk). Yonkel kept going and never complained; I, on the other

136

hand, always griped, but went on working, too. On February 28, 1948, when I actually celebrated being fifty years old, I changed the saying "Never say 'die,' say 'damn' " to "Never say 'stop,' say 'go.' " Besides, I had something to keep me going at my half-century mark: Chez Shmendrick.

One of Chez's new delights for us then was landscaping, and we hit every local flower show and nursery, buying like insane city hicks: tools, seeds, trellises. We fell for roses and mimosa and learned names of flowers we never even knew existed.

But always, after that brief bit of sane activity, it was back to our unbelievable profession. Off we'd go to concerts in Altoona, Pittsburgh, Rochester, and when we returned, the weather was 70 degrees and we raced back to Chez to see our first four crocuses pop up. And just like any Broadway production, spring meant lining up its own special crew: a man to clean the gardens, someone to paint, another to macadamize our dirt road, another to do carpentry.

In the months that followed, I divided my time between short concert tours and longer stints at our oasis, where every time I returned, there was something new to see: flagstones on the walks, new doors and posts, daffodils in bloom, and Yonkel, unbelievably, out at night pruning the trees. We both left Chez reluctantly, but we had to make lots of money in the city to pay our bills in the country. Eventually we put over one hundred thousand dollars' worth of improvements in our once tiny home, including adding twelve acres, an in-ground pool, a guest cottage and my very own *shvitzbud* built under the house.

Because we were spending so much of our time at Chez, we decided to sublet our New York apartment to a French actress. She found everything there *charmant* except for our twin beds with the night table between them. "Ah, the beds I will push together," she said, "*à la française.*"

Home was now the country from May to September, and it was a little strange at first not having a year-round pied-à-terre in New York City. But driving up to Mahopac grew quite relaxing: no bridges, no tunnels, parkway all the way to our little village and home, really home.

On May 14, 1948, Jews everywhere got a homeland. The United Nations declared a Jewish State in Palestine and renamed it Israel. It was an incomparable moment. Ever since I was five years old, I had chanted "Next year in Jerusalem." And finally, finally after forty-five years, after two thousand years, it was happening. But nobody shot off firecrackers. With the Holocaust behind us and Arab armies ready to invade before us, and the British pulling out, we just prayed: God help us. It would take a miracle to make it work. But as Ben-Gurion said, "In Israel, if you don't believe in miracles, you're not a realist!"

So, we held our breath and went back to cleaning, sweeping, mopping and polishing our dollhouse. We planted a vegetable garden, added begonias to the front of the house, and Yonkel hammered and pasted our forty years of theater posters all over the garage walls. When you walked in, the effect was striking. I, meanwhile, bought seventy dollars' worth of shrubs to transplant, and I learned that I have a sinister attraction for anything that bites or stings.

But Broadway was a puzzle. Whenever we had to go into the city, it was impossible to get a room—all full up. Often we'd land at the King Edward, where no king ever lived, only third-rate actors. Yet the theaters were empty and the cabbies were complaining. Who could figure it?

One thing was certain, however. I would have to stay on the road, and I did. To Wilkes-Barre, Swan Lake, Stevensville and Bear Mountain. During one quick trip to Montreal, a nice concert, I was introduced to a little boy who had seen us in Poland a couple of years before. He thanked God to be on our side of the ocean now.

And whatever I made went into Chez. Septic tanks, water pumps. Who knew from water pumps? And everything cost twice what we were told. So I *shlepped* to Forest Hills, New York; Manchester, New Hampshire; Stamford, Connecticut.

Meanwhile the mouths to be fed grew in one furry leap. King, a beautiful dog, came to us from my cousin Helen Rossenberg, the national president of ORT (Organization of Rehabilitation through Trades). ORT worked to give vocational training to Jews who had been uprooted. Years before, Yonkel and I had donated a thousand dollars to its formation, and thus inaugurated the Golden Circle. Now, my cousin had introduced King, and amazingly, Yonkel fell for him at first sight. Competition for me! Mama also took to King and so did I. Whenever we'd return after a trip away, King would go crazy with joy, and it was such a nice greeting.

Mama had started getting feisty. One day I returned from a concert tour to find her battling with Yonkel. She insisted that she be given a salary like any other housekeeper would get, and that she didn't want to cheat to be able to buy stockings. Of course she could have had anything she wanted. But, to her, a "salary" meant earning your way, and she got it.

I was also not above pitching in (although I didn't ask for wages). When the cleaning lady would go on vacation, I scrubbed floors just as I did in the days when Yonkel had come wooing me. So I scrubbed again, and he was still wooing. And we started having real country Sunday dinners, ten guests at a time, with Mama always a big hit. She said she didn't know where to hide the salary Yonkel gave her so no one would steal it.

We were slowly settling down, and I guess that was why I agreed to tackle another Broadway show. After the *Morning Star* disaster, my skepticism about me and Broadway was keen but Julie Berns, a young playwright, had seen me in concert and was favorably impressed. She wanted me for her new play, *For Heaven's Sake, Mother,* which would open in Philadelphia that October. Nancy Carroll would star, with me in the second lead.

The plot involved a Hollywood actress who for various reasons decides to tackle the stage. Carroll, who was a 1940s screen star, a truly shimmering beauty, seemed almost too perfect for the role. I played her wardrobe mistress (and, with Mama's past, could also be considered cast to type). My part was small but colorful, and I was anxious to begin.

Trouble started with our first rehearsals. Nancy and director Harry Gribble had heated arguments from day one. Carroll was insecure to begin with, and her flighty attitude didn't help. She couldn't learn (or wouldn't learn) her lines, kept everyone waiting, and continually made wasteful demands. One of them was that she have her own costumes made to order. She insisted that several of them be completely black (and this was supposed to be a comedy!). Her boyfriends were all over the place, and she couldn't take direction. Gribble, on the other hand, didn't know how to handle Carroll. They'd get into shouting matches, Carroll would stalk off, and Gribble would leave to get drunk. Julie Berns and I would remain to do the work. I shrugged my shoulders and went off to Klein's to get clothes for my character, buying what I thought was perfect and funny for my Madam Rubin.

The battles and delays continued, and ten days before the play's opening, we had yet to have one run-through. While everyone quarreled, I went to Chez and planted irises. I'm afraid most film actors are not used to stage techniques. And the foolish among them refuse to learn. We started grueling twelve-hour rehearsals trying to make something jell and we didn't even have a last scene yet. I finally blew up at Carroll and she apologized, but we were getting nowhere.

Somehow, we opened *For Heaven's Sake, Mother* at the Walnut Theater in Philadelphia on November 12, 1948. I felt I came on too late and the play was too long—actually we had no play—but I tried to shoot what I had to the sky. The following day the critics were brutal on the play. So now what? Where could we find a George Kaufman to cure this invalid?

Gribble was befuddled, the cast couldn't remember their lines, let alone new cuts, and Yonkel said there was no hope and that was a shame.

Finally, Gribble stepped out and Julie brought in another director. Moods went up and down like an express elevator, but mine stayed at a happy medium. My part had more laughs than I'd ever gotten in any play, and that with no help from nobody! We did $6,700 in business despite the bad press, and Julie decided to take it to New York.

Believe it or not, we opened. We played the Belasco Theater and gave one of our worst performances but the critics stayed to the bitter end, even George Jean Nathan.

Not surprisingly, the play got some of the worst reviews in the history of theater, but I came out with good notices. We now played to five hundred dollars in business, panic set in, and we closed in a blaze of ridicule after eight performances. That had to be the most amateurish venture I'd ever been in, and I vowed it would be a lesson to me forever after.

I was still pretty mad. Chez Shmendrick never looked saner and more serene, but soon I had some concerts to do, so it was back to the city apartment where Frenchie, we found, had done no cleaning for six months. She was a tomato, but I was stewing!

Winter was upon us and money was still going out for the house—or should I say into the ground. We now had a new gardener, Angelo Paniconi, and Yonkel had evergreens planted on both sides of our road, à la Versailles.

My mood brightened, however. King, our dog, survived a dangerous operation. At a concert Yonkel and I gave in Boston for the Home for the Aged, Rabbi Nedich said, "As long as we have you two, we have something to look forward to." Louis Nizer's book *Between You and Me* had come out and it included a loving commentary on me that almost made me cry. Later on, he also wrote, "Molly breaks down the barriers of resistance. Her comedy then seems funnier and her tragic sense more profound. She can disarm a listener in a few minutes—sometimes seconds. In this sense, she literally captures an audience and its emotional responses then become full and uninhibited." I was truly moved.

Television had come to me, and at fifty-one I found myself full of new plans. Our sponsor was Rokeach Soap and we signed to do eight weeks. This time, however, they didn't put purple goo on my face (as they did to me in London years before). The cameras are much more sophisticated, which forced me into a mad scramble for clothes. It appeared that none of my dresses "televised." I called Wilma's on Fifty-seventh Street and she agreed to dress me for a credit on the program.

On my first show, which took place in February along with my birthday, I sang some songs in Yiddish and English and generally kept things light. Everyone seemed to like us except Rokeach. They wanted no Yiddish! After the second show, however, they changed their minds, and our TV shows got better and Wilma's gowns more stunning. And maybe I could have been the female Milton Berle, but I decided against it.

Why? Because Yonkel and I still had our theater, the National; I had signed with Columbia Artists for concert tours, and with other agents for nightclubs; and television just wasn't for me. Nothing could replace performing onstage in front of a live audience, and my beliefs haven't changed to this day. Even though I did go on to do films, and now even do a TV show or two, I still have to go on tour and meet my audience face to face.

On top of all our work, including our radio programs, we would also be welcoming home the little boy we had adopted during the war through Foster Care. We had paid for George Weinstein's education since 1942 when he was orphaned by the war and had fled Belgium for London. Now, he was quite a grown young man on his way to study science in America. (George stayed with us while at Hofstra and M.I.T. and is now a physics professor in Brussels, with children of his own. So I'm a grandparent, even!)

But then I was digging pinks and portulacas—new words in my vocabulary—the agents were calling with lots of work, and I had to tear myself away from the gardens. Yonkel, in the meanwhile, showed me his new play *Abi Gezunt* (*As Long as You're Healthy*). He only had the first act, but it sounded perfect for Second Avenue and I couldn't wait for him to finish it.

I was playing more and more nightclubs and I didn't like it. I was being held over, and I still was unhappy. Although the bosses were very nice to me, too many bad guys seemed to run them and I felt unclean. I'd usually do the first big show to a family audience, but by the second show, their gang would be in and I'd want out. But in clubs you often don't wrap things up till 5:00 A.M. and that's not so nice for a Jewish girl like me!

Instead, I rushed back to Chez for my nephew George's seventeenth birthday. Helen's son was off for Brooklyn College, the first generation in our lives ever to be able to go so far.

Yonkel and the composer Joseph Rumshinsky, our partner, were dug in, writing in the wilting heat to finish *Abi Gezunt*. Part of the plot, Yonkel informed me, called for me to do a number on roller skates. As long as I have my health, as Mama said, I'll try it. Off I went to the Gay Blades Roller Rink, put on my first pair of shoe skates and managed to stay upright.

In the midst of all this, some of Yonkel's distant relatives who had survived Hitler arrived from Norway and we had to take care of them until they got settled. Our foster son, George, also came to visit. He had always written beautiful letters and he turned out to be a poetic young man. Sadly, however, he told us he was still "afraid of being Jewish" and informed us he had decided to change his last name to Severne.

I'm not one to philosophize or psychoanalyze, so I just kept digging in our vegetable garden that Angelo had planted. But the garden wasn't "vedging" (Yonkel's word) so Yonkel said, "Angelo, a pool would cost me less." The next day, Angelo raked up the garden, brought in a bulldozer, and his mason relatives began on a nine-by-twelve-foot pool. Again Yonkel protested. Nine by twelve feet? Not big enough. "But you're only two peoples," Angelo reasoned. "But," Yonkel explained, "we have lots of friends so I want you to make it thirty feet by sixty with steps to walk down." "Ah!" Angelo smiled. "Scala de Milano?!" And we just nodded and hoped for the best.

Back in the city, I started limbering up for Second Avenue at Michael's Gym on Sixth Avenue. Yonkel had hired a professional skating troupe for me to work with and every day I'd practice on my skates, then they'd spin me around, holding me by my ankles while the blood rushed into my head. And at fifty-one, who starts learning acrobatics? Me, like a fool! I should have taken that Arab acrobat's marriage offer back in 1917.

We said good-bye to the country house, hating to leave. It was Labor Day and we labored on *Abi Gezunt*. The plot itself escapes me now. Many of the things we did then were alike: I was usually some sort of ragamuffin who always found fame and fortune (and a good husband). What made things click was that Yonkel knew our audience and wrote for them. He also always included a catchy gimmick involving yours truly. One time I even threw rubber sausages out to the audience (heaven knows why) and I meet people today who tell me they still have the sausage I tossed them fifty years before!

Yonkel's greatest gift, however, was as a play doctor. He could take someone else's fractured, sickly piece of work and mend it into something fine. My job was adding the lyrics and then work, work, working to make his scripts and my songs come alive. *Abi Gezunt* was no different. Back in town, I had another apartment, rehearsals, interviews, more skating and a full dizzy day.

Maxwell House gave a big luncheon at the Ritz at which I told my stories and was a hit. The bosses said we'd be on the air fifty-two weeks a year. Later, however, at rehearsal for the play, I got scolded because I blew my lines in the second act. Irving Jacobson, a very funny comedian and my co-star, blew his, too, and also caught Yonkel's wrath. So we both worried, but I, at least, could limp back to Chez, and lo! the pool was finished. It looked like La Scala and the earth smelled good. A day at Chez and I'm okay. Only now Angelo had plans to build a guesthouse near the pool. "You'll drive us into the poorhouse with your pool house!" we lamented, but let him go on building.

Back at the salt mines (a.k.a. show biz), I began a new Maxwell season, went broadcast shopping, had rehearsals, skating, dinner, more rehearsals. Who said theater is an easy profession? We would start at 8:00 A.M. and end at midnight. But our advance sales were terrific. Everyone who didn't come to see *For Heaven's Sake, Mother* was coming now.

After our twelve-hour days, the play was beginning to shape up but it was still forty minutes too long. Yonkel immediately began to cut, and we called him a regular *mohel* (freely translated, Yankee Clipper).

There were other problems, too. One look at the scenery

and we knew it was bad. Typical Second Avenue. For the same money we could have had something newer, more modern. But it wouldn't have been union, and that was the bottom line. Luckily our actors were all excited about the play, and that lifted our spirits.

We opened *Abi Gezunt* on October 3, 1949, at the Second Avenue Theater and the actors were right. We had a hit. Yonkel had chopped off thirty minutes more and the show was smart, gay, clean, with the music singable and the audience singing it. We opened to a benefit crowd, who are, traditionally, difficult to please. They loved the show, me, and Yonkel. They waited outside to compliment us; it was Yonkel who deserved all the praise for keeping us in line. The Yiddish press was also mostly wonderful, writing that we had resurrected the Yiddish theater. One man said we "gave the theater a dry cleaning."

The only sour note was that some of the Yiddish press was still unkind to Yonkel. Yonkel had been known as an intellectual. The Yiddish press never forgave him for going into popular culture. It was pure snobbery. The Yiddish critics wanted pure literature and pure Yiddish and they couldn't care less if the results were entertaining. Yonkel, on the other hand, incorporated the American musical into our Yiddish plays, got rid of a lot of worn-out actors and choruses, and brought in young people and young ideas. And, the audiences loved it. But the Yiddish press never gave Yonkel any recognition for what he did. Even today, they never mention his name. He felt bad, but we couldn't do anything about it except comfort ourselves with our audience reaction and our friends. David Sarnoff, J. S. Seidman, all the cantors and actors loved the play and Yonkel. The box-office boys said they never had a more exciting time as everyone was calling for tickets, including Harvey Stone and Mr. Simon and Mr. Schuster. Amid such cheering, I got a whopping cold in my throat and so went on full of doctors, penicillin and silver nitrate. I worked every trick I knew, more dead than alive. Louis Nizer, who came to see the show, sent a lovely letter so I knew I succeeded.

On Saturdays we had to add twenty-four extra chairs. On

Sundays we rested. One Sunday we sneaked in a day at Chez and found Angelo building the guesthouse despite the autumn chill. The work gave him a job for the winter when all gardeners are usually idle. He said it was good for him, and we said he was good for us.

I also went back to my Ludlow Street Baths, so good, too, for my weary body. I invited all my little old cronies in for a Saturday matinee of the show. Meanwhile, Mischa Elman and Peggy Wood came backstage, full of praise. The Sunday *Times* had a big spread for our fiftieth performance. On our wedding anniversary, which followed shortly after, all the papers were full, the house was full and we were thankful. Nothing succeeds like success.

Nevertheless we were already reading new plays to do. Our benefit audiences had seen *Abi Gezunt* twice over and we needed a replacement. It was Indian summer and a good time for me to write new lyrics, but Yonkel was very unhappy with the plays available. Instead he decided to rewrite *Sadie Is a Lady.* He was fifty-eight, looked forty-five and felt twenty-five. We celebrated his birthday at the Café Royal and I thanked God for everything.

Despite our good fortune, 1949 had been a bad season for the Yiddish theater. Many theaters had closed for good, so we were grateful to still be on top with *Abi Gezunt.* Greta Garbo came to see the show one night, and we were all on our toes. Later, Yonkel and I went to the Copa for some toasting, and we saw Jackson, Clayton and Durante. Jimmy was one of our most genuine talents. He was funny and warm and ridiculous, and his walk was as famous as Chaplin's. It was also phenomenal how he handled a nightclub audience. I don't ever remember anyone ever heckling him (and in those days they even heckled Jolson in nightclubs). We went backstage to see him and he kissed us both!

Gezunt was into its ninth week and was healthy and thus so were we. *Sadie,* still now in rehearsal, looked impossible. The play seemed all odds and ends, which I hoped would jigsaw together. Irving Jacobson, our producer now, was pleased with my new songs and gave me a thousand dollars for my lyrics. That was the first time I was ever paid for my writing—and I had written the lyrics for almost all of our plays. But in the past, old Edelstein had never paid anyone extra for anything—we just did it for one lump sum, and often little lumps at that.

The year ended with us breaking all Christmas box-office records. Now if only *Sadie* would really prove to be a lady and be equally kind!

We certainly worked hard enough on the gal. We began 1950, a new decade, playing *Abi* and rehearsing *Sadie*. We smiled and said, This, too, shall pass—but the passing was not easy! Weary and overworked, we opened *Sadie Is a Lady* and held our breaths. The first act wasn't good, but the second seemed terrific. Frankly, it was a hokey, incredible show, another rags-to-riches story. But Yonkel snipped there and snapped here, and some people liked it better than *Abi Gezunt*. As we said on Second Avenue, *So go know!* It looked like another success.

But, back at Chez, terrible news. Angelo had had a stroke and was in the hospital. His wife, Mary, would take care of the house and their son, Joey, the grounds. The bathhouse would have to wait, hopefully, until spring.

We premiered *Sadie* on January 27, 1950. We had a new opening number; and I sported new flaming-red hair, courtesy of hours in the beauty parlor. The show built and then rolled on to a mad end. I didn't believe it, but we had pulled it through. Some critics even compared it to *South Pacific*. Our comeback to the Yiddish theater was a solid success, and Jacobson asked us to sign for the following season. We accepted and got a raise and a bonus. He was happy and we were happy, despite the Yiddish press, which blasted the heck out of us. Again, it was just the Yiddish audience that loved us, so somebody must be wrong! What I truly felt, though, was that to have made a success out of such stupidity was a tour de force all to Yonkel's credit.

And we were clicking despite a disastrous February full of sleet and rain. Business was off everywhere. Even the National canceled its show with Moyshe Oysher. Adding to the woes were a brownout, a coal shortage which we felt in our bones and our box office.

But I did have one special treat that month. On February 28th, according to City Hall, I was officially fifty-two. I say "officially" because until the records showed me otherwise, I had always been told I was born June 1st. That had been my birthday for years, so I only accepted February reluctantly. Actually, as I've mentioned before, I celebrate them both. Why not? Anyway, that's only the beginning of my story. On that date, I had an appointment with the great Kate Smith. She had been asked to appear before a largely Jewish crowd and she wanted me to teach her "My Mama" in Yiddish. Now, I have great respect for Kate, but she had no training musically. When she sang, it was out of God-given, instinctual talent not note-learning. When I asked her what key she sang in, she had absolutely no idea. Also, Kate was monolingual and it was difficult for her to learn foreign words. But she was dedicated and determined not to let her audience down. After I saw it was useless to try to teach her by note, I decided to do it another way. I had a recording made of my singing "My Mama" in Yiddish and I gave it to Kate to listen to. She proved to be an ideal mimic. Kate had a good ear and she taught herself to sing it identically to how I had recorded it. She duplicated my every inflection and was a great hit. It became one of her most famous songs. When she brought the house down with her rendition, I sent her my own special citation praising her skill and she was thrilled.

Sadie was now in its twenty-third week and business was beginning to slip. And there was always the tendency in a long run to slip a bit in your performance, too; but Yonkel watched us closely and we knew it and behaved.

We were now in combat with a new threat for the theater: television. Especially when the weather was bad. Everyone stayed home and kept warm by the set. Even the restaurants were empty. We, however, chose to have a holiday. It was our twenty-fourth week so we gave a big party on stage for two hundred people catered by Moskowitz and Lupowitz. There was food and drink for everyone, even John the watchman. Somehow, we kept on and survived right through to April and Passover, when we finally brought *Sadie* to an end. At Chez Shmendrick we enjoyed a lovely seder with our family and closed the Second Avenue Theater. We had had a bountiful season both financially and morally and felt we had injected new blood into an anemic Yiddish theater.

Of course, only half a season was ending for us. Now we were to hit the road with *Abi Gezunt* beginning with the Shubert in Philadelphia, my hometown. There, we met a refugee girl, the daughter of Foigel Gonif, Yonkel's mother's rather easy-going husband. Over and over again, we would run into Holocaust survivors and we were always glad to see them.

Our next stop was Boston and Yonkel and I walked to Florence Street where we had lived thirty-two years before. And our old landlady recognized us! But our old house was torn down, the Grand Opera House was down, the whole neighborhood was down, and Boston let us down. We went back to New York without any smash successes on the road and hoped for better breaks in Montreal, but the story was the same. Ticket prices were high, a lot of refugees couldn't afford to pay them, and in spite of exciting performances and rave notices, business was disappointing. We finished to an SRO crowd but were still forced to close.

So back to Chez where spring was budding forth with one color more stunning than the next. But our Angelo wasn't there to share it. His stroke proved completely debilitating and Mary had to have him cared for at a special home. He would sadly linger for ten years, but we kept Mary with us and helped her to pay for his needs.

With the warmer weather, Chez's needs also demanded two masons, two carpenters, two gardeners, a new power mower. But we were hooked, busy, happy.

I did the American Radio and Press luncheon at the Brevoort and was *très* witty, then did a concert in Forest Hills, Queens, and was *très* Yiddish. All in one day. And I am so grateful for our life. We were spending our third summer in our very own home and we had good prospects for the following theater season. But, Yonkel said, instead of burying our money into shows, we were better off burying it in the good earth which at least gave us back scallions and radishes!

Yonkel, the city-slicker who said he'd never move away

from its hustle and bustle, was now busy rearranging huge boulders into a new wall and doing the gardens as if they were scenery in a musical comedy where the bride walks down a rose-strewn path to a flower-covered canopy during the second act. We celebrated our thirty-first anniversary there, enjoying our first swim in our first pool and we were having the time of our lives.

Gray clouds, however, tarnished even such shiny silver linings. The news from Korea looked very bad. It all seemed so ominous and we couldn't understand why. The country's spirit seemed to sag, our guests were thinning in number, and even Mama left us for a while.

It was just Yonkel, King and I, and that was nice. Yonkel had been working on something new which he called *Mazel Tov, Molly*. The plot was a spoof on Yiddish weddings but included some beautiful numbers. I had to engage three girl singers to accompany me, so you can see it was a big deal! Yonkel had finished the script, so Rumshinsky and I went to work on the score. During a break, we went to Atlantic City for the Jewish National Fund show, an exciting bill. It included a Hungarian tenor with a colossal voice and an Israeli war hero who'd lost both of his hands and played the piano with hooks!

Mazel Tov, Molly rehearsals began with a run-through, as did our radio broadcasts, a few commercials, then back to Chez and our pool. We dove into play because, *comme toujours,* everything else was sticky with *MTM* and much work was needed to unstick it. So we work, work, worked, breaking only to help celebrate Abe Kahn's ninetieth birthday at the Hotel Commodore with 1,500 people, the ILGWU and Dave Dubinsky. I wrote a number about Kahn which I did in my *Yonkele* costume (a play Kahn hadn't liked back in 1923). But everyone enjoyed my new rendition, including Kahn.

Mazel Tov, Molly opened at the Second Avenue Theater on September 25, 1950. It was not a great play, a bit too long, but with solid, beautiful productions. Yonkel had taken a piece of calico and made a silken gown for me. Despite its flaws, the play had glamour, beauty, good taste. *Variety* came out with a rave notice for the play and success was in the air, again. With it went nine shows a week plus five radio programs. Not easy, but rewarding.

We were in our nineteenth season with Maxwell House radio. We opened with songs from *Circus Girl* and it was a good send-off. I also did my song "Grandma's Shawl" on Kate Smith's television show and even Yonkel was pleased. Alas, the same TV was also taking our theater audience away and we had to come up with another show to finish our season. Adding to our woes was a very bad storm. Glass windows all over town were smashed, marquees blown down, and our house seats empty. We closed after only ten weeks. Yet, the Show Must Go On (though I've never found out why!) and I started writing lyrics for our next production.

Our President had his troubles, too. Truman said he would use the Atomic Bomb against the Koreans, if necessary. He warned the nation of the great dangers involved and talked of declaring a National Emergency and here we go again. I can't believe it. The sword hangs over us again! Our armies were in retreat in Korea and everyone was barking at each other at the U.N.

Our new play was called *Pavolye Tate* (*Take It Easy, Pop*). Yonkel took one of our old plays, *Hello, Molly,* and gave it a face-lift. Both the *Times* and the *News* gave it rave notices and we needed them. Everyone screamed "Molly Triumphs!" and no one remembered the old *Hello, Molly.* Again, that is show biz.

We started 1951 back at Chez chopping ice, all ruddy and hungry. I rehearsed MGM's "Cavalcade of Jewish-American Stars," which featured the Barry Sisters, Jan Bart, Michel Rosenberg, Moyshe Oysher and me, the Mistress of Ceremonies. I also did two songs, but for whom? So far, we had no sponsor. Would we have done better with all the great Jewish stars of that day who were no longer known as Jews?

But, as I said, I don't philosophize, don't psychoanalyze. I went down to my Ludlow Street Baths for my first steam bath of the year and enjoyed my old cronies. They seemed to go on forever and they credited their longevity to the steam room. I also saw Odets' *The Country Girl* and it was powerful theater. Later, I met Margaret Truman at Sardi's and found her a very unaffected girl. Just like her dad.

Meanwhile, the critics were really reaching deep to describe *Take It Easy*. *Variety* called me Mary Martin, Ethel Merman and a bean-sized Bernhardt. What, no Duse? Eddie Cantor was in to see us and many years had passed since we'd seen each other. Back in the 1920s, Cantor had taught me how to do an imitation of himself singing in blackface. Now, he was back a bigger star than ever. Yonkel introduced him to the audience and all Cantor talked about was himself. A pure, kosher ham!

Good news. Streits Matzohs would sponsor "Cavalcade" for television, but only for a fifteen-minute show. And I was still being seduced by the little box. On February 18th, I did the Ed Sullivan Show, "Toast of the Town." Afterward, our union called to tell us that Nina Abramowitz, our greatest character actress, was dying and had asked to see us. We drove down to the Old Age Home, and I asked her what she had been doing there. "I try to bring them a little theater," she replied feebly. "But they can't see and they can't hear and what they do see and hear, they don't understand." How brave and funny she was, even at the end!

February brought my fifty-third birthday and an exquisite gift from Yonkel: a diamond ballerina, as beautiful as a Cellini piece. After dinner, the family and I all went to the ballet because Yonkel, from the Rabbi's court yet, was a balletomane. Truly, it wasn't bad getting old that way!

Meanwhile, back at Chez, our adopted son, George, was visiting. Mama asked him what he did, and he said, "I'm a physicist." So Mama said, "A what?" and George answered, "Actually, I'm a nuclear physicist." To which Ma answered, "Oh, I see."

I began to do a series of big Israel Bond rallies, the first with former Ambassador MacDonald and Bess Myerson. The second one was at the Jewish Club (our local golf club wouldn't take in Jews, so we had built our own). We raised over $90,000 with Yonkel buying $3,200 for our thirty-second anniversary. A good investment and a good deed. Jews were buying all over from Narragansett, Rhode Island, to Poughkeepsie, New York.

In between the bond rallies, Yonkel and I tried to sneak some time in at Chez but there always seemed to be company. Maybe we were too cordial. But, suddenly, there was no room for us and everyone used the phone in the guesthouse to call California. That was a bit much. We put a lock on the phone. Otherwise, we entertained until the last guest left, then Yonkel and I did some nude bathing with Mama and she actually swam.

We were coasting. Maxwell had renewed our program, there were no immediate theater plans to slave over, and the Israel Bond rallies gave me the occasional exposure needed to stay in the public eye.

Our only enemy was the unpredictable fortunes of age. I was in Youngstown, Ohio, with Senator Kilgore for a rally when I learned Yonkel had had an arthritic attack and was in the Polyclinic for treatment. He had never been sick, and I was really frightened. I flew back to New York to the Polyclinic, but there was little to do. Yonkel was better, but arthritic. The doctors said he could come home and I was relieved. Lindy's restaurant had been sending him food, so his hospital stay hadn't been too uncomfortable. But I was anxious to get him home. Please, I prayed, may this be the last illness for all of us.

We went back to Chez and it was Indian summer and the leaves were coming down. We turned down all hard work and just planned a concert or two. Yonkel was undergoing treatment and I continued tour-hopping: Philadelphia, Brooklyn, Portland. I'd make a pitch, then be home the next day to rake leaves. The toilet comics were on again and it just sickened me. But I'd do my bit, fly back to Chez and plant spring bulbs. The "comic" routines I'd heard would have made good fertilizer.

CHAPTER ✲ 11

AT THE END OF 1951, Yonkel was sixty years old and I, fifty-three. For a brief moment, we might have thought of "slowing down," especially when Yonkel's arthritis had seemed so bad. Yet, when the Morris office called and asked me to go to Korea to entertain the troops, we accepted immediately.

Two big reasons prompted our decision. One was that Yonkel had made an incredible recovery. There was no trace of the arthritis and he was basically healthy. The other reason, a more self-centered one, was that no Jewish celebrity had gone over to perform for our boys in Korea and I wanted to be where the action was!

Our troupe would consist of Paul Douglas, Jan Sterling (then his wife), Piper Laurie (a much-heralded "starlet"), and a newcomer named Raymond Burr. The initial idea was that together we would constitute a variety show, but I remained skeptical. Although Douglas and Sterling both enjoyed very successful film careers, neither of them had any kind of stage act. Piper and the other girls we'd be taking along were mainly window dressing. Each of them was given one funny joke to tell and then told to prance around seductively. But it was Burr who was in the worst shape. His fame had been created on the screen as a tough guy, and he hadn't the slightest idea how to either tell a joke or MC. Such a skimpy lineup did nothing to inspire my confidence, particularly when I learned we had to be broken up into *three* touring troupes. I started preparing material to cover at least an hour's show.

I didn't have too much time, however, to really worry about what demands touring Korea's very hot war zone might make. I still had commitments to fill all over the country for the Israeli Bond office. In between injections for typhoid, smallpox and typhus, I flew to Washington, Denver, Chicago and every other compass point trying to raise money so our new homeland could stay on its feet. In Los Angeles, the Army doctors gave us the once-over and said we were okay. But, back at Chez, our own doctor knew about our far-flung bond activities, and he ordered us to bed to rest our nerves. While we were at home, a man called who had a son stationed somewhere in Korea. He wanted us to be sure and meet his son so we could tell Papa how he looked. Would you believe it? And in a war yet!

We took off for Korea from Burbank Airport on December 20th, at 9:00 A.M. There was no question we would be flying into battle. The Army had outfitted us in fatigues, combat boots and helmets. As if half a dozen typhoid shots weren't trouble enough.

We all left together, Douglas, Sterling, Laurie, Burr, the starlets and me. There were movie and news cameras to give us a proper "Hollywood" send-off and then we were in the air, in our roomy army plane, flying over the Pacific.

We arrived in Oahu, Hawaii, eight hours later; but it was too dark to see or do much except walk the beach and breathe in the orchids. We then flew on to Wake Island and signs of shooting. We had breakfast, refueled and were off again. We were sixteen hours in the air and somehow lost a day. We arrived in Tokyo at 12:30 P.M. and rushed right through to the Yokasuku Naval Base and our first show.

I never did get to see much of Tokyo, but through no fault of mine. Paul Douglas had had some bad bouts with the bottle. His wife made him take an oath not to drink on this tour. And I don't suppose he did. However, Paul took Yonkel to the bar in the Imperial Hotel and got him drunk to compensate for his staying sober! So while all the company went sightseeing in Tokyo at night, I stayed in while Yonkel said, "Just a minute, Malkale," and fell back to sleep. It was the only time I'd ever seen him besotted!

Yonkel slept it off and we were up at 5:30 in the morning, dressed in our fatigues and off by convoy to an airfield in Korea. We passed Mount Fujiyama, covered in snow, and then saw our first glimpse of Korea: dusty, barren, full of poverty and fighting.

Our one-third of the touring troupes consisted of Burr, three pretty starlets, and me. The girls had no acts at all, but the boys whistled as they came on stage bursting from their sweaters and I guess that was treat enough. I followed in an oversized General's outfit and my first words were: "Boys, sex takes a holiday!" Then I did a striptease out of the General's coat and big boots and went into my show. Before going on, I'd find out what songs the soldiers were singing in the barracks and then make up my own version. My material proved just right and the boys cheered every story. It was the biggest compliment I had ever gotten and Yonkel and Raymond had their hands full getting me off stage three times a day.

Burr, I must add, also proved a huge hit. He knew his stage ability was minimal so he stressed face-to-face contact with our boys. Raymond would go right down into the foxholes in order to visit and his courage was greatly appreciated. (And this was before his Perry Mason character made him invincible!)

The experiences we had happened too fast to savor, however. We flew to Pusan and did an airfield show for the Marines and before the applause died we were on our way to Seoul. We found the city gutted and Yonkel had to bunk in our Ladies' Quarter. Of course, the girls didn't mind. Neither did I.

On Seoul, we did four and five shows a day. I sang *corazones particulos* in Spanish to some injured Puerto Rican soldiers, English tunes for some hospitalized nurses, Yiddish songs for Jewish sailors.

At one base, one of our pilots had parachuted out of his plane under intense enemy fire. He was so unnerved the doctors couldn't calm him down. So they brought him to our show. Slowly, he relaxed and by the time I was through, was out of shock. He came to me and said, "Lady, you saved my life and I want to give you something that also saved me." He then handed me his parachute! (Which I treasured right back to Mahopac, where I took it.)

One tall, thin Western kid said, "Lady, may I kiss you?" I said, "Sure, fella!" Then he added, "You remind me of my mother. She's little and round like you!" No wonder I sang and sang.

Except for some unexpected short circuits. At one show, I was doing my "Woiking Goil," which is a fast-patter song. Yonkel was standing backstage, as always, when an officer rushed up and said, "Tell her to stop!" Yonkel looked at him as if the man were crazy. "Stop?" Yonkel said, "In the middle of her best song?" "Get her off!" the officer yelled and Yonkel yelled back, "Not until she's through!"

They stood there arguing until I came off and the officer went on and announced, "Company so and so report to base!" All the boys from that outfit got up immediately, cursing. And they marched off to fight and I stood there in tears: Will they come back? Will I sing for them again?

U.N. "advisors" flew us in old Samavars, planes we had given to the Russians, who had given them back. Our pilots often didn't understand English. Or directions. We occasionally flew over enemy territory, lost contact with headquarters, and always wore our Mae Wests just in case.

We played the Mosquito Outfit, that was the enlisted men, and at night, the Officers' Club. I would often fall down tired, but the eager young faces kept me going. The best compliments on my ears was hearing the boys shout, "We want Molly!" We ended the year praying for an end to the useless loss of our Youth.

The following day, January 1, 1952, we froze all night and further cursed the fates. Our heating stove had smoked up and blackened us all. I felt sorry for our poor platinum and blond starlets. They all had black hair now and wouldn't go on until they could wash it out! But we were up at seven, flew to Pusan, did a show at two, jeeped to another base for an outdoor performance, and the girls still had dark hair.

We flew back to Tokyo to rejoin the other two units and the finale of our tour.

We were staying again at the Imperial Hotel so our accommodations were vastly improving and I finally got to see some of Tokyo nightlife. At one stage show, the Japanese girls were all in men's clothing and imitated the West with exaggerated dances. Who knows why? But I did enjoy their traditional Kabuki Theater.

The following day we had lunch with General Christenburg and I got a special medal for my job. But I only felt I earned it after that night.

We were scheduled to do a show at the Ernie Pyle Special Hospital for Amputees. When we arrived, I glanced around and felt like I was back in the Camps. Except now I wasn't seeing ravaged buildings which could be resurrected but looking at young boys maimed for life. We were overwhelmed with the sacrifice they had made and tried to give them the show of our lives. And they kept cheering for more and we gave it. I reached a height I don't think I'll ever reach again.

The next day, we flew off in another huge airship, big enough to walk around in. We arrived at Midway at noon and found the Island uninhabited save for the new trees recently planted and our air base, where we were shown the gooney birds, the area's chief attraction. Then it was off to Honolulu, refueling, then Hollywood and *almost* home.

Once back at Chez, we began calling the relatives of boys we had met in Korea. Whether Boston or Denver, we sent blessings flying over the wires from our hearts. And we had a lengthy list. Yonkel had made a point at every stop to seek out whatever Jewish service people were around and jotted down their names and addresses. And one woman told us her son had written: "It was worth going to Korea to hear Molly sing!"

Chez was covered in snow and we sat by the fireplace in our dollhouse, relaxing and reliving our Korean experience. We were resting and working, scripting new radio programs. Korea began to seem eons away. That in one world there could be so much beauty and so much heartless devastation at the same time! It was incomprehensible.

It was also painfully true. And while there was very little I could do to turn Korea's dismal situation around, I rededicated myself to piling up bucks for Israel, the more the better.

I started at Riverside Plaza, a concert for a hardware

group I think, and raised $18,000. Then it was back to WEVD and our radio routine. While there, I visited Hattie Carnegie's seamstress, a Negro, whose son we'd met in Korea. I gave her his regards and she cried.

I also taped interviews in Spanish and English at the U.N. to report about our trip, visited U.S.O. Shows, appeared on CBS. All to let the rest of the world know what we'd seen and felt.

Then it was back to pushing bonds: Indiana, $29,000; Columbus, $40,000; Portland, Oregon, $45,000. And I'm getting famous as a saleslady. But never famous enough. Mama went to the Palace in New York to see Judy Garland and gave the cashier my picture. No dice. She still had to pay money!

Mama was keeping the home fires heated and our workmen working. We came back to Chez and found the last of the artist-masons, Romolo Giannini (the name still rolls on my tongue). He was building a new addition to our guesthouse and there were plans to build a new attic for Yonkel's overwhelming collection of books. There was a small party to celebrate my fifty-fourth birthday and I received a rather special gift. A letter from the boys in Korea announced that I had been chosen "Pickup Girl," the gal with the personality most likely to cheer them. And at my age!

Soon, however, it was back to Lakewood with Israeli Attorney General Shapiro and $40,000 in bond sales. Very nice. Back to the city, and the lower East Side we knew was slowly disappearing. What next? No Jews! No Theater!

And worse news. Helen's husband, Bill, had a severe heart attack and it looked very bad for him. We were very frightened because he was only fifty years old, and may never be able to work again. Then we visited Sarah Adler, mama to all the Adler greats, and she must have been ninety and complained about getting gray hair. Such is life.

Mama, too, was having her problems. She told us she had to go to New York to visit her doctors for "an understanding." She will tell them what is wrong with her. They sent her back pleased with her general condition. Just a few, as she called them, odds and ends: a little diabetes, a little rheumatism, and so on.

To counteract family worries, I kept going: to Fort Worth, Wichita, St. Louis, Michigan; $197,000 in bonds and each one another stake in tying down Israel's security.

But, at every concert, there were always doubters: in me, in my cause, and it seemed I had to prove myself over and over. So I lunched at the Biltmore with some pressmen, did a television spot with Betty White, dined at Ciro's with a press agent, did more TV with Paul Coates, and squeezed in two recordings in Yiddish for the radio. Yonkel cried, "Take it easy, Molly!" And I shrugged and said, "How can I?"

I don't know if people understand just how much like an athlete a performer is. Rest means slow death. As they say, you had to use your talents or lose them. And in performing, your body is a great part of that talent. To this day, I must continually watch my diet, exercise, limber up before every concert. And it was never easy, not even when I wasn't a hundred years old!

Sometimes, I would propel myself on years of built-up steam, but even that evaporates and then I would look around for something less strenuous. At one point around this time, we had Selma Diamond, Chuck Lewin and David Polin (great writers all) visit with us at Chez to try and create some television format for me. They came up with nothing, nil. Three negatives and, in other words, no TV.

Yonkel sensed my frustration and decided to build a new cellar under the house with my own *shvitzbud*. Now I wouldn't miss Ludlow Street, which had closed down with the rest of the Jewish East Side.

Romolo's men were digging our cellar, the autumn colors were in and it was good to be there and leave all the hangups behind. The last time I had seen Giannini, our artist-mason, I had complained about how long it was taking to finish things. "But Missa Pick," he answered, "everyting she's a getta done!" And by golly, I couldn't believe my eyes when we returned. The cellar was finished and we could've actually lived in it, the workmanship was so fine. Unfortunately, now the attack began. Five workmen were in chopping down old walls, putting in new ones, and pipes were scattered everywhere to drain off water away from our new underground Chez.

So it was fly, fly, fly to sell bonds, plus earn a few bucks to pay for the pipes.

And there's a first time for everything. Winter was on us and so I took to the trains. And, somehow, I arrived in St. Louis with my accompanist and found we were a day early. We had ridden on a dank, drafty train, caught colds, and no one was there to see about a room. A local contact took us to a hotel and we sat out the day, sneezing. After our concert, I *shlepped* back to New York, nursing my cold all the way. That evening, Yonkel and I did a concert in Brooklyn and I must have looked splendid, runny nose and all.

But at least I could now go soak in my steam bath. It was finished and proved a local attraction. David Dubinsky, the ILGWU head, was over to see it with his lawyer. Dubinsky wanted to buy a house and he wanted one with a *shvitzbud* like ours. When his union finally bought him a place near Montauk Point, Dubinsky called us for all the details on how to build one; but we never heard how it turned out.

I inaugurated my hot tubs only briefly, however. The blistering winds of January, 1953, blew just as bad for work on the East Coast as the winters before. The streets on Broadway were dead. We went to see the great Melvyn Douglas in *Time Out for Ginger* and the house was but a third full. Even Beatrice Lillie, whose show was a delight, had trouble battling the weather. We surrended and went south to the Jews' second homeland, Miami.

We were on the bond belt and it would be difficult to sell to Jews from every state and Canada who'd already bought in their hometowns. But we jumped in, nonetheless, working the Sorrento, Governor, Atlantic Towers and Shoreham hotels. Often, we were given a bad room without a stage, so I'd stand on a chair and sing while Yonkel pitched bonds to the crowd. Sometimes, there wouldn't be a room at all. At the Catalina, we had to work in the lobby. People kept walking in and out and I kept singing. Somehow, we managed to sell $1,950, but it was torturous.

Then we hit what we had been most afraid of. We played the Martinique, a swell, luxurious, uptown place and nobody came to hear us. They saw "Israel" on the sign in the lobby and stayed away in droves. So at last, we'd met them (or didn't meet them): the anti-Israel Jews. They wanted nothing to do with a place they preferred not to exist. Only sixty people eventually drifted in, but we gave them a damn good show for only $700.

Mama was now with us, and she helped. She had never been to Miami, had never seen the hotels. At the Tides, Yonkel introduced her to the audience. She bowed and said, "Thanks for helping my children to help Israel." And she walked off with the show.

Mama brought with her a letter from our adopted son, George, asking us to come to Paris in March. We had been hitting every corner of the States, and welcomed the chance to travel. As one old man put it in Miami: "Molly and Yonkel? They're known from edge to edge!"

George had gone to the Sorbonne to study, met a Dutch student there, and married. Since he was back in Europe, he decided to check into what remained of his life in Brussels where his parents had died in the war, and from where he had been forced to flee.

His father had owned a factory in Brussels which the Nazis had confiscated. Now, in restitution, the new government was offering it back to George. It was a raincoat factory with its own store, and, for a while, George and his wife took it over and managed it.

We, of course, had wanted him to stay in America with us. What parents wouldn't. But, when we saw him in Brussels, we knew he was too much of a European now.

I did some concerts in Paris and was surprised to find myself under attack. The Commie press tore us apart for going to Korea! Yonkel replied, "We don't act to the tune of Moscow, but to the tune of Jewry."

Otherwise, we were treated grandly. There was a big reception at the Hotel Moderne attended both by French actors and press. I was invited to do some French TV, *toute en français,* and really enjoyed it. We ended with a concert at the Beaux Arts in Bruxelles, the starting point for our DP camp tour seven years before. We were joined by Renée Solomon, who had played for us back then. We left damp-eyed. On to London, we met my cousin, Leon Picon, who was cultural attaché. He lived with a nice wife and three beautiful children and it was all *veddy* homey. London then still had much war destruction, especially around the Jewish East End. I gave a concert at Scala and felt terrific, at ease in both English and Yiddish.

But I can't leave Europe without telling the story of my hat.

We were back in Paris, briefly, and at Les Halles, the marketplace where the truckers brought their produce at 4:00 A.M. and had their onion soup at the bar in front. We were right up there with them and they all turned to admire my hat. It was one Frederick had made for my last African trip, a tiny brown thing full of feathers to match my mink coat. Well, the truckers all turned and said *"Quel chapeau!"* and applauded as we ate our onion soup with the swank 4:00 A.M. crowd.

Well, this hat had had mixed reviews. I was wearing the same hat (and mink) that Sunday in Johannesburg watching the Zulu women parade by. They dressed to the hilt in their colorful blankets and crazy red mud hairdos. One woman walked by with an enormously high clay bun full of buttonhooks, can openers, shoehorns and pencils. "Look at that woman's head," I said to Yonkel. And, of course, right at that moment, the same woman turned around, pointed at my feathered head, and burst out laughing! It's all a matter of background.

One last hat chapter. In New York, on Fifth Avenue, a taxi went by as I was walking with said headgear. The driver took one look at me and with typical singsong Yiddish inflection said, "This is a hat??"

I gave a farewell concert at the Alhambra in Paris and said *au revoir* to it and to George and his Dutch lady. We knew all were in good hands.

But back at Chez, no rest even for those wearied by planes and bonds and people. We hit both the north and south with one extraordinary rally in Fitzgerald, Georgia. Seven Jewish families had moved there, over two hundred people, and we sold $53,000 in cash! The first time in Bond history. And what an audience: displaced persons from the

Bronx, Brooklyn, Queens and Second Avenue all homesick to hear an *oy!* So I *oyed* and had them laughing and crying and buying.

Fly, fly, fly. And I was now fifty-five and for my birthday, Yonkel gave me the new steam bath and a new road. But who has time to use them? One dip and it was back to pushing bonds: in Montreal, Gary, Newport and Flatbush; $134,000 to strengthen our five-year-old State.

We flew until our heads were cloudy and then would drop down to Chez for a *shvim, shvitz* and *shnaps*—a swim, a steam and a good, strong drink!

And we had a new project. Once again, the *goyish* theater dangled a lure and we bit. The play was by George Boxt and called *Make Mama Happy*. Jan Julien would produce it and even Yonkel landed a part. He read and impressed everyone, so—in between bond rallies—we were learning lines and hoping we'd hit something good.

Hannah Appel also joined our cast, and, frankly, every one was cast well. Except me. My part kept turning straighter and straighter, veering away from whatever special quality I could bring it. Any actress could have played my part. But, everyone seemed keen and up and maybe we had a play.

We debuted at the Monticello Playhouse before a small crowd. Julie Harris, Julien's wife and Eli Wallach were in from New York, but the play had little going for it. So where were we? Nowhere. Yonkel was the Barrymore of upstate New York, but with a new cast the play went merrily to hell. And we were burned again.

So it was August and bonds. Old Orchard, Long Beach, the Club Caprice. We stopped only once in September for Mama's seventy-sixth birthday. We cheered *biz 120* (live until 120 years)!

She didn't even last a month. After never having been sick a day, Mama was suddenly struck with a heart attack. On October 8th, we rushed her by ambulance to Mahopac Hospital clinging to life. Two days later, I left her at 5:00 P.M. and she was joking and laughing. Helen, saying she was lonely for Mama, came in at 7:00. Forty minutes later, my phone rang and she told me Mama was dead. Dead? No! It was unreal, a dream! I could still hear her voice! See her smile! How could Mama be dead?

My Mama, who still went swimming and still tried to climb trees, was gone. Helen said she asked for a clean handkerchief, then gently rolled over and died. I thought, Only an angel dies like that.

A service was held in the Schwartz Funeral Parlor and all of show business came to have one last look at their greatest friend. We buried her on October 12, 1953, in the Hebrew Actor's Union plot, at rest amid the theater world she loved.

CHAPTER ☀12

MAMA WAS BURIED and I had my hair done, put on my greasepaint, and did a show for Bonds for Israel. And it was all an illusion to me. I couldn't believe it: a world without Mama and me doing shows every night? It can't be, I pleaded. But it was.

Yonkel filled in beautifully as I stood numbly by. Anyone who has lost someone dear knows that during those first few days of loss you are too shocked and grief-stricken to truly feel or do anything. You go through the motions of arranging a funeral, selecting a plot, meeting with friends; but it's as if you're traveling in someone else's dream. It is only later, after the service is over, the friends have gone and the phone stops ringing that you awake to discover that the sad vision is really true. Then, you cry your heart out.

Everyone who knew Mama was shocked at how quickly she died. Hundreds of letters poured in full of sympathy and surprise. Mama had only been hospitalized for two days, supposedly with a "mild" attack. She was never a burden, always the lady who knew when and when not to interfere, who found joy in knitting gloves for incurables, loved by everyone, and now gone. After the burial service, my sister Helen, Bill, Yonkel and I came back to our house and our hearts were broken. The place seemed absolutely cheerless without Mama there and I shoveled snow all day like a madwoman because I was afraid to go into the lovely room we had just built for her. For one entire year, I couldn't sing "My Yiddishe Mama." To this day, I still can't do it without crying inside.

Angelo's wife, Mary, who had been working for us part

of the time, now moved in for good. We gave her Mama's new room because we wanted life there. Together, we sorted Mama's clothing and her little bits of jewelry and gave everything to ORT to sell for Israel.

Make Mama Happy, given up for dead in Monticello, was resuscitated briefly and we opened at the Parsons Theater in Hartford. The play worked better, but still not good enough. We rehearsed some more, welcomed a new director and took it to the Walnut Street Theater in Philadelphia. Again, we opened to laughs but no excitement. Plainly, we still didn't have a play. And when you ain't got *wit wot*, you close. Another Broadway flop. At least pre-Broadway this time.

We crawled back to Chez, I had a good cry in Mama's room, and then we slept. Both of us were emotionally pooped! And, once again, we began to feel that maybe it was time for us to retire.

Unfortunately, Ed Robbins, our agent, didn't agree. He insisted we were not ready to retire. So, why argue with the man! We gave him the okay to arrange more bond rallies and we started to plan our first trip to the State of Israel.

Yonkel, also re-energized, decided that since we weren't retiring from life it was high time we began writing about what we'd enjoyed of it so far. Actually, it would be more my autobiography but written by the person who knew it best: Yonkel! His working title was "I'm Talking About Molly."

So we began 1954 full of plans and covered with snow. A queer-looking man stopped by the house and sold us something he called thermal underwear. We got into them, went out in the cold, wet stuff, and they worked. We were nice and warm.

While Yonkel wrote, I went back into the kitchen for the first time in maybe forty years. Every day I learned something new and was getting a kick out of it. It was like playing house, which I never did as a kid. To me, it's such a luxury to be able to do nothing and take your time doing it! But, what a *baleboosteh* (housewife) I became: washing clothes in the washing machine, cooking, baking, pasting little decals in the closets, ironing quietly while Yonkel wrote in his handsome den. Lucky for us, his writing was zestier than my cooking!

Throughout that February and March, I also began reading my diaries to Yonkel and found them very revealing. Full of work, success, exhaustion and travel, travel, travel. It all reminded me of a story about a deportee. He was asked where he wanted to go and then shown a world globe. Africa? No, too hot. South America? Sorry, he couldn't speak Spanish. The U.S.? Too much noise. Finally, he returned the globe and asked, "Maybe you have another one of these?"

With spring, Yonkel bought the usual new Chrysler. But instead of breezing around Mahopac, we breezed off to Texas. We were going there to do a concert for Ben Proler's Testimonial Dinner. Once again, it conjured up stories.

The first was about a similar testimonial only the Honored Guest had a heavy Jewish accent. The M.C. told the speakers to stretch out the evening so the old "Honored Guest" wouldn't have much time to talk. So each speaker started with ". . . and that reminds me of a story" and then went on and on, until after midnight, when they introduced the Honored Guest, who was no fool. He arose, looked them all over sharply and said, "Tis reminds me of nothing," sat down and got the biggest applause of the evening!

Proler then took us to the Shamrock Hotel, which was the source of a second story. It seems there was a rich Texas lady who wanted a room there, but they wouldn't take her in because they said she wasn't elegant enough. So she built a hotel right next door which she made sure was a bit higher. Then she could spit down on the Shamrock.

After Texas we went back to Chez for our first Passover seder without Mama. I didn't think I'd ever get over losing her. My heart cried out for her. When I went on to Goldman's to perform for a noisy seder crowd, my enthusiasm wasn't in it. I gave a good show, but when they asked for "My Yiddishe Mama," I broke down.

My moods told me to lay back a bit, and I did. Apart from helping Yonkel with his book and an occasional concert, the summer went by with no work, no rush and no people. I went back to being domestic and even shopped in the local Jewish butcher store. There, the owner told me Mama had always tipped him twenty-five cents! He shared some other funny Mama Picon stories and even gave me a recipe for *tsimmes*, a pudding of meat, sweet potatoes and prunes.

In July, Vivienne Segal, a school chum of mine from Philadelphia, came for a swim with her new husband, Hubbell Robinson. I had never heard of him, or what he did, but when he began talking about the Hyman Kaplan TV show (based on a book of the same name), I listened. He then asked me who I thought would be right for the part of Hymie. As if on cue, Yonkel came over to the pool carrying cocktails. "Yonkel would be just right," I said jokingly, "only he's lazy and he don't want to work!"

The next day, the William Morris office called asking if Yonkel wanted the part. "Isn't it a coincidence," I said. "Vivienne Segal was just here with her husband and when he asked me who I thought would be good for Hymie, I said Yonkel . . . who is her husband? an agent?" And Ed Robbins, my agent, laughed, "No! He's only the president of the network!"

Yonkel got the job and did very well in the role. All the papers raved about him, even though it was his first appearance on television and in English. I tell this story for all the young people who want to get into the business. All you need is a swimming pool and an old friend with pull.

Yonkel's TV triumph spurred us both into reopening our own Second Avenue theater. But before our plans took shape, we received an offer to dub our 1937 film *Yiddel Mit'n Fiddle* into English, London English. We grabbed at it because maybe it would get to Israel, at long last.

We began preparations for more travel by, of course, traveling. The September hurricanes were upon us, Carol and Edna, and there was millions of dollars' damage. Trees were torn up, phones down, lights out, refrigerated food ruined. Havoc! However, we still drove up to our concert in Jackson, New York, guided by police with flashlights. Sixty-five percent of our audience were less foolhardy. They stayed home!

Thankfully, things were better up at Scaroon, Pine View and the Catskills. And a new thrill. People recognized Yonkel from his "Hymie" show and came up to him wherever we were. What a medium television can be! Over twenty-four million people saw that show.

We were now back wintering in Miami and I did four *vodvil* shows a day as if I'd never been out of it. At one of them, a Korean war vet came over to give us the fifteen cents we spent on our call to his mother! And, to say "Thanks." Yonkel was now getting fan mail and more recognition on the streets and he was so pleased. Me too! He was with me, I was happy, and I could still do four a day!

One quick story from that tour. We were in Allentown, Pennsylvania, selling bonds and I made a sale to Charles Klein, an eighty-two-year-old eccentric millionaire. We found that he kept $10,000 (petty cash?) in his apartment. He told us he was bored with doing nothing, so took a job collecting rents. He would walk up all four flights and when people went to help him down, he'd brush them off with "Don't worry. My chauffeur is waiting!"

We wrapped up the year by spending most of November and December in the air. Literally. We played Detroit, Cleveland, Grand Rapids, Seattle, Detroit again, Windsor and Steubenville all in one week. We went from coast to coast with planes fogged in, trains late, but the show always went on.

We celebrated Yonkel's sixty-third birthday somewhere over the United States and touched down only to drink in the New Year, 1955. Waiting for us was yet another daughter of Foigel Gonif, Yonkel's stepfather. Seems she had lost two husbands and was in America looking for a third. Also on her list, we learned, was some money and a Frigidaire! We wished her well and I thought, Watch out! men everywhere!

Israel awaited. I made out a new will, got new shots, bought a new hat and flew the new El Al. A group of Hadassah women were on the plane with us and they sang all the way: from "Rabbi Elimelech" to *The Mikado*.

We had to exit at London first. And Joe Green was waiting for us. We discussed plans for dubbing *Yiddel* and then went off to see Margaret Rutherford in some review.

The name escapes me because that night I had a terrible

fright. Yonkel, who had been nursing a cold, simply fell over and fainted. We got him back to our hotel and I was plenty worried. Yonkel, on the other hand, brushed my concern away. He seemed to bounce right back and made my cares look silly. It was a pattern we would follow again and again.

Buoyed by Yonkel's recovery I put extra zip into a concert I had been asked to do at the Dorchester. We had a warm Jewish crowd full of elegant women in Paris gowns and millions in jewels. I was a bit surprised when a waiter commented that he'd never seen anyone keep them so quiet. (A compliment, I think.)

I got a good fee, and, despite a cold of my own, set out with Yonkel to find the best French restaurant in town.

We decided to do London in style, this time. One night, Covent Garden; the next, *Richard II* at the Old Vic. Yonkel wore his tux, and I got equally done up.

Unfortunately, our dubbing of *Yiddel* didn't fare nearly so well. We listened to the first playback and realized we were attempting an almost impossible task. Here we were dubbing a Yiddish play and all the actors sounded British.

The working conditions were equally unpleasant. We worked from nine to six in a cold movie house. While crystals of chilled air drifted from our mouths, we tried to loop each sentence by watching our lips on the screen and trying to say something similar in English. It was a long, difficult job, aggravated by what should have been obvious shortcomings. Although the orchestra, choir and conductor were excellent (and improved the film), as soon as the first British accent was heard, all improvements were undone. What we needed were some experts with *sachel* (horse sense). None were around.

We did the best we could, staying in London until it snowed, when we should have been in Israel for Purim. We finally finished, put *Yiddel Mit English* in the can, and flew to our new homeland.

The sunshine at Lydda Airport was our first welcoming sign as we touched down in Israel. Although I had performed in Palestine, this was my first time setting foot on sanctioned, bona fide, State of Israel soil. Believe me, it *was* a thrilling moment. The Israeli Bond office sent us a car and driver to tour Tel Aviv and Jerusalem. We toured five different synagogues within the hour: Persian, Sephardic, Bukharan, Yemenite and Hungarian. All were orthodox Jews who each prayed in their traditional ways to the same God.

We visited a war cemetery and the Knesset. A member of the Knesset recalled a concert in the Rivoli in London, a listener recognized Yonkel from Czernowitz, and two American visitors knew me from the Arch Street Theater in Philadelphia! So we were at home in Jerusalem.

Our next stop was Haifa, the city we liked best: with Haar ha Carmel, mountains and the sea. In the evening, Mayor Aba Hushi gave us a reception in his two-room flat. Mrs. Hushi baked us special cakes and both of them made us feel very much at home. He and I had once done a bond show together in Pittsburgh. Now, he was giving me the grand tour of what was being done there. The scope was tremendous. In Israel, in order to see all that was being done, your day had to begin at 6:00 A.M. New buildings were going up, the beaches were crowded, the young were everywhere and from Upper Galilee to Shabbat in Tel Aviv, all was beautiful, strong and free.

It was during this visit that our second adopted child came into our lives. My stepbrother (child of that wife in Poland Papa never let us know he had) had married an Israeli. When we learned his wife was pregnant, we had sent them money to survive. Now, the wife had died and we were quite taken with their child, Meira. She was seventeen years old, a Sabra, with black eyes full of life. Her goal was fashion design and we wanted to adopt her and send her through high school and college. Meira was smitten with us also and we quickly made plans for her to eventually come to America.

We gave our first benefit concert in Israel at Ramat Gan for the Israeli Red Cross, the Mogen David Adom. Our audience was small but their response was terrific.

Their job ahead was an overwhelming one, its enormity underscored for us daily. We met so many people we had known once in their prime and who were now impoverished, cut off from their families, living on charity and hope. Among them were the daughter of Yonkel's rabbi, the son of our Polish impresario (who was slain in Russia), and numbers of once-wealthy Romanians now reduced to rags.

Each of these people had fled to Israel as refugees. None of them were allowed to take any valuables with them when they ran. So many of them were people who were too old to start their lives over. They had no money, no language, and few of their own people. They were completely isolated.

Saddest of all was that many of the Yiddish actors knew how hopeless their plight was in Israel and looked to America to cure what ailed them. However, they hoped that cure would be a place for them in our Yiddish theater. How could I tell them that Second Avenue had died in the meantime?

Our visit was quickly coming to an end and we tried vainly to see, hear and absorb everything. At night, we got on the Habimah Bus to Herzlia to see a desert company do *Tea House of the August Moon*. Splendid. Up at 7:00 A.M., we were off to the Negev, Beersheba, the Cave of the Dead Sea. At Beersheba, the mayor spoke very seriously, very afraid that it might be too late for Israel unless America helped.

Our finale was a reception given by Prime Minister Sharett at his home. The entire Knesset was there and I sang. They listened and approved. We then gave a concert for Ezrat Nashim (Women's Aid) and President Ben Zvi himself received us with his wife in the barracks hall. Very impressive, despite the locale! We did three tapings for our American radio show, lunched in a mental hospital and didn't let up until our rumps hit the cushions on our airplane seats.

We flew via Rome and Iceland, two nights on a plane, landing at Idlewild (now Kennedy) at three in the morning amid a raging blizzard. Just as we had left it!

Once again, we had traveled far afield and were back at our doorstep trying to sort out what was behind us and what lay ahead. It would take a long time to digest what we had absorbed in Israel, of course. But, in the meantime, we had to decide what was going to happen to our lives in the States.

First, however, we went to Mt. Hebron Cemetery to see Mama's tombstone, which we had ordered months before. It said simply "Mama Picon" and I couldn't believe she had been gone for over a year. I smiled at the lettering and said, "We've had to go on without you, Mama. And it's just never been the same."

Chez Shmendrick seemed a bit unkempt in our absence, especially with Angelo no longer there. We searched around and hired a nice old gardener, Mr. Tompkins, a gem who did everything. By June, he was filling up the pool again and we celebrated my second birthday (my fifty-seventh) by dining on champagne and love.

Idyllic? Yes. But not as a diet for every day. I guess we were at that certain age: certainly no youngsters but hardly ready for the grim reaper! I wanted to walk on the stage again. Even play a child again! Play anything.

My spirit was willing. Only the offers were weak. Finally, two producers from the remnants of Yiddish theater conned Yonkel into writing them a play. In Brooklyn. For next season.

Yonkel got right to work on something he called *Farblondjete Honeymoon* (a snafued honeymoon, in loose translation)! He read me his first act, which sounded fresh and playable. And what was I doing? Freezing beans!

July and August were the hottest on record so we took a breather (Yonkel from playwriting, me from beans). We toured Cape Cod and Provincetown (or, actually, its one street). The landscape was a juxtaposition of Portugese fisherman, gays, psychiatrists and folk singers. And some certified Bohemians, or as Mama called them, *Behaymas* (cows).

We returned to Chez unrefreshed and to find our beloved King very ill. Our faithful friend for eight years had to be put to sleep. The old dog was full of tumors. Everyone was so upset, but Yonkel most especially. The man who had grown to adulthood fearful of even the tiniest pup, who knew dogs only as snarling animals sent by the Poles to growl after young rabbinical students, dearly loved King. He would deeply miss him.

Yonkel committed himself to finishing *Farblondjete* to compensate for his loss. When it was done, he read it to his producers and they both said: needs more "heart" (translation: they want it sticky-sweet). Well, maybe for Brooklyn. So Yonkel went back to goo it up.

While he reworked, an early fall hurricane hit. This one was named Connie and she created a five-state disaster. Our cellar was flooded up to the sills and the new macadam road caved in. After she mowed over us, it was Operation Clean-up. Tompkins and I labored to get the grounds green again. Shortly afterward, I was still able to exhibit my vegetables at the Firehouse Flower Show. And won Second Prize.

The hurricane had cost us $5,000 in damages so when our producer, Jacobs, asked me for lyrics, I quickly agreed. I had no idea if we were even insured for hurricanes.

We started the September season with rehearsals, costume fittings, interviews, music cues and prayer: let this play please come to life.

As usual, the plot of *Snafued Honeymoon* was no intellectual challenge. This was comedy at its simplest level of farce. I played a young girl (what else?) who worked as a maid in a fancy house. Naturally, the lord of the manor fell madly for her, she fends him off rather unconvincingly, and they marry. The rest of the play involved all the obtacles blocking the consummation of their wedded bliss.

It had been five years since we had played the Yiddish theater and I had absolutely no idea what greeting awaited our return. We opened September 26, 1955, in Brooklyn at the Palace Theater (which was anything but the Palace). And, hard to believe, we did it again. A hit. The biggest box office in Brooklyn, ever. The audience gobbled us up.

We were back and, for a while at least, so was Jewish theater. Our matinees were tremendous, our nights SRO. Other theaters were doing $80 an afternoon, we were doing $800. And getting paid $850 a week on top of it. We were champs (along with the Dodgers, who won the World Series that year). Bravo, Brooklyn!

We now rented a furnished apartment near the theater and left Mary back at Chez, where she quickly called us with the good news: our cellar was flooded again, right in the middle of rehearsals. Yonkel was yelling at the crew (who were yelling back), I was starring in one play and trying to learn another, and the bottom of my house was washing away. A nice quiet life.

As soon as our producers had read *Farblondjete,* they asked us to write a second play to be performed for special benefit groups, many of whom would have seen *Snafued Honeymoon.* Now, we were trying to fulfill their wishes, but everything was difficult in that penny-pinching operation. We had no scenery yet, no costumes. In a desperate attempt at a run-through, we performed our new play before a *Farblonzet* crowd and the audience rioted. They had come to see *Snafued Honeymoon* and got snafued instead. It was a nightmare. Yonkel went out and spoke to them and eventually the audience quieted down and was satisfied. But the entire experience was very upsetting and for the first time in a long while I had to take pills to fall asleep.

Slowly, slowly, things did begin to take shape. By the fifth week of *Farblondjete,* all was well enough for us to sneak a half-day's rest at Chez. There I just smelled the green earth and lazily talked to Tompkins about manure. By our seventh week, we were coasting. November was upon us, and Yonkel turned sixty-four. Next year, social security!

With winter came the seasonal slump. Our business was way off. One woman asked to go in for half-price. She said she'd only look with one eye! With that line, Yonkel let her in free.

Christmas would bring the opening of our English version of *Yiddel,* now titled *Castles in the Air.* We previewed it with no great expectations and booked it at the World Theater.

We were starting our eleventh week, yet my nervous stomach wouldn't let me relax. I began to have severe stomach pains, had to watch my diet, and after each show it was fruit, tea and bed. I was getting injections for colitis, vitamin B_{12}, ACTH, and hoped it all helped. We were the only Yiddish theater still open. And I was full of medication. Worse, it was Christmas, and our Scrooge-bosses had signed over all of $200 for presents for everyone.

We were now drawing crowds on sheer merit. There were no ads, nothing. And as 1956 was screamed in by half-a-million people on times Square, I was also screaming—in pain.

By now, I suspected something was wrong inside me. But the only advice the doctor gave me was take hot baths. (Was that a subtle way of saying "Go soak"?) Finally, Doctor Feit, my internist, suggested a radiologist and, maybe, surgery. The radiologist found nothing major—just a minor case of very bad hemorrhoids. Feit said "operate" and I agreed. "Feit, I know you'll do all right." Then, in Yiddish, I added: *Die Sonim oif Zelaaches*, roughly, try to fix my *taaches!* (A literal translation is not for print.)

Off in a private room, I was doped all day and then it was over. Nurses crowded into my room, one to tell me we had entertained her ten years ago in a D.P. camp. There were cards, flowers, and pain with a capital P. The after-effects were excruciating, numbed only by sitz baths, wet packs, all messy and painful except for Yonkel who was by my side until they threw him out at night.

I went home, weak and in agony, and—as they say— maybe I should have stayed in bed. *Castles in the Air* opened and the notices were not too kind. Only the *Herald Tribune* was good to me. All the charm of the original got lost in translation.

Everything was bothering me and poor Yonkel stuck to me despite every *kvetch*. But he was tired and we were grateful to Mary, who decided to sell her little house and move permanently into ours. It would be good for her and for us.

Still mending, I agreed to take *Farblondjete* to Miami and it was the right decision. We did 100 percent better than Brooklyn, I was having a vacation, and we were getting paid for it all. On February 28th, the managers held a party for me in the lobby (a first!). I feigned surprise and we all had a good time. Even Jacobs, our Brooklyn producer, sent flowers (another first).

The birthdays and anniversaries were piling up for Yonkel and me. And on every occasion we exchanged gifts according to whim. One year Yonkel bought me a Royal Red maple tree and a Pink dogwood. Our thirty-seventh wedding anniversary followed shortly afterward, and we gave each other two more Royal Reds which further brightened up our garden with their flaming leaves. When several Polish refugees came to visit, they took one look at the foliage and said, "The President of Poland doesn't live so nice!"

At other times, especially when we were in a hit show and feeling flush, we'd both run about planning extravagant secret surprises. During *Farblonzet*'s run, and with Yonkel scoring on TV, he bowled me over with a luxurious black diamond mink coat and another $1,000 bond. I, meanwhile, had been working with various jewelers fashioning what I hoped would be a unique series of gold cuff links, each set representing an aspect of Yonkel's creative life.

Throughout 1956 and 1957 we just enjoyed our countrywide tour and even took *Farblonzet* to a *goyish* theater. We opened at the Somerset Playhouse, where Tallulah Bankhead had opened the week before. Extra chairs were needed for our run. Our audiences were young but very responsive.

Encouraged, we moved on to the Wedge Summer Theater in Atlantic City and again, sold out. The first Yiddish play to do the Straw Hat Circuit and break records, too. Even Mom Samitz, a Romanian restaurateur, and a sort of Polly Adler on the side, brought thirty of her girls.

But with Chez so attractive to us, we would find ourselves accepting work which kept us near home. We even got a new dog to sit with us by our hearth! (How more domestic could we get?)

Prince joined us rather reluctantly, at first. He was a lovely, taffy-colored Collie mix, part of a litter from a friend in the Bronx. After we had put him in our car and driven him to our house, however, he refused to eat or drink. He just sat quietly in a corner and looked homesick and unhappy. Two days later, he ran away so we called his former owners and asked them to take him back. They arrived and joined us in a fruitless search. We just couldn't find him. Finally, our friends left, we gave up hunting and went to bed. At 6:00 A.M., Mary called up to our bedroom, "He's back, Prince is back!" We tumbled down the stairs and found this ragged, wet dog waiting for us. Yonkel went right to the kitchen, took out a big chunk of steak from the fridge and gave it to Prince.

He ate and drank with gusto then fell asleep, all muddy and tired. In the next few days, he slowly began to follow Yonkel around and we began to grow hopeful that he'd stay. As it happened, Prince grew old along with us. We had passed some sort of test with him. We had proved faithful and he did likewise.

With Prince at his side, Yonkel began working on something called *Ghetto Gayeties* while I translated the songs. He had agreed to do more work for Jacob Jacobs but he had taken the assignment without having any heart in it. Yonkel felt Jacobs and his partners were too passé, part of a world long dead or dying, and it was depressing to work for them. Their theaters were old, dirty, and moss-covered. They ran no advertisements in the press, not even cardboard window posters. But their audiences always proved responsive to anything we did. They were the ones who kept us returning. Deep down, however, we both yearned for something better.

But what? I was now fifty-nine years old and the offers were coming in, but most often from South America, British Columbia or Cleveland. We had fans all over the world and were grateful they still wanted to see us again, and again. But I found we were pursuing our travels just to keep from getting bored. Granted, with every audience we would rise to the occasion; but we were itching for something different to test our skills.

Just at this time, a Mr. Warren walked into our lives. He had a summer theater in Atlantic Beach and asked us to do *The World of Sholem Aleichem* for two weeks in July. Unlike our previous work in the theater, however, Warren already had a script written by the author of *Fiddler on the Roof.* Yonkel would not be needed as a playwright, and I wasn't the star. It was Yonkel who would play the lead!

His character was "Mendele," a bookseller who narrated the play's stories by Aleichem and his contemporaries. I had a smaller role and mainly would work on songs which needed to be added. Yonkel, however, would be stage acting for the first time in many years and he threw himself into studying his role.

It was a script both of us could enjoy. The characters

were warm and tender but, most importantly, human. Our delight in the play made it easier to fly about and finish the concert and play commitments we still had while rehearsing *Sholem Aleichem* at the same time.

Right through June, we did benefits, concerts and toured with *Farblondjete*. And it did get a bit crazy. Once, we opened at the 8th Street Playhouse in Chicago and our child actress couldn't make it. Yonkel did some quick surgery and, re-arranging the script, cut out her part just before we went on. Meanwhile, Michael Michalesko, the once-handsome Yiddish matinee idol who now played second lead, was old and sick and we had to fly him back to New York and bring in a replacement. In the middle of all this, Yonkel was learning his lines for Mendele which would be spoken in Yonkel's most difficult tongue: English! Yet he knew almost his whole part and auditioned it for me. His voice was tender, his inflections charming and funny. I felt he was beautifully fit for the part and couldn't wait to see him in it.

Full rehearsals for *Sholem Aleichem* began with Stanley Warren directing. The cast was uneven (the youngsters particularly bad) but everyone was eager. What bits of scenery and props we saw seemed ingenious. We trained it out to Atlantic Beach every day full of enthusiasm.

We also threw ourselves back into the New York City scene. In one typical day we had morning rehearsal, took the train back to Manhattan, walked to Broadway to see *Rock 'n Roll Madness* at the Paramount, had guests in town for dinner, and ended our night at Madison Square Garden listening to Billy Graham.

The World of Sholem Aleichem opened on July 9, 1957, at the Capri Theater in Atlantic Beach. As I expected, Yonkel was magnificent; we had a big house and a very good week. I was less happy with my performance at first, but I worked to get it better and better. Our friends from the city and Mahopac all said it was worth coming 170 miles to see. What a compliment coming from an otherwise jaded group! A bigger thrill, however, was when over one hundred teenagers came and were a wonderful audience. They loved the play and crowded backstage for autographs. (So who needed Elvis? We had Yonkel!)

Our two-week engagement passed in a blur. We had a very good last show which went beautifully, but it wasn't big enough to encourage a return. We begged off and everyone was sorry to see us go.

Arnold Perl, the author, had been taken with Yonkel's performance and now wanted him to play Tevye for Perl's version of *Tevye and His Daughters* (later made famous as *Fiddler on the Roof*). We raced back to Chez, unloaded all the food we'd bought at Sam's Deli in Long Beach, and began to read Perl's script.

We disliked every page. I didn't like the script or the part and neither did Yonkel. The role was too long, unfunny, and the entire play seemed labored. We called Perl and turned him down. And there we were staring at twelve weeks with no work.

But we needn't have worried. Yonkel had his book to finish and I could have filled my days just tending to Prince. Our faithful friend had discovered sex and now went roaming. Eventually, he'd come back full of burrs and cuts and I'd have to clean him. Poor Prince, he was paying the price for puberty.

Our country idyl didn't last long, however; at least not for Yonkel, the new star in our family. Despite his success with Hyman Kaplan on TV, Yonkel was still reluctant to speak, let alone perform in English because he thought his accent mangled the proper pronunciations. He had worried needlessly. He had done only two roles in English but the offers were coming in. His first was for a television comedy-drama called "The Littlest Leaguer." It was for "The Goodyear Hour" and Sal Maglie, the Dodger great, would star. Yonkel's role was as kindly old Gramps and he got third billing.

The show aired on August 25th, and Yonkel sparkled. Although his part was small, he appeared so genuine and natural that everyone called to compliment him. *The New York Times* gave him a rave notice, and only for him, and his director said he deserved an Emmy for what he did with a line.

Well, I was tickled for him. He had stolen the show with only twenty lines. I had a lovely champagne supper waiting for him at home. The phone was ringing with well-wishers, and he deserved every single wish. The next day, the fan mail began coming in and the offers with them. Art Carney wanted him for a new play and Lee Tracy for his "New York Confidential" TV series. Me? I took two prizes and three honorable mentions at the local Garden Show!

CHAPTER ✻ 13

Yonkel and I saw Arnold Perl's version of *Tevye* and we walked out after the first act. Yonkel had been smart to avoid getting involved in such a failure. However, there were no other New York offers for us and fall and winter loomed without a hint of local work. As always, we had to hit the road: a bit of *vodvil* here, and tours of our past successes opening everywhere.

In Montreal, at the Monument National, we did one act of *Molly, Dolly* and one act of *Yonkele* and it was a hilarious evening. There I was, fifty-nine years old, making Yonkele (a thirteen-year-old Yeshiva boy) believable. And I didn't feel a bit silly doing it. *Yonkele* was our Peter Pan and always was a joy for me to do. Deep, deep down within me, I *was* Yonkele. I still am!

We zigzagged a bit—Philadelphia, El Paso, Chicago—and then planned a tour of *Farblondjete* (to be done in English and Yiddish) which would take us west right to the Coast. There, we opened at the Carmel Theater in Hollywood, a new experience and a traumatic one.

In the first scene, a child was supposed to pull me backward. The theater—a former movie house—was in dreadful condition, and when the young actor tugged at me, I tripped on some shabby carpeting and fell. Crack! I landed smack on my right wrist. Somehow, in shock, I got up, held my right hand up with my left and kidded my way out of the fall. I did a piano solo with one hand and then finished the show in a daze.

As soon as the curtain fell, I was taken to a hospital where I learned I had broken my wrist completely. I wasn't surprised, the pain was horrible. The wrist was set, I was given some sedation and left to sleep.

A bone specialist was brought in the next morning. He took one look at my X rays and decided to completely reset the bones. By six that evening, I was on my feet, full of sedation and wearing a cast from my fingers to my elbow. Yet, I went on with the show. Edward G. Robinson was there and said it was an experience to see what I did with only my left hand.

The show was a hit, but I was helpless. I couldn't wash, dress, even comb my hair without help. Yonkel assisted like an angel but I was dead-tired, my every movement an effort. It would take at least eight weeks for me to mend. As we rang out 1957, I prayed the New Year would heal all wounds.

However, 1958 in Hollywood proved hot and dreary. There was no rain, and between the heat and my broken arm, I was down. Our business was very good, but, as it was always before, I wasn't happy in that city. People seemed to be nice, but I sensed an insincerity which made me irritable. Everyone seemed afraid that others were lurking, ready to pounce on them and take away their jobs. Nobody trusted anyone, especially outsiders like us. No one ever let you know this directly. Instead, we came to Hollywood, met all the top people, sang and danced at their parties, and everyone said they loved us. Then fifteen years went by and we still hadn't been invited back. What craziness. At least in our Second Avenue theaters there was no need for paranoia and we had a healthy life.

Aggravating my already moody situation was the fact that I had to stay put all day so I'd have the strength to go on at night. While the rest of our company went out and had a ball, Yonkel stayed by my side to dress and even feed me. All my costumes had to be button-fronted and I looked like the latest doll, "Poor Pitiful Pearl." At the theater, the girls took turns making my changes; and the only thing I had to cut out was the Yonkele scene which had been my encore. I couldn't do my somersault! Otherwise, our business remained good and I shouldn't have complained about anything because the rest of the theaters there were in trouble. Eric Porter, the English actor who recently starred in *The Forsyte Saga* on NET, was then doing a superb job in *Separate Tables*, yet his audience was meager. The nightclubs were also empty. Even the famed Brown Derby shut down at midnight. We were grateful to have finished a month.

The only good side effect was that Yonkel had been able to continue reading his book to me. I thought he had done a masterful job. The book had grown into his autobiography, but one full of humor and humility and I was anxious for him to complete it so that a competent translator could be found. Yonkel always wrote in Yiddish and I knew we'd have to find someone special to do justice. (As it happened, Yonkel spent the rest of his life polishing his opus, so I'm still looking for that special someone.)

We had a brief run with *Farblondjete* in San Francisco, but I was exhausted and on edge and screamed, "I wanna go home!"

We flew back to New York and taxied to Mahopac. The countryside was full of snow, but we made it up our hill and shouted *Hurrah!*

Prince was frantic with joy and Mary had hot soup to welcome us back. It was good to be home, even with my broken arm still in a cast. Now it was just a matter of waiting patiently and forcing myself to rest until I healed.

Sitting tight wasn't so easy, however, despite Mary's fussing. To regain use of my right hand, I began squeezing putty with my fingers.

The month of February passed in a blank. I was seven weeks in my cast and straining at the leash. Part of the cast was cut off at my elbow but it was still painful and clumsy to try and straighten my arm. By the eighth week, I was desperate to have the rest of the cast removed because we had three concerts booked. Yet when it did come off, my wrist was swollen and tender and I would have to be careful. Grrrr!

I played Flushing, Oceana and the Eastern Parkway area in pain. But these were captive audiences for us and the evenings were ours.

Then we rushed back to Chez and just in time. My sixtieth birthday fell on February 28th and blew in about a ton of snow for each year. Mary was out, and Yonkel and I had celebrated with a bottle of champagne and cheered every snowflake, just loving being together. By morning, we were surrounded by white and completely snow-bound. Drifts were five feet high and rising. The blizzard stretched from Maryland to Maine and we were glad to be home and safe. That day, Mike Todd had died en route to a Friars testimonial in New York. His private plane crashed during the storm killing him and three others. I listened to the news and kept squeezing my badly bruised putty ball.

The snow passed and after a white winter, I welcomed the sight of our first red robin. I was mended and so was the weather. We began to work our way up into the Catskills and I had two new numbers which looked good. Yonkel had scenes from his Hymie Kaplan TV show and was also ready to go.

We did Fallsview, Ellenville, Laurel, Lakewood, Browns, Lock Sheldrake and Kutschers—the tops. We had an older audience and worked hard to warm them up. They were sweet, despite their ages. One old man told us he had asked his father to come and the father (who must have been ancient) had said: *"Men ken chapen a drimmel dort?"* (Can you catch a nap there?)

Whenever the weather warmed up, we hit the road. We played Newark, Johnstown and then Phoenix, Arizona. We sold bonds and sang and then were off. I stopped at Chez only long enough to transplant some Mexican poppies and a rose tree. Then we were back in the air again for Tucson. After a seven-hour flight, we joined the locals in a restaurant-club and told our stories and pushed bonds until 2:00 A.M. It was all a bit rough, but we sold $40,000 all in one day.

We were now back on our fast track: sliding through spring and summer from Florida to Fallsburgh and every point in between. We would have kept right on traveling together but the Morris office called to tell Yonkel that he had the part on Lee Tracy's "New York Confidential" television series.

The script was waiting for Yonkel back at Chez and he eagerly began studying it. He then went off to the city to rehearse and shoot the telefilm while I rested. Yonkel needed the applause and deserved it. He had been treated badly in the Yiddish press and pretty much overlooked by the *goyish* ones who had no idea how much he contributed to my success. His efforts at keeping the Yiddish theater alive were never fully appreciated so I enjoyed having him singled out to do television roles.

He filmed all day in the city then called to tell me that a casting director had seen the rushes and wanted him for a Goldwyn film. I welcomed my TV star home with a hearty, late-night dinner and listened as he complained about TV filming just like a trouper: too much hard work, too little money, and no glory!

I spent much of my time in my gardens. September was upon us, and Mary and I started canning tomatoes and cukes, running everywhere to pick and pickle. Yonkel had gotten a call from CBS to do a segment of "Look Up and Live" and was off to the city.

Mainly, however, I was working just to keep busy. The concerts were always as good as I could make them, I continued to try and wow my audience so they'd be pleased, but my work was now so routine I could have done it while asleep. And the time of the year also got me down.

It was five years since Mama died, but I could still feel her presence in so much of my life. Her spirit filled every corner of our house which made me miss her all the more. But we had to keep going on and we journeyed into the city for an elegant Adler affair.

Stella was giving a party to celebrate a new nephew, the child of Luther Adler and Sylvia Sidney. It was *très chic*, with two butlers and everyone in evening clothes. Yonkel brought a twenty-volume set of world drama and Stella was thrilled. Sarah, the family matriarch, was also present and still magnificent in her dotage. She was called upon to say something and at first begged off saying, "But I'm not prepared." Then she left the room, composed herself, and returned to recite a poignant message for the newborn. She exited, of course, as *the* star. I sang and the party broke up around 3:00 A.M. We spent the night at the Astor and then visited Mt. Hebron to see Mama's grave again. The grounds were crowded with new souls and I thought, "There's no place even to die these days." Then I had a good cry and went back to town.

Waiting for me was a piece of good news. Ed Robbins, my agent at William Morris, called about a new play Dore Schary was directing. It was the story of a middle-aged Jewish woman who falls in love with a middle-aged Japanese man and was titled *Majority of One*. It sounded interesting and an appointment was made for me to meet with Schary and the author, Leonard Spiegelglass, the following day.

We met, talked about the play, and only Schary was reluctant. The woman was supposed to be sixty, my age exactly. But Schary thought I was "too young." So go figure? Nevertheless, they gave me the play and invited me to read for Schary.

I had never auditioned for anything, especially for Broadway. Early in my career, it had been made clear to me that I was thought of as "too Jewish." (Today, they would say "too ethnic.") And even when Broadway had come to me (i.e., *Morning Star*) my rave reviews never seemed to encourage any further offers. Now, here was a woman my race, my color, my creed and my age. I went to Schary's apartment convinced I could easily do the role. After I read, Spiegelglass agreed. He kissed me and said, "Molly, that's it! That's just how I wrote her!"

Yet I walked out knowing the part would probably go to Gertrude Berg. Why? Well, Schary was pretty specific. "You just don't *look* like a *Yiddishe* Mama," he told me. "You're too young, too small, too blithe, too lively."

Well, maybe he was right. It's hard to argue when you're being eliminated with compliments! But, of course, they never give you an outright *no,* so while I waited I answered a call to meet with Paddy Chayefsky. He was making *Middle of the Night* into a picture with Fredric March, and he wanted to look at me and Yonkel for possible parts in it.

We met with Chayefsky, Delbert Mann, the director and some other fellow. Each looked me over (all four feet, eleven inches) and were very sweet. To me and to Yonkel. So now we had two projects presented to us and I felt neither one would come through.

As I thought, Gertrude Berg was signed for *Majority*. And, again, I was told it was my "youth" which worked against me. I tried not to care at that point, but I still couldn't help feeling that I wasn't given a fair chance to show my stuff.

Winter was upon us and our "youthful" bones were achy. My doctor advised me to try the Safety Harbor Spa in Florida. After a bond rally in Minneapolis, we returned to Chez, packed our bags and left for Tampa on December 16th.

Safety Harbor was a completely Jewish *kuhrort*. It was tucked into a sleepy village, all very quiet and restful. A Dr. Baranov headed the spa, assisted by five other doctors. Both they and the guests all knew us, so we fell into a friendly routine. We were examined and found in good shape but a little overweight (I tipped the scales at 114¾). We were given 800-calorie diets, took mineral baths, got massaged. And in the evening, someone played on the balalaika and we all sat around and sang. Then we retired early, a bit tired from so much health activity.

One thing about the place seemed rather queer. There was a steak dinner on the Sabbath, a big deal, and then dancing. It was here we got to meet the other guests, who were all millionaires and grossly overweight. Each was trying hard to reduce, relax and have fun, but they only managed to seem sad and lonely.

To perk ourselves up, Yonkel and I got out and toured the countryside. We enjoyed the big red kapok trees, the lovely little village and the easygoing life-style. There was no pressure as in Miami and in just one week, Yonkel and I began to feel rejuvenated.

Before we left, we had a surprise guest for lunch. The famous silent film star Olga Petrova joined us at table. She was seventy-five and, after ten facelifts, had a face like a mask. But she was alert, intelligent and a definite personality. We had always thought she was Russian, but her accent revealed she was British and bullish. She lived in Clearwater with her husband and drove her own tractor on their farm.

So we finished 1958 in Safety Harbor on a strict diet. Yonkel said he never paid so much for so little. But, now we were aware of *Health* and hoped we wouldn't forget it the minute we got back to Lindy's or the Royal.

Back home, we ventured out for a concert or two, filling Hunter College Auditorium with 2,500 people and almost as many turned away. We did "Motel Payse" and narrated "Oif'n Fiedel," a story by Sholem Aleichem. Everyone seemed aglow and we were gratified, but we felt it was a shame there couldn't be more such audiences for the Yiddish tongue.

We would soon begin preparing for another Jewish Theater season but we felt no great rush. Yonkel worked on some play ideas, I contributed some songs, but we kept a slower pace. For my sixty-first birthday, we celebrated with a bottle of Burgundy and a nice dinner. The National Company for *Majority of One* wanted me for the road company, but Yonkel turned it down. It would mean a year *shlepping* around without him and that wasn't for me. I trusted his judgment and we continued to enjoy our quiet dinners and fine wines. We were growing old, gracefully.

Yonkel went to town and read the first act of his new play, *Kosher Widow*, to Irving Jacobson, our new producer. He seemed excited about it and felt the benefits would sell well. Meanwhile, we were preparing for summer in the country. Our 115-year-old ash tree became diseased and began to deteriorate. We had to cut it down and were left with a terrific mess. Yonkel was right to name our home Chez Shmendrick, after our traditional fool. You begin to feel like a *shmendrick* every time even holes in the ground cost money! But it was our home, we loved it, and it paid off in beauty.

I began to feel I was merely marking time in my career. All my concerts seemed predictable and routine. Frankly, I was bored with myself and yearned for something new. Two offers provided just the spark I needed.

First, I was asked to introduce the role of Mrs. Jacoby in the London premier of *Majority of One*. I would be facing a very different crowd in a very different atmosphere. It was just the challenge I needed, yet I held back. I was still stung by Dore Schary's negative appraisal of me in the lead, and so didn't leap at the London offer. Yonkel, however, knew how badly I wanted something fresh and we scheduled it in for after the New Year.

The London Theatre Guild soon called that Robert Morley, my London co-star, and his partner were on their way to "talk" to me about doing *Majority of One*. Having had such "talks" before, I thought the idea was crazy but said, "Let 'em come!"

I took to my gardening and Yonkel worked on his play. In between, we both set out to surprise the other with a special wedding anniversary gift. We had spent forty years together, and each of us had been secretly meeting with jewelers in order to fashion a unique gift. I worked with a silversmith and had him sculpt the *shmendrick*'s clown face on a pair of solid silver cuff links. He worked to duplicate the *shmendrick* face of a painting Yonkel loved. I was sure Yonkel hadn't suspected my gift and would be overwhelmed.

He was, but not as much as I. Unknown to me, Yonkel had been working with Jack Maltz to create a bracelet out of forty antique gold hearts, each heart representing one of our years together. There isn't another one like it in the whole world, just like there isn't another Yonkel!

Majority of One had opened on Broadway with Gertrude Berg and Yonkel and I went to see it. Berg was a "personality" not an actress and it showed. She brought no color or variety to her part, but acted pretty much on one level. Yet she was clever, and skillful enough so that she sold the little she had. And she had a hit. After seeing what she was doing, and getting raves for it, I had a change of heart and told the London people I didn't think *Majority* was for me. They were very upset and asked me to forget what I saw and to reread the play. (I was flattered by their concern. Later, I learned that Morley had stipulated that he would only do the play if I co-starred. It seems mine was the only Jewish name known in London. Over there, I was still considered a Palladium star.)

I went off to Philadelphia for a bond rally at the Warwick Hotel and thought about what to do. Finally, back home at

Chez, I reconsidered and told Morley's people that I would do *Majority* if they would start rehearsals in February. Everyone was very happy and set off for London to work out a contract.

Our fortieth anniversary fell on June 29th and from Belgium our adopted son wired: "Life Begins at Forty." The following day, a Mr. Langner of the London Theatre Guild called for an appointment. He wanted to come up and "see" me, and that's just what he did. We were swimming and sunning ourselves when he arrived. He said he just needed to "look" at me. It was nutty.

Yonkel had polished *Kosher Widow* and then got a brilliant idea. He wanted me to play two characters, the wife and the sweetheart, each a very different type. "Molly, you can do it!" he chimed his favorite line. Well, we talked and thrashed out the character of the wife, our kosher widow, and the play sounded exciting. We were giving birth to the characters together.

Back in New York, I met (again) with Schary, Mr. and Mrs. Langner, Peter Davis and some Guild people. And it looked like I'd be doing Mrs. Jacoby even if *Majority* meant a year away from home. I was still doubtful, but Yonkel liked the idea. So, as Grandma used to say, "I'll try mine best."

We were now into August's heat, and I got ready for our Second Avenue season with two bee stings which swelled my arm into a baseball bat. I needed special shots and was drowsy for days. I had put Yonkel on our two-day steak diet (because I was overweight for *Majority*) and, nasty from hunger, learned that offers and counter-offers were crossing the Atlantic over my fee. When it rains . . . etcetera.

But, I was going to be stage acting again and growing more excited with each day. I had been looking for something different and my second new deal arrived. Jerry Lewis was doing *The Jazz Singer* for TV and wanted me for the part of the mother. (So maybe I did look like a *Yiddishe* Mama, after all.) Jerry's producer called and said he and the director would be coming into New York to meet me and "look" me over. What, again??!

We gathered at the Barbizon Plaza and I guess they liked

what they saw. After much nonsense, they made us an offer which was double what they had started with and we accepted. Now we had to work fast. We needed costumes for *Kosher Widow,* new duds for our Hollywood jaunt, and heaven knows what else for a year in London. I had an upset stomach from the heat, insect bites galore and pressure from Ocean to Ocean. But, we were back in Show Biz!

I had no script yet for *The Jazz Singer* but was getting plenty of publicity. I bought a mink stole and two new suits, had my hair and nails done, got a fresh dose of poison ivy just to keep me humble, and with Chez bursting out in the reds and yellows of autumn, I set off for the Golden Coast.

In Burbank, I immediately walked into madness. I met directors, actors, secretaries, ad agency people: "yes" men and "no" men and errand boys. Everyone but Jerry or his producer. They were both "busy" so I observed the scene at NBC Studios, glanced at a script, and that was that.

Until Jerry arrived. Then bedlam took on a stranger form. Lewis was bright and opinionated and demanded center stage. Everyone danced to his tune. On the set, Jerry smashed oranges against the wall, fenced with his valet, did bellyflops over tables, burst out into song and dance routines, everything but rehearse. We sat on our derrières all day reading and rewriting our scripts to Jerry's conception.

It all seemed quite crazy but Jerry, in spite of his antics, knew his business and asserted himself. He got things done his way. Part of his problem was that, once he got his way, he was afraid to begin. He took me aside at one point and said, quite seriously, "I'm in awe of you." Meaning, I think, I'm in awe of what you represent and I want to measure up to those standards. For an hour, he tried to impress upon me how dedicated he was to his work despite the clowning. But we still sat and sat while Jerry clowned and re-wrote. I gave Yonkel a call and listened to the Dodgers beat Chicago 3 to 1.

Adding to Jerry's nervousness was the fact that his wife was about to give birth. After a long, tiresome day, he said he had to go home and hold her hand. As sort of a peace gesture, he brought me a blowup of a Loew's State program from 1945 when he was listed number two on the bill and I starred. That day, we were in the studio from twelve to twelve and the hours were interrupted only briefly when Jessel, Berle or George Burns would drop by.

Lewis wanted very much for this version of *The Jazz Singer* to be very different from Jolson's. One of his creative decisions was to play the last act, when he rushes to his father's death bed, in clown makeup. The scene, of course, was one where the jazz singer gets reunited with Mama who had hoped he would be a cantor. To ease her sorrow, he sings a Jewish spiritual to her. The moment was made for high drama but Lewis insisted on introducing a weird sort of low comedy. He chose a huge fake nose and garish makeup for his clown's face and threw everyone into an uproar. All his "yes" and "no" men advised him against the outfit, but he insisted. Later, the critics would rip him apart over it.

The lights for color television were three times hotter than anything I'd experienced, so the filming left me pooped. But we'd rehearse, shoot, see the results, then shoot again, and finally we finished. Everyone praised what I'd done and Jerry gave me a diamond lavalier and a *shmaltz* award. I just hoped what I did made sense and was worthwhile, then I packed for home and flew away. Never, never was I so glad to see Yonkel's face. I fell into bed with the aid of pills and kisses!

I was back in my own world: legitimate theater, and our show looked promising. We watched *The Jazz Singer* on television and I thought it was a good show. Jerry was convincing, his acting was restrained, and I felt I had done a lot with my small part. Unfortunately, everyone hated Jerry in the role. It was a shame because he so wanted success.

We opened *Kosher Widow*, unofficially, with a benefit show. The audience was sticky and we started slow. The second act was better but not too good. There was a half-hour speech between acts plus a collection. All the old evils. We needed to make corrections.

We reworked and repolished and the entire company began easing up. We had been concerned because *Widow* was our first completely dramatic play. And Yonkel had written an ambiguous ending. But the audiences were waiting for us, bless them, and we began to smell a success. I only hoped that Yonkel's work would be appreciated because he really gave this one his all.

We officially premiered on Saturday, October 31st, at the Anderson Theater. Afterward, we went to Moskowitz and Lupowitz (our Sardi's) and Lenny Lyons was there, the Cantors were there, the Abrams, the Franzblaus and every table applauded. A smash.

The next day, the *Times* critic was equally wonderful and now we had the blessing of both camps: Yiddish and English! Yonkel got a very good notice in the Jewish *Tag;* even they gave in this time. And the *Forward* also wrote us up lavishly.

And something new in Yiddish theater: we were getting mail orders! Even the benefit audiences cheered. *Time* magazine squired me to Sardi's for a big interview. Richard Tucker, Leo Roslyn, even Dore Schary, Langner and Spiegelglass were full of praise. Lenny Spiegelglass bubbled to me, "You have nothing but talent!" Each part really had not been too difficult for me, and with our success, what every actress dreams about had come true for me.

Amid all the cheers and shouting, the contracts for *Majority of One* were in and I suddenly realized what a commitment lay ahead. Yonkel, despite *Kosher Widow*'s success, was still just as eager for me to do this. When our lawyers made too many suggestions about my contract, Yonkel said: "Gentlemen, don't let's be beastly to the British!"

We celebrated Yonkel's sixty-eighth birthday on stage, after the show. The theater's managers gave him a portable television set and the audience joined the show orchestra for several choruses of "Happy Birthday." We all saluted with *oif Lange Yuhren* (for many years)!

In the middle of our fourth week, I broke away from the theater to meet Robert Morley at Sardi's. He insisted on my having champagne and was very warm and outgoing and huge! It looked like it would be fun to work with him and, for the first time, I didn't have doubts about signing the contracts.

But Yiddish theater was never easy. We had Anne Bancroft and Arthur Laurents calling for tickets, yet we had to squeeze in performances of *Farblondjete Honeymoon* for the benefit crowds who'd already seen *Kosher Widow*. I ended up doing nine shows a week. But, since everyone had been saying for years that Yiddish theater was dying, it was a feather in our hats to make it come alive again. Of course, try and tell that to the woman in the Bronx who couldn't buy two seats to *Kosher Widow* because we had sold out. She answered: "That's why the Yiddish Theater is dying!" After one performance an elderly man had said, "This is the biggest thing since the Zionist Movement!"

We had the biggest hit the Yiddish theater had ever had, and our Hebrew Union gave us a big shindig to say "Thank you" and "Good Luck in London." Our poor union was in trouble; it had no money. However, the Four A's wanted to absorb it and that seemed a godsend. Other lunches and parties followed and everyone was heartbroken that we couldn't have lingered at least a dozen weeks more. We closed *Kosher Widow* on January 10, 1960, and everybody shouted "Please Hurry Back!" Every matinee and every evening show had been SRO. Every performance was a holiday. This had been the show of our dreams. How could we leave it all behind?

Part of the reason was that I felt I could go at *Majority* fresh, discarding what I had seen and disliked on Broadway. Deep down, however, I mostly couldn't wait to begin a role for which Dore Schary had turned me down!

CHAPTER 14

WE SAILED FOR ENGLAND on the *S.S. United States,* upper deck, and for the first time went first class. We were off in style for a new adventure in the theater.

On the Yiddish stage, I felt I was set. I knew I could do whatever was asked of me. *Majority of One* was something very different. The play had been conceived for non-Jewish audiences. There was no way one could fall back on Yiddish *shtik* and get by. Jenny, the leading lady, was Jewish but she was also an American. Her romance with someone Japanese had to be played as a clash of many different worlds: Jew and Japanese, White and Yellow, West and East. And on top of all that, she had to be warm, human and funny! *Oy!* I was certainly walking into the challenge I had been seeking. And I was scared.

We arrived in Southampton, took the boat train to London, and made arrangements to meet Morley for dinner. As we sat together, I marveled again at his great size and thought: "My God, how can he play a Japanese? How's he going to get up and down on those floor cushions!" Morley, on the other hand, kept looking me over and listening to my English. We were sizing each other up, but in the friendliest of atmospheres.

The publicity people for the play had joined us and we learned that Morley had changed our billing. Instead of "Starring Robert Morley and Molly Picon," he had insisted that it read "Starring Molly Picon and Robert Morley."

"Oh, but the woman's part is the lead," he said in his jovial British accent. "I deserve second billing." Since he had bought the rights to the play and, in effect, owned it, his thoughtfulness was doubly generous. (But not unique. I found that throughout the British theater even stars as great as Olivier were not afraid to take smaller roles if the play was good. Such professionalism is what's kept their theater alive. There, if you don't get a good play, you at least get good acting.)

The following day, we met Wendy Toye, our director and designer, and I saw the sets. Lovely! We were introduced to more of Morley's partners, had a nice lunch, returned to meet the rest of the cast, mingled a while, then were off for dinner and a show. Everything seemed so leisurely paced, so very unlike our rehearsals in New York. Morley had even sent flowers to my hotel room, another phenomenon.

At our first rehearsal, we blocked most of the first act and Wendy and Morley seemed pleased. I began to feel my way into Jenny's shoes but I was mostly trying to come to grips with all the easy goings-on. At five, we held a press conference where I met, among others, Morley's mother-in-law, the great English character actress, Gladys Cooper. She was in red tights and a sweater and equally easy-going. The next day, a picture of Morley and me dancing together appeared in the *News-Chronicle*. We were an odd couple, but cute.

Our second rehearsal met to block our Japanese scene where Mrs. Jacoby visits Mr. Koichi Asano's "humble" abode. Everything we did seemed raw, but a beginning. We then broke for a leisurely lunch of kippers with Morley, Wendy, the PR people, Mr. Fox, a backer, and Yonkel. Afterward, Wendy and I shopped for clothes for Mrs. Jacoby and found four good dresses. Yonkel and I dined at the Caprice, an excellent meal, and I kept waiting for the other shoe to drop. Two days of rehearsal and I hadn't gulped down a sandwich once!

Everything was so mellow, it couldn't last long and it didn't. I was having trouble getting used to the British English. I wasn't picking up my cues and Morley finally complained. So I told him I couldn't understand *him*. I think he was in shock, until he finally blurted out, "Well, then, what do you want me to do?" And I answered: "First, you can take that cigarette out of your mouth (he always had one hanging halfway out), then you can speak slowly, more articulately, and preferably in Yiddish!" Morley roared with laughter and after that we understood each other. The shoe had dropped, and now we could move on.

We still kept an easy pace, but with Wendy only working us from 11:00 to 5:30, we still had the play all blocked in three days. We were on our feet, with no scripts in our hands, and now I had to memorize my part and find myself in the character. Morley was still a bit vague about Asano and it seemed the younger members of the cast were way ahead of either of us.

In between, it took our hairdresser, Renée, four hours to undo my kosher widow–red hair and bring back my original brown. Exhausted from such a messy ordeal, we went out to see Margaret Rutherford in *Farewell Eugenie*. I found her very funny but a bit weird. She had a look that was a little bit out of this world and a tiny laugh which wasn't quite human. But, she was a delightful eccentric (that wonderfully British kind!). Afterward, at dinner, a South African recognized us, and he had purchased tickets for *Majority*. Our first customer!

We were rehearsing at the Queens Theater and making progress. We discussed how to say every line and Morley proved quite helpful. We were both still reaching in a fog, Morley especially. After each rehearsal, I'd walk back to our little service flat on Jermyn Street (just two rooms and a kitchenette), have a light supper, study my script with Yonkel cuing me, and then to bed. Morley, however, would go in and out of character and often wasn't up on his lines. Yet, Wendy was observant and soon all our characters were taking shape.

I began to feel relaxed enough to take a short break and visit our adopted son in Brussels. We had spoken to George by phone and he was anxious to have us come. We rehearsed until noon on Friday, then Yonkel and I flew to Brussels. One hour. Modern times.

George was waiting for us, and after checking our things at a local hotel, we were off to his flat to see Lizbeth and their two little girls. Yvonne was one and a half, and Carol Ann, one month. We spent two full days with them, talking and talking, and getting to know them better. We visited their raincoat factory once held by the Nazis, shopped in the local markets, watched Lizbeth cook very sensible, hearty meals, and just enjoyed. George was still working with other top physicists at the Brussels University and we were delighted to find him so brilliant and yet so warm.

We, regrettably, had to leave them on Sunday afternoon, and after leaving a check for some children's toys, we kissed each good-bye. Hopefully, they would be able to come to London for one of my performances. George had never seen me on stage and I very much wanted that.

We had terrific press in the *London Star*, the Newcastle papers and others. Such publicity spurred us all to polish the rough spots in our portrayals. And I was beginning to feel the long, long thread of English theater. I had a kimono fitting at Nathan's Theatrical Company and learned Dickens had been their customer!

Watching Morley work at his Japanese characterization was especially interesting. Wendy Toye, who was also a dancer, had to teach Morley how to sit on the floor and, tougher still, how to get up gracefully. With his great bulk, Morley was better suited for sumo wrestling than the delicate life-style of an elegant Japanese aristocrat. But he persevered and soon was sitting and rising with the grace of a Kabuki dancer. Although Morley liked to kid around a lot at rehearsals, ad-libbing and one-upping everyone, watching him work so intently to train his muscles to do the impossible convinced me he'd come through beautifully in performance. But it wasn't just Morley I was watching. Every chance I had, I went off to see as much English theater as I could from Margaret Lockwood in *Suddenly It's Spring* to Flora Robson in *Aspern Papers*.

I was intensely trying to look, learn, absorb and, despite all the outward signs of ease, my stomach knew my struggle. It got very badly upset. The doctor diagnosed it as mild dyspepsia and said not to worry, but I felt sick and woozy. That night, Morley took us to the home of a Japanese family living in London. He wanted us to study their mannerisms and customs. But when they started serving about six or seven different kinds of raw fish and Morley asked me what I wanted, I answered: "A doctor!"

We had a "Dress Parade" to try out our costumes and all my clothes seemed very good. But poor Morley now had to learn how to sit and rise gracefully in a long kimono!

We traveled to Newcastle upon Tyne on February 14th, one day before opening, in a pre-London tryout. It was a dreary, dank town, but our sets at the Royal Theatre there looked beautiful and ticket sales were even prettier. Lots of locals would be there opening night, but plenty of friends would come later. Hebrew University had bought the entire second night!

We previewed on February 15th. We had a very good house, and the play went well. I did a curtain speech and got lovely applause. Gladys Cooper, Ian Hunter, the whole crowd congratulated me. I was thrilled, and, amazingly, completely relaxed. Nobody is ever as tense as they are for a New York opening. But in the outskirts of London, I didn't have those feelings because I knew it wasn't a life or death thing. My first few lines were sticky because the audience needed a few minutes to adjust to my American English. Afterward, however, there were flowers and wires and I felt we'd done it.

Most of the local press agreed. The dailies were keen on all of us, and were especially nice to me. In fact, the only criticism I got was from a Jewish critic (it figures) who felt I used my eyes too much!

Otherwise, all was golden.

Leonard Spiegelglass was also there. I had supper with him and Morley and Lenny told us what he felt needed fixing before we opened in London. Nothing involved me! Even Schary called from New York and called me "Darling"??? Spiegelglass changed a few things and the performers got tense and a little low. Morley and I worked to lift the show's spirits and we ended once again on high. I was then giving a speech every night after each performance, telling my stories, and the cast loved it.

We finished the first week with a full house every night. And Morley was nicer than any actor I had ever met. We were working beautifully together and at the last show of the week I introduced Morley to speak but he passed to me. So, instead of stories I told the cast to all sit down and I sang "Hands." It went over wonderfully. There's nothing like having a bag of tricks to dig into!

On Sunday, we went with Morley to Harrogate. There we lunched at an old inn by the Thames where the mice nibbled at the legs of our table. Wonder if any of them had dined with Dickens? We spent the night at the Majestic Hotel, watched some of the BBC on the telly, and went to bed. So restful.

The next day, I had both a Turkish and Russian bath and a hairwash and set. It proved the highlight of my day. We had a poor dinner in the hotel and Morley, sick with a bit of the gout, stayed in his room with his swollen foot and pouted. Still, he managed to be amusing anyway, sending us three books to read in bed.

Just as most American plays open "out of town" before hitting Broadway, so we were taking *Majority of One* on the road before opening it in London. We played the Manchester Opera House and the New Theatre in Oxford and we did well every night.

In Oxford, we had two big shows which broke all house records. I celebrated my sixty-second in Oxford with champagne sent to our table by our hotel. It was interesting country, a fascinating town, with all races of people and the students in the bars dressed like Beatniks. My only problem was that we had no bath. Only a *teppele* was provided. (I think that's potty pan in translation!)

Wherever we played, we seemed to have similar audience reactions: they appeared to struggle with the first half then suddenly come to life with the second half and finish cheering on high. Meanwhile, many of the English theater greats stopped by with compliments. I was overwhelmed.

By the beginning of March, we felt ready to tackle London.

We drove in from Oxford by car, back to our flat on Jermyn Street opposite Fortnum and Mason. We unpacked and went to Isow's, our favorite Yiddish restaurant. Over dinner, Isow told us that reports from our road trip were very good and it was welcome news.

The weather was cold but Yonkel and I bundled up and took a walk around London. Yonkel knew each mew and alley from his youth, and so we tramped around buying gifts for the company.

By the last dress rehearsal, some sticky things began to come apart and feelings were low. We had a small stage which was very cold, in capital letters. I had been nursing a cough and Morley a cold, and at the last dress, he didn't show up. Even though the understudy tried valiantly, the play came apart. The sets were hard to move and everything seemed odd without the audience. I had seen our rehearsals scale the heights and plummet to the depths. Morley had been brilliant at times, careless and lackluster at others. Sometimes, I had hit with our preview crowds right off, other times they seemed to strain at my every word as if my language needed translation.

Making matters more difficult was the fact that *Majority* really doesn't build until the second act. Sheer force of will was the only thing that kept the audience attentive during the slow opening scenes. Would London's sophisticated, knowledgeable, difficult-to-please theater crowd stay with us 'til the end? Opening night, among my wires was a note from Gertrude Berg, and I thought: "Yup. I'm going to need all the best wishes I can get."

Majority of One opened at the Phoenix Theatre in London on Wednesday evening, March 9th. Everyone was in evening dress, a very classy affair, and their reaction was universally terrific. We got a great reception and an ovation at the finish. There were flowers, more wires, gifts, and everybody glowed. Yonkel said I gave a "real top" performance. Beatrice Lillie, whom I had seen and loved in New York with Noel Coward, sent flowers and we arranged to have tea together. It was the start of a mutual admiration.

The next day's press was wonderful, save for one. There was even a great write-up in the *Times* in New York. My biggest thrill, however, was that George and Lizbeth were coming in for the weekend. I was so proud that they would be seeing me on such a prestigious stage. They got Lizbeth's mother to come from Holland to babysit for their children in Belgium so they could come to London! That was international baby service, for sure! George and Lizbeth were thrilled with our show and we introduced them to Morley and Wendy—and *Finis* our first London week.

We were on high until we read the Sunday papers. Morley and I both got very good notices but they tore poor Lenny Spiegelglass and the play apart. I feared for the show. But, George and Lizbeth were with us and we roamed around Hyde Park looking at an art show. They bought a picture from a local artist and we all tried to keep our spirits up. Like Scarlett, we just told ourselves, "Tomorrow is another day."

For our second week, the house averaged fair: good in the evenings but poor for the matinees. However, the show's managers seemed happy and "Sir this" and "Lady that" were in and out telling us how wonderful we were doing. We did enjoy one swell dinner at the Claridge with Spiegelglass, Van Johnson, Estelle Brody and I as honored guests.

I did an interview with the *Telegraph* (typically British journalism: coffee and cakes and a few questions). We were getting better houses, lots of Jews, including Mrs. Izakowitz of the Yiddish theater. She was eighty years old and came alone, but said she loved the play. Friday night, the house was down, and I suspected all the Jews in London went to synagogue. But the crowd we had was very warm.

The show seemed to get better with every performance and I began to hope that we might have a run. Not a New York run maybe, but a run.

On Sunday, a day off, a reception was held for Yonkel and me by the Jewish theater community. There were writers, actors and many, many old people. Yonkel spoke and I did my "Hands" routine and everyone was delighted. We then moved on to the Grand Palais, the Yiddish theater in Whitechapel, an old, cold place. The cast had put a great deal of effort into an Israeli play, but they didn't have enough combined talent to save it. We were invited on stage and made some cheering comments but the evening left us blue.

We had bigger troubles with *Majority*. Morley's cold had worsened and his doctor wouldn't let him perform. His understudy, Ivor Dean, went on for him and didn't do badly, no one took their money back; but we didn't know how the audience would react to a prolonged absence. David Opatashu, on his way to Israel to film *Exodus,* stopped in and read us our notices in Hollywood.

Business stayed good for a few days, but began to drop when the agencies couldn't sell tickets without Morley's presence. He was still out and people knew it. I spoke to Morley and he sounded better, but his doctor wanted him home all week. It was messy, but Morley tried to help out. He sent over a very droll letter, which he asked me to read to the audience. He said that he hoped the audience would enjoy his understudy (but not *too* much!). "Enjoy him," Morley wrote, "but then please come back when I return so you can see how the part *should* be played."

We went from full evenings and great crowds to off-nights and bad feelings. People in the audience wanted to know why Morley's absence wasn't publicized in the papers. I never knew whether our show was in or out.

On Sunday, I performed in a First-Nighters Reception for Rodgers and Hammerstein held at the Criterion Theatre and filmed for British television. I sang some of my favorites, songs I'd written that were most identified with me: "Grandma's Shawl," "Hands," "Busy, Busy." Yonkel said I stole the show. And even if he was lying, it felt good to hear him say so. Richard Rodgers gave me a kiss and that helped, too.

As for *Majority,* we hung on and held our breath. Wendy, the director, sent me one rose in a vase, Japanese style, every week, and kept our spirits up. Morley finally rejoined in our third week and we looked more promising. Business was picking up and Morley said we'd really do better after Easter.

Morley and I started pushing for publicity. We had a wonderful write-up in *Theatre World* with a great photo of the two of us. We also did a Palladium TV show and initial reaction seemed good, but we continued to go up and down.

On the down side, Morley was also in the middle of a film and his performance for us grew tired and slow. We had our flat broken into on Jermyn Street and my new mink stole was taken. I took a vault in a bank to secure the jewelry the thieves overlooked and laughed sourly that I was now famous enough that the gangs knew me.

March was just not our month. It was cold and rainy and the biggest crowd we saw was a "Ban the Bomb" march of young people whom we watched from Knightsbridge as they passed in the thousands. But Morley was optimistic. He said, "*Edward, My Son* took ten weeks to get started—so why not us?"

Morley always managed to cheer us by word, deed or food. On Saturdays, when we had a matinee until 6:30 P.M. and an evening performance at 9:30, Morley arranged for a complete dinner to be served at 8:00. Well, I had always been used to taking a few small bites on a roll and then nap, so I couldn't bring myself to sit down to a four-course feast. Morley would dive right in, of course, and mumble through his bites: "You Americans are nuts!" On another occasion, a friend from New York came to see us and she brought a box-load of cookies Helen had sent. I told Morley they were also for him and he ate every boxful! Later, when Helen sent more of her cookies, her famous *rugelach* rich with prune and nuts, Robert saw them and said, "Is that all she makes?" Then he ate them all, again!

I fretted about our poor matinee crowds but everyone told me no one in London has good matinees. And I didn't know what to believe. However, April came in and brought beautiful weather, at last. Yonkel and I took to the streets and walked and walked. In the Garment Center, one woman yelled out, "Good old Molly!" We laughed and went to watch Princess Margaret's wedding along with a hundred and fifty thousand other uninvited guests! We were now in our ninth week and Morley said we were doing better than others. Besides, Morley said, the British were now anti-American because of the Francis Gary Powers spy plane incident in Russia.

The Summit Meeting between the two superpowers broke up over it and Khrushchev demanded that Ike apologize for the plane incident. The world watched and waited. A lot of us still thought we could blow up in a minute.

It was around this time that my father's relative, Unikov-ski, visited us from Israel and told us he wanted to send his daughter Meira to college in America. We volunteered to pay her full tuition and he almost cried. And our audience reaction also brought surprises. At one performance, when I said to Morley: "I hope you like chopped liver?" a voice from the audience shouted: "And who doesn't?"

Morley's film, a portrayal of Oscar Wilde, opened with a big premiere at the Carlton Theatre. He was magnificent in the role and there was a big party for him afterward with lots of actors, champagne and Helen's *rugelach!*

We were now into our thirteenth week and Morley was giving a straight performance so Wendy wouldn't give him too many notes. After so many weeks of work, Wendy knew we needed to be kept on our toes, so she'd keep track of our performances and then call a rehearsal to let us brush up. Those little notes kept us sharp.

We had been gone from the States for nearly six months, but even our neighbors from Mahopac dropped in to see our London show. And Mary wrote to tell us everything was under control at Chez Shmendrick. So maybe I could stay here for a long run! In the meanwhile, I was getting veddy British. Morley and I did more BBC and we received an invitation from Laurence Olivier for the "Night of the Stars Benefit" for actors' children. Morley said we must accept and then invited us to the Henley Regatta on the Thames.

We watched that renowned race from Gladys Cooper's house, which overlooked the river. It had beautiful grounds, although her house was old and unpainted. It seemed cozy but I never got to peek inside. Gladys warned me not to go in. "I haven't cleaned it up yet," she said.

Morley's home was far more glamorous with sculpted grounds and a swimming pool. But with his wife and three children running about, it always had a zany atmosphere. Morley contributed to the mayhem, of course. He had a valet with whom he enjoyed arguing constantly. And as Morley argued, he'd keep undressing while the valet would argue back and keep picking up after him.

By our eighteenth week, we were enjoying our best Monday in weeks and the whole thing seemed puzzling to me. We had a play which never hit the top but never reached bottom, either. Even Margaret Leighton's play closed after twelve weeks, yet we were still going and covering expenses. And this with no publicity. In London, they didn't paste the town with billboards. Your play either made it on word of mouth or didn't.

We just hung in there with a crazy kind of low-key success. We had stars from the Yiddish theater in at matinees and Queen Elena of Greece at night. One evening, we had both the King and Queen of Sweden in the audience plus a Portuguese contessa. By our twentieth week, Morley was relaxed and started cutting up again. He made one of our actresses break up during a serious scene and I scolded her. Then Robert let everyone know I wouldn't stand for disrespect on stage. It was our first quarrel, but not a serious one. It had rained every day that week and I think we were all sour and damp.

The first time the sun came out was for our "Night of the Stars" at the Palladium. Over one hundred top British actors, among them Olivier, Vivien Leigh, Robeson, were invited to perform while Morley and I M.C.'d in kimonos. We had nine acts, it was the most elegant show of the year and so much fun for me to be on top. We ended our twentieth week with our biggest Friday ever (and all *goyim*). I never thought we would have gotten that far.

To keep us going, a publicity man was brought in from New York and as we reached our twenty-third week, Morley began talking about running a year after, which I'd have to carry on without him! Yonkel thought it would be a stunt to have Peter Finch take over, but I had my doubts and just glowered at the weather, which was consistently bad. Finally, Morley decided to close in September and I at least knew we had a specific run.

To break the routine, Yonkel and I journeyed to the Glyndebourne Festival with friends to hear *The Magic Flute* and then returned to the Palladium to catch Judy Garland's incredible act.

Judy was fat and magnificent. She still had beautiful legs but was round as a barrel and perspired constantly. Yet she sang like an angel, reaching one level higher than the last. She was totally controlled, every gesture had its meaning and these were things nobody had taught her. She was just a pure, natural talent (very similar, I thought, to the ragged genius of Piaf).

Many years later, I was playing in Paramus, New Jersey, when I had a chance to meet her daugher, Liza. Liza was dating one of our stagehands then. She was just a teenager and not yet a theater star, but I remember she told me, "Don't say anything about this to my mother, Molly. She'd kill me if she knew!"

We would end with twenty-nine weeks in London plus the management asked us to do a five-week tour. Three of those weeks would be near London and one in Liverpool and one in Leeds. We had to accept in order to cover production costs.

Yonkel and I celebrated Jewish Children's Day with a luncheon at the Royal Festival Hall. Sybil Thorndike and I spoke but it was Yonkel who stole the show. He listened to everyone else who spoke, then took bits and pieces of what they'd said and would comment. He always knew what to emphasize and how to build to an emphatic conclusion. When he finished, the audience sat in stunned silence.

Dame Sybil, then seventy-eight, came to one of our matinees with her husband, who was eighty-eight. She came backstage and was full of kisses and "darlings" and they were both so quaint. She had this rather rakish hat on and I complimented her on it. "Oh," she said, "but I never buy hats. I just wear what friends give me!"

We ended our last week in London amid a pouring rain but a full house. We brought a magnum of champagne to Morley's Saturday-night dinner, but there was little sentimentality like Second Avenue. I guess we knew we still had those weeks left on the road.

That Monday, we opened at Golders Green Hippodrome to a very good house. The majority of the audience was Jewish and I got a very good response. Later, I made a curtain speech and mentioned that my co-star had told me it was customary in their country for the visiting star to make a speech. Morley interrupted me and said: "No, Molly, it's your country." And I replied: "No, Robert. It's your country; it's my neighborhood!"

Business was terrific there. We filled all 2,500 seats and left rather reluctantly for Brighton. Our hotel was filled with old, sick people and we took a little walk in the rain to cheer ourselves. Yonkel was very depressed about Israel's clash with Nasser of Egypt, and we brooded while the big powers barked.

Thankfully, our opening at the Royal went well and the entire week was good. Meanwhile, we sent two bags off to the French Line and I began to feel we were homeward bound.

Our next stop was Liverpool and we had to drag our bags to the Adelphi Hotel because no taxi would drive in the fog. We opened in the luxurious Royal Court, and after the usual slow first act built to a strong finish once again. Business was good, but the weather—*yech!* The town was gray and sooty and full of squalor. It was a sad city with a sadder climate. It was strange to play in such a pleasant hotel theater amid the drunks and poverty. We finished the week in a blaze of applause and left feeling sorry for those who had to live there.

Our travels were getting silly. In an attempt at comic relief, Morley took us to Stratford-on-Avon to see Peter O'Toole in *The Merchant of Venice*. We found it very anti-Semitic and that disappointed us.

We wrapped up our London experience with a farewell party at the Plow and Harrow. There was flooding all over the rest of England but we had one, big, luscious party and just sang and sang.

We said our adieus and, as in any shared experience, you do leave a little bit of your heart behind. But I was glad to be finished.

We were sailing from Paris so we crossed the Channel, moved into the Grand Hotel, then walked the Parisian boulevards under the stars. It was such a joy just to walk the Left Bank. At night, we took in the Folies Bergère with its 1,400 costumes and not an inch of talent!

We spent one day in Brussels with George and Lizbeth,

then raced back to make our ship, the elegant *Liberté*. On board, we learned that John Kennedy was our next President by a very small margin. He seemed like such a young man, but with a tremendous smile and just the right temperament for those very touchy times. It seemed he had minted the word "charisma."

CHAPTER ✺ 15

I HAD LEFT NEW YORK determined to prove that I could succeed on the non-Yiddish stage. Word of my success in *Majority of One* had reached the States and offers were streaming in. How ironic! Once again, just as I had done forty years before, I had to go to Europe to make myself famous in America.

We arrived home on November 14, 1960, and before my luggage hit the docks, the phone calls began. My first offer was to do the play *Come Blow Your Horn* on Broadway. There was a very funny part for me—not the star role—but one which could be outstanding. However, my intincts told me the play wasn't important enough for Broadway, so I turned it down.

Our press agent, Max Eisen, wanted me to do *Majority* in the tent theaters and a film agent wanted me for a Stanley Kramer picture. There were also offers for commercials and various television series. All kinds of offers but nothing attractive. So I did what I most enjoyed: worked on Chez and waited.

There were leaves to rake, gardens to mend, new bookcases to build and a cellar's worth of memorabilia to sort. The weather was cold but clear and healthy and we worked with zest. I hung wash in the sun to dry, Yonkel cleaned the flagstone walk, and we talked about the future: to work or not to work?

Yonkel had just celebrated his sixty-ninth birthday, and he was satisfied to stay home and do nothing. I, however, still had the urge to go on. But where? And doing what? As we used to say on the East Side: "If you ain't got *wit wot,* you're in trouble!"

We spent November and December close by the home fires, dieting off our European eating excesses. We had checkups and the doctors said we were in good shape except for what Mama used to call "a few odds and ends": a little diabetes, a little high blood pressure, a little arthritis. Otherwise, we were able to work—and ready.

We found Mahopac about 30 degrees below zero so we counteracted with a hot *shvitz*. Meanwhile, our plowman was stuck for nineteen hours in a huge drift. It was like living in an igloo. We had four days of snow and the worst cold in eighty years. Our bond rally in Miami was canceled, the city was paralyzed and the only one moving was a little chimpanzee who was orbiting earth in a space capsule.

The weather broke just enough for me to get to town and do a big concert at the Brooklyn Academy of Music. George Jessel was the host and there were cantors, Israeli dancers and I, on last, but WOW, what a reception.

Don Appel and Jerry Herman had put together a new musical they initially called *Shalom!*, but later changed to *Milk and Honey*. It was written against an Israeli background and they wanted me for a comedy part. They both had been at the Brooklyn Academy the night before and now were more eager than ever to sign me. Herman told me he would write an extra number just for me, plus they seemed genuinely interested in a new number I thought the play could use. I told Ed Robbins, my agent at William Morris, to say okay and they were elated.

I also signed on for a segment of "Family Affair," a popular television series. Yet, with so much work cooking, I wondered if any of it would really materialize. No performer counts her chickens until not only are they hatched, but walking around with chickens of their own! So I went on with my own plans, which included a big celebration for my birthday. Myron Cohen, the Barry Sisters, and many international friends helped me slip very easily into sixty-three. I hoped I wore the years well.

But things around me were beginning to get hectic. Roman wanted to discuss my song, and Jack Paar's producer wanted to discuss me.

The last was sort of a peculiar thing. Jack Paar had *the* hit nighttime talk show and I had been invited to be pre-interviewed about getting interviewed. The show's producer spent over an hour chatting with me and I had the feeling everything rested with the opinion of the Great God Paar, whom I never met. Who could figure it?

Rokeach, at least, I could understand. They wanted me to push their *matzoh* balls and chicken soup and I went off to a mosque in Newark and taped the entire bunch.

My contract to do *Shalom!* arrived and, after signing it, I began to feel that it would be a reality. We had a reading of a reworked version of the play and its tone was much lighter and my part a lot better. Appel had a new song for me and everything seemed to be falling into place. I restrained myself, however, because I knew I couldn't leap into *Shalom!* until I had done my twelve-week touring stint. We were booked into the Coconut Grove in Miami with Yonkel directing. He had all of one week to get us into shape.

Everything worked against us. Scenery fell apart, my leading man didn't know a line, the rehearsals were just god-awful. Somehow, Yonkel managed to growl and cajole in just the right proportions and our opening night went beautifully. By the end of our first week, we needed extra seats in the orchestra and my performance was up. We felt we would breeze through our run with *Majority* and I'd be primed to begin *Shalom!*

Max Eisen had other ideas. In a letter to my agent at William Morris, Eisen spelled out how much work he had ahead for me after our tour of *Majority*. We *were* selling out every performance and the audience wanted us back. However, beyond playing *Majority*, I knew Eisen hadn't another thing for us. Yet, he insisted that releasing me to play *Shalom!* would cost him future bookings. He wanted $25,000 to let me go. Meanwhile, Eisen's local manager in Miami still owed us over two thousand dollars in back pay! I shrugged my shoulders and left the lawyers to fight it out.

It was June and a Hawaiian boy had had a lei of orchids

made for me for my second birthday of the year. Rehearsals for *Majority* were in progress for a tent theater in Lambertville, Pennsylvania. Martyn Green was to play Asano and I loved him on first sight.

My happiest news, however, was how well Appel and Herman reacted to my song. The character I would play in *Shalom!* was a genteel widow who had been without her husband for many years. She had been ever so faithful to his memory, but now she was in the new land of Israel and had a chance for new love. I wrote what I called "Hymn to Hymie," where the widow pleads for an "okay" from her long-dead spouse. We all had, as they say, good vibrations about that song.

Spring came and with it my first dose of poison ivy and my first shot. The two seemed inevitable. Less expected were some severe stomach pains and violent vomiting. My doctor gave me some shots for the pain and warned that I had a gallstone and needed to watch my diet and take it easy. I, of course, took his advice by immediately taking off for St. Louis. I had promised to make an appearance before a big Hadassah crowd, 1,150 "girls," and couldn't let them down.

I wanted to keep busy while the plans for *Shalom!* brewed. Max Eisen booked *Majority* for twelve weeks on tour and I accepted. Apparently, Jack Paar's producer sold me and I was invited to do his talk show.

Unfortunately, Paar wasn't there to talk with me. He had broken his toe and Hugh Downs took over. The evening passed in a nervous blur. All I remember was that I had to fight my way into each line. After my appearance, the producer said, "May I kiss you?" I had to assume I had done all right. Frankly, however, sitting on a couch, fighting for five minutes of exposure, wasn't for me. I went back to my rose garden, our first astronaut went into orbit, and I found a nest with three baby rabbits under a shrub.

Green had lost a leg in an elevator accident and limped badly. We had to rework many of the scenes to accommodate him, but Green was a pro and read perfectly. He knew all the acting angles and flashed a precious smile. He and I had a ball in the round!

Meanwhile, the battle between Eisen and the *Shalom!* producers raged. As part of his volley fired in our direction, Eisen began calling with all kinds of future offers for us. At one point, he even wanted Yonkel to play Asano in Miami. We thought him crazy but shrewd. And he was both. William Morris and Actors Equity were both on my side and their big-gun legal staff, too. Yet they couldn't come up with a workable solution. Eventually, everyone stopped trying to reason and just let Eisen sue, which he did. And he ended up getting paid a percentage all through my run of the play.

Maybe I should have fought him harder, but all my thirst for battle evaporated with one event. In the middle of all this legal wrangling, my sister Helen's husband died. I went to spend the day with her, but she took it all very calmly. We had a quiet funeral for Bill, just a few friends, and buried him near Papa's grave.

In our profession, you just keep going on, in this case, to the Colonie Summer Theater tent in Latham, New York. And more summer tour problems. We had a shabby stage, an impossible crew, and a manager who was careless. Props fell apart, the audience was bad. What a mess. Yonkel yelled and I *kvetched*. Icing this cake of misery was a torrential downpour. And when you stage-act in a tent during a rainstorm it looks like a silent movie. Somehow, we got through that one, even celebrating our forty-second wedding anniversary, June 29, 1961, amid all the *mish-mosh*.

When we opened in Nyack, I acquired a lifelong anecdote. We opened at the Tappan Zee Playhouse with a top show. Helen Hayes was in the audience and she came backstage to see me and say hello. We greeted each other with a kiss and I told her I was often called the Yiddish Helen Hayes. And she answered: "From now on, Molly, I will be proud to be called the *Shikseh* Molly Picon!"

We finished our twelfth week at the Westport Playhouse where we broke all records. Eisen made a speech to the cast promising future bookings, but Yonkel squashed him and we ended the run feeling high.

Jerry Herman had brought me my script for *Shalom!* while I was still on the road. Among the changes was the new title: *Milk and Honey*. This was Herman's first musical, and it had problems. The biggest one was its identity crisis. Herman wanted both music and drama but the blend emerged as strictly melodramatic.

The plot, even then, was a mite corny. Phil was a builder who had retired in Israel. Ruth was a forty-ish single woman, part of a large group of American widows who were touring that country. Clara Weiss was their wisecracking guide. All of them were lonely and looking for love. And all eventually find it but not without some problems, the biggest of which was Phil's wife. Today, an affair is not so shocking. In 1961, however, adultery was still a sin and so became the dramatic crisis in our play. It would not be easy to turn such events into a musical.

What gave the play its strength, however, was that it would be played out against the backdrop of Israel: the new country for new dreams. A lot of its best moments involved singing and dancing about her great future. Somehow, both Yonkel and I felt, it could be made to work.

Rehearsals began for *Milk and Honey* at the Martin Beck Theater. Years before, when I did *Morning Star* on Broadway, Beck, a producer, had come backstage to see me. He told me he liked the play, but personally wouldn't have touched it with a ten-foot pole. He explained: "Who wants to see a Jewish play on Broadway?" Now, we were beginning a play about American Jews in Israel and would play it in his theater. Beck's words came back to me, of course. I wondered whether we would prove him wrong. I desperately wanted to.

Robert Weede, a great star with the Metropolitan Opera, would play Phil. Mimi Benzell, a beauty who was also an opera singer, was Ruth. My name, as Clara, was third on the bill. With these great voices, the show's songs would be boomed out powerfully. Weede, especially, was absolutely meticulous. His technique was flawless, he perfected every note. What he needed to develop was warmth. Although he had a big success with *Most Happy Fella*, Weede was uncomfortable on a musical stage and it showed. Mimi was actually stiff. We began our rehearsals full of perfection but looking for heart.

I, too, was struggling. I was learning my "Hymn to

Hymie" but hadn't gotten it down yet. The song needed something flip, especially when Clara cried: "Look Hymie, I'm young!" Finally, I negotiated with Jerry and I worked my somersault in! It was my best move.

The rest of the dancing was less successful. All we widows had a *horah* to dance and we seemed to be getting nowhere. The dance routines ate up hours, but we still seemed confused. At one point, I put in my own step and soon the entire company was doing my *pas de Picon*. At another point, I was to be tossed in the air and so spent hours going, literally, up and down! Meanwhile, in between dialogue coaching and costume fitting, Eisen's lawyers handed me a summons. He wanted an injunction to stop me from rehearsing.

Thankfully, the singing ensemble emerged magnificent. And with the *horah* and "Hymie" numbers, my role was getting V.I.P. treatment. After the first week, *ça va*, it didn't look so bad.

We rehearsed from eleven to seven and we had lots of work to do just with machinery. One of our props was a genuine tractor. We also had to work around bales of hay, plows, and real, live animals. In one scene, Phil had to milk a goat. That meant getting one star goat, fully equipped with milk, plus one goat understudy—who also had to be bulging at the teat! The producers paid a small fortune for what was perhaps two minutes of stage business: about $750 a week for one laugh.

The music and dancing were emerging as spectacular, but the plot still got in the way. I thought we still had too much of a sad story between Phil and Ruth. And it seemed I was offstage for hours between the first and second act. However, we kept making changes, I opened the second act with "Hymie," my part seemed better, so maybe they knew what they were doing. And, in the middle of the summer, we had tickets being sold for January.

We took *Milk and Honey* first to New Haven, along with the sheep and goats and a fortune in costumes and sets. I figured we'd have to run a year at SRO just to cover expenses. Money kept being poured into tinsel even though we still needed a healthier tree to hang it on.

I watched the goings-on in amazement. Our costumes were especially intriguing to me. All of us widows (I guess out of our pensions?) were somehow able to afford dresses right out of *Harper's Bazaar*. Each was more elegant, more flowery, more lavish than the next. But, worst of all, they were impractical to dance in. And as for the sets, everything was set to roll on and off stage. Our show was a stagehand's holiday.

We rehearsed from noon to midnight and I struggled with my sets, my songs, and my dresses right out of *Roberta*. My biggest problem, however, was finding my part.

Don Appel kept talking to me about keeping Clara "sweet" and the idea just gagged me. Clara was anything but sweet. She was bright, vital and funny. In fact, she needed to be played broader than they wanted her. The real problem, I suspect, was not so much that the producers didn't want Clara to be too funny (although, God knows, they needed the comedy); they were afraid I would be too "Jewish." They kept cautioning me about using my hands and even removed a rhinestone buckle from my hat because Hadassah might find it gaudy!

But, I've always taken direction, good or bad. So I was struggling trying to give them what they wanted. However, where I could, I tried to work my points. Appel knew there was no way I could use my body unnaturally. As my role increased, little by little, so did my gestures and comedic interpretation. And if it seemed "Jewish," so be it.

The rest of the cast was equally frustrated. We were in the dog days of August with no air and less air-conditioning. The dancers' body makeup ran over their costumes and ours in one dirty mess. The props were cumbersome and I just hoped we had a show as big as our sets!

We opened in New Haven on August 26th, at the Shubert Theater. I got a big ovation on my entrance and after my *horah* and "Hymie" song. The play didn't do so well with the critics, however, and we waited for the expected changes.

It had finally become apparent that the show was weak. It hadn't worked as heavy drama so changes were made to lighten it up. The first to go, thankfully, was a synagogue scene which had never worked. Mimi had been given this long speech where she went to temple to beg God's forgiveness. That was out. With it went the Jewish wedding scene where they had (to everyone's shock) introduced a dancing rabbi. Out! Out! (and $100,000 for scenery with it.)

As for Weede and Benzell, little could be improved on. Neither of these fine voices was suited to musical comedy. Their characterizations were weak but the singing, dancing and dizzy props which sailed around them strengthened whatever they did.

Our boss, Martin Beck himself, was in and was excited. Despite his own dire prophecies, he felt we had a success which just needed time and work. When the New York seers, play doctors, and agents started to see the show—Jerome Robbins, Milton Goldman, big ticket agents—the word *Hit* was in the air, even though they spelled it with an asterisk which listed our limitations.

We took the show to Boston for one more tryout before Broadway. We opened at the Colonial and the critics had good notices for all the performers. What they still didn't like was the play! So more changes.

We worked on a new finish for our Widows number, adding a marching chorus, which seemed bright and funny. The weather was now hot as Hades and some of the "girls" were tiring. I blew my top at them, then couldn't sleep that night from nerves. We were down, then up. A new "Chin Up, Ladies" chorus was added for the Widows and it was a guaranteed showstopper. Now, I had three numbers made of pure electricity. Weede and Mimi had none and I felt sorry for them both.

We kept making changes but still had to lick Mimi's big "asking forgiveness" scene. Instead of going to a rabbi or temple, it was decided that Mimi confide in me. I played it straight for her and Mimi's song went much better. Even with the confusion of different lines and different scenery, we still had SRO audiences in Boston, 80 percent who weren't Jewish. (Not that these figures stopped the critics from chastising our script. Local critic Eliot Norton pulled the play apart by saying it was only for limited audiences. And I said, "I get most of my mail from unlimited audiences.")

Not even a hurricane seemed to affect us. One blew up the coast, canceling our matinee. That evening, we went on despite the fallen trees and downed power lines and our audience was still a sellout. We braced ourselves for New York. Our first preview on Broadway was on September 28th and it moved like a dress rehearsal. The benefit audience was tough, but the scenery was tougher: noisy and slow to move. Yet, by the second act, the audience was pulling for us and we closed to bows and applause. Critic Phil Adler said, "Thank God for Molly!" Jennie Grossinger, of Catskill fame, came backstage and said she was thrilled. We had lines at the box office but the changes grew along with them.

Some of them reflected opening jitters. At one point, someone decided I should speak without inflections. "But the dialogue is written that way," I reasoned and, thankfully, prevailed.

To ease the tensions, we went back to Chez. We melted into our old easy chairs with a sandwich and a beer. I wanted some relaxing and got it. I spent the whole weekend just prowling around the grounds, where I found a cat with six toes under our patio. I named her Honey, took a *shvitz* and unwound.

Weede, however, wasn't so lucky and the day before our opening, was out sick. His understudy went on, but couldn't carry the load. Everyone was very upset and no one knew if we'd open at all. Weede's doctor would decide in the morning. I prayed to Mama for help.

And she pulled the strings for me. *Milk and Honey* opened on October 10th at the Martin Beck with everyone, Weede included, in top form. The performances were brilliant and the reaction to my numbers even more thrilling. We bowed to much applause and excitement was everywhere. Yonkel and I briefly joined in the good feeling at a big party our backers threw at the Four Seasons. Then we slipped away and off to bed.

In the morning, we awoke to rave notices for me, for the play, for everything. I'd never gotten such reviews. Whitney Bolton of the *Telegraph* wrote: "I've waited fifty years for Molly to come to Broadway and she captured me in five minutes." Our box office did $16,000 in one day, topping even *My Fair Lady* in sales. Noel Coward, Danny Thomas, Myron Cohen, Billy Rose, Milton Berle all sent their congratulations. Hurrah, we were a SMASH!

Maybe now I'd get a publicity agent. Early on during rehearsals, I had discovered that Mimi had two to plug her, and Weede had one. Naturally, I had asked where was mine. Oh, you don't need one, I was told. But the real message I got was that nobody wanted to publicize me too much for fear it would scare away the gentile crowd. They had been proven wrong. Very wrong. The play got good notices, but I got the best ones. The audience was coming to see me.

I had had a taste of uptown success when I was held over at the Palace forty years before. But, now, I was a legitimate Broadway star and that was thrilling. People stopped me on the street, there were wonderful write-ups in the *Times* and *Newsweek*. Even Broadway's gay audience adopted me and streamed in to see the show. I did the Paar show again and Jack, himself, was on!

Yonkel, of course, was elated, even if he hardly ever saw the show. He had two house seats but was forever giving them to our Jewish actors. I wanted him to know just how much I still cared and so arranged a huge party for his seventieth birthday.

Samye Van, my hairdresser, worked with me on every detail. He arranged for a fantastic smorgasbord for each table at the Picadilly Hotel and sat with me while we wrote out 250 invitations, including stagehands. I wrote a funny song for Yonkel, but Samye stole the show.

Van had been a female impersonator and on the night of the party, he dressed himself in a costume identical to the one I wore in my "Chin Up" number. Surrounded by the two female singers who actually joined me onstage, the three emerged with Samye doing a screamingly funny version of "Chin Up, Ladies!" Everyone from Oestreicher, our producer, to the boy who took care of the sheep was there. It was fantastic, amusing, touching, heartwarming. And Yonkel deserved it. We went back to Chez on a cloud, just to talk and relax and thank God.

By our sixth week, we were the hottest ticket in town. Arthur Laurents was in and had tears in his eyes. The author of *West Side Story* grabbed my hands and said I was a Great Lady of the Theater! John Raitt, Tommy Manville and others all crowded into my dressing room. A woman brushed them all aside and shouted, "Morristown Loves You!" then breezed out. Yonkel and I walked to our hotel from the theater and we couldn't keep count of the people who recognized me. After sixty acknowledgments, we stopped keeping track.

Someone, of course, should have told my stomach. My gall bladder began giving me trouble and my doctor had to give me a shot for pain. I was so weak I could hardly stand, but I went on to do my somersault and flips. Ed Sullivan was in the audience and said, "You have them eating out of your hands."

Nevertheless, the two enemies of a hit show lurked on the sidelines ready to come into our game: boredom and illness. After weeks and weeks of rehearsals and the high from SRO nights, there is a tendency to get a bit lax, to play at less than peak intensity. By our ninth week, the performances were getting sloppy. I spoke with Weede and Benzell and we all agreed we needed to pull together. Even the cast pitched in to keep everyone on their toes.

I think for the first time in the theater the stagehands gave a cast party for Christmas. Everyone's feelings were good because, with the holidays, while the rest of Broadway was half-full, we were still selling out. The party was held right after a Saturday matinee and was filled with presents and laughter. I wore a red-nosed reindeer mask and Yonkel played Santa, ho-hoing with a Yiddish accent. It was a merry party laced with camaraderie and love.

After the partying, however, came the dues paying. All the winter sneezes and sniffles were upon us. Six members of the cast were out, including Tommy Rall, our second male lead and a fabulous dancer. But me, the old war-horse, kept going on and on. Mimi was battling a virus and her throat was gone. Weede canceled another night, but I *shlepped* and Handlesman, our stage manager, came back to say, "Thank

God for Molly!" How could I not go on? I was ringing out the old year with the biggest success of my career.

We opened 1962 without Mimi but our full houses held up. I did an extra benefit after one show for the Yiddish actors who seemed mostly old and sick. Many of them had talent, but few of them had taste. The benefit left me feeling very depressed and I wondered: Am I going Broadway or what?

All of us were taking vitamins and shots, hoping to keep well. Helen Hayes came in during our twenty-first week and said I was her dream girl. Every time she became discouraged, she came to see me and I encouraged her go on again. Meanwhile, I performed "Chin Up" and "Grandma's Shawl" for "The Mike Wallace Show" (following Ava Gabor, Cyril Ritchard and Johnnie Ray). Everyone bravoed and Helen Hayes sent flowers and a card: "Cheers from your fan!"

Mimi and Weede, however, were still *kvetching*. The score was a very difficult one to sing eight times a week, and they didn't have my Second Avenue tricks to fall back on. Ed Sullivan also booked me for his show and I think they resented that. Of course, with my luck on TV, Sullivan was ill so George Gobel M.C.'d. But I went on during the first half of the show, sang my "Hymn to Hymie" and even did my somersault. To this day, people still talk to me about seeing that show!

Now, I was traveling with the *crème*. Mary Martin and Ethel Merman came backstage and the famous Lou Siegel sent over kosher food for us to party on. I was ready, but after a round of picture-taking, they all left. This is success?

I was also invited to be part of an evening for Danny Thomas at the Waldorf given by the Jewish Theatrical Alliance. Jessel, Berle, Murray, Bishop, Carter and I entertained. I was the sole female performer. Samye did my hair and I dressed up in a Chapman gown, then was forced to sit next to Zsa Zsa and a line of other beauties. But I vindicated myself by doing my "Yiddish Lesson" to great applause.

I celebrated my official sixty-fourth birthday that February 28th, and the stage crew gave me four dozen American Beauty roses. We had a party in our cellar, I in my bugle-beaded gown, and Yonkel wearing a rooster on his head, making a grand entrance. We had cases of Burgundy and lots of cakes and an excess of love.

Yet, somehow, I was getting very tired. After six months of doing a show every night, plus television and my Rokeach shows and benefits, I needed some time off. Yonkel and I had a book in the works which would be "as told to" Ethel Rosenberg, the author of *Go Fight City Hall*. To us, it would be a *mish-mosh* book, a little of this and that. But we met with Ethel and began telling her stories. She seemed to have a feeling for comedy and her own book was very funny. We hoped for more of the same.

Meanwhile, I entertained theater folk. Gladys Cooper was in New York to do a play and we invited her for dinner at Spindletop. Gladys ordered fish and we ordered steak, which we couldn't finish. We asked Gladys if she had a dog who might eat it and she said yes. We had the waiter put our steaks into a bag and when we came out of the restaurant, Gladys said, "You know who the dog is? Me! You Americans are too extravant, leaving a half-pound of steak. I'll eat it!"

By our thirty-fifth week on Broadway, we were still doing over $50,000 a week in sales. My biggest thrill, however, was getting nominated for a Tony Award along with Diahann Carroll, Anna Maria Alberghetti and Elaine Stritch. Neither Weede nor Mimi congratulated me on my honor but Tommy Rall did. By Easter week, we were breaking our own records, but I did not win a Tony. Carroll and Alberghetti tied for Best Actress in a Musical. Still, Yonkel said I looked gorgeous in my new gown, while Brooks Atkinson invited us for cocktails and raved about my show. Those were awards enough.

However, I was ready to stretch myself even more and Hollywood presented the opportunity. Paramount wanted me for the film version of *Come Blow Your Horn*. Frank Sinatra had the lead, with Lee Cobb playing his father and I his mother. Me, an Italian mama?? Bud Yorkin and Norman Lear, the film's director and producer, respectively, seem to think so and the film's telephone scene would be a natural for me. Would I fly to Hollywood to test with Frank? I tell you, Is this a Life?

Joining Sinatra meant leaving the show for ten weeks. However, Sinatra offered $40,000 and two fares just to tempt us. We were also starting our forty-third week and the best Monday in months. It was contract renewal time and the temptation was also there to just stay and sign on again.

Yonkel and I celebrated our forty-third wedding anniversary and tried not to give the immediate future much thought. Yonkel had an exquisite diamond watch-bracelet made for me, and then tossed another party for the *Milk and Honey* cast. Rumors were circulating about the contract renewals, with Weede confiding to us that the producers wanted to replace Mimi. Word also got to us that people were being sized up to replace me. I don't even know if such things were true, but when Yonkel tossed our cast party and neither Jerry Herman nor Don Appel came, we got suspicious. The next day, Yonkel told the show's representative that I wouldn't sign a contract for another year. We left them stunned as we took off for Chez loaded with food and Helen and Samye Van.

Weede, who had signed a new contract, joined us at our pool for a delightful swim. After a nice dinner, our guests left and Yonkel and I relaxed and looked at the stars and planet Mars (which Mama called Morris). Suddenly, Appel called, then Jerry Herman. Everyone was full of apologies to us. Flowers were sent. The producers came to smooth over any ruffled feelings. I was their cookie! All of them pleaded with me to remain or they'd have to close the show.

Norman Lear and Bud Yorkin also applied their own pressure, including deciding to recast the Italian characters back to Jewish. I was selected for the film. Now, I had to work on the new film role *and* keep Broadway in tow.

We were in our forty-sixth week, with Weede out sick and Mimi tired and unhappy. I had a feeling then that something was wrong with her. As it happened, her health began to deteriorate and she died only a few years later. Whether she was seriously ill then, I never knew. But she was always weak and sickly and not at all happy about co-starring with Weede. Adler and Appel and Oestreicher, all the show big-wigs, pleaded with me to try and have Hollywood film my

part in three weeks—at the most. Our audience was dropping
with Weede sick, and where would it go without me?

My role in *Come Blow Your Horn* had now reached the
papers. Mimi kissed me and told me she had sent the managers the name of someone to replace me. Thelma Ritter, I
believe. Weede was still out sick, and Adler was in my dressing room threatening to slash his wrists if I left. Other stage
managers began raiding our best dancers to use in their new
productions. Finally, *Milk and Honey*'s producers agreed to
give me a leave of absence with Hermione Gingold coming
in to do my part.

I squeezed in some shooting for a segment of "Car 54,
Where Are You?" while Oestreicher mused about signing
me on our old terms. It seemed he still didn't know if I was
the star or Weede or Benzell. Yonkel and I decided to let it
ride until we all found out.

Gingold was in a box seat for the last week of my show
and I felt sorry for her. She was very frightened. She couldn't
sing or dance and she knew it. *Milk and Honey* really wasn't
the play for her, but she was taking over the part just the
same. My book of stories, now called *So Laugh a Little,* had
been published and was doing well. It was a good time to
take off for a new venture.

Yonkel and I jetted to Hollywood on September 4th and
the royal treatment awaited us. We had a lovely suite at the
Chateau Marmont, and flowers from both Yorkin and Lear.
We made ourselves at home and I took a pill to bring on
sleep.

Once again, as soon as I got to the Paramount Studios the
business of looking me over began. Everything seemed okay
and I moved on to meet the dress designer. The poor gal
didn't have the slightest idea how to dress my character so
the two of us sat down and I told her what I should wear!

Once it had been decided to return the film's family back
into Jews, I felt more in control. The wife was a typical *Yiddishe* Mama and I slipped into the part like an old shoe. Still,
this was to be my very first Hollywood picture so I was feeling just a little apprehensive about the whole thing.

Our first day on the set involved blocking our scenes and

getting to know each other. Lee Cobb was an old film pro while Yorkin, our director, was not too proud to listen to suggestions and even accept a few. I observed them and tried to learn.

This was also Tony Bill's first picture and he seemed rather cocksure of himself. But then, he had been handpicked by Sinatra himself, even though Frank Sinatra, Jr., had wanted the part. Frank didn't think his son was right for the role. When he saw Tony Bill's photo, he said: I want him. So, one step out of college, Tony was now on our set.

Lee J. Cobb and I were now meeting to read our scenes and we were off to a rough start. Cobb, although Jewish, couldn't get the right inflection. He hadn't played a Jew in years and his delivery was flat and humorless. Yorkin suggested we work around him for a while and we did. Sinatra still hadn't appeared on the set, so we worked around him, too. And I thought *theater* was a crazy business!

Everything went easily. No great demands were made. Yonkel and I hit Chasen's and Romanoff's, Disneyland, and even took in a massage and *shvitz*. Filming just wasn't all that hard, so we took advantage of the free time available.

By about the fourth or fifth day, Sinatra finally made his appearance. He had been hospitalized for something, but looked fine. He was immediately charming and seemed genuinely pleased to meet me. He knew all about me and my work and asked me to tell him stories about the Yiddish theater.

Many stage actors have found movie-making a bit strange (and vice versa, I suppose). In film, you do little bits of your part and then do that same little bit twenty times over. Sinatra, however, worked differently. We would only do two takes. Otherwise, he said, the acting is labored. So we'd shoot a second take and he'd say, "Okay, Boys. Put it in the can."

Frank's other quirk was that he didn't like to wear makeup. It took too much time in the morning. Consequently, I was informed that I wouldn't be wearing makeup, either. I guess so Frank and I would "match." Which makes my first Hollywood film really *cinéma vérité!*

It was music, not acting, which seemed Sinatra's greatest love. He was always listening to playbacks of records he was making—and he always seemed to be making records. Yet, on the set, he was a thorough professional, always the first one on the lot, took directions (and gave them), but was never adamant about anything.

He was a gentleman, but on top of that, he also liked to have fun. We had some time off from filming and Sinatra insisted we go to Las Vegas in his private plane. Yonkel and I had never been there and figured: it's now or never, and so we flew!

One hour later, we were in Vegas and on our way to a plush hotel, the Sands. All we caught was a quick glimpse of the desert, then we descended into a clockless world of roulette, craps and slot machines (even in the bathrooms). Frank had arranged for everything. Dinner was taken care of, as were our seats for the late show. We saw and enjoyed Nat King Cole, and Sinatra paid all the bills.

All our lives we had heard of Boulder Dam, so we dashed off to take a look at that. We saw it amid a stormy rain, full of lightning and flash—but what a magnificent sight! Then we rushed back to fantasy-land. We caught George Burns with Carol Channing (unfortunately, no Gracie). Juliet Prowse was also on the bill, and was Sinatra's current flame. Frank had a gift for her, which he asked us to deliver and we did. She sang and danced with great skill, but she lacked that one little thing that would have made her Great. I was introduced to nice applause and clearly it went to my head. The singer in the lounge teased me into joining him, and we dueted until 4:00 A.M. *Mazel tov,* Molly!

Yonkel and I left, still feeling as giddy as kids. We were on our way to Western Airlines when we were paged at the airport. Sinatra's plane was there waiting for us. And so we flew back, just Yonkel and I, in Frankie's three-million-dollar plane. It had a piano, a bar, and a pilot who once lived near Mahopac! A car was waiting to take us back to the hotel, and so we concluded our grand treat in a grand way.

I could get used to such red-carpet treatment, and, maybe I would have to. *Variety* was very unkind to Gingold and my dresser, Bertha MacDuncan, wrote to say the show was falling apart and might not last.

At that point, however, I wanted to finish my first film

and finish it with skill. Yorkin was very patient and cooperative and gave me full leeway. He'd listen and say: "Molly, what do you want to do with it?" My biggest scene involved me and a telephone. I had been left in Frank's bachelor apartment and ended up taking all kinds of weird messages. As a Mama I was also preoccupied with my sons, and all this had to come through on a few minutes of film. When I finished, the whole crew applauded and Lear said, "No one could have played it like you." The next day's rushes showed the scene was funny and natural, not too pretty but rather cute.

But this was a kind of job I had never had. You worked one day, then rested a week. So, naturally, we filled in with our *shtick*. We did a Hadassah luncheon in the Valley, played a studio party, and entertained at an old age home. The place was real Hollywood posh, and its guests real Hollywood old. A 105-year-old man presented us with flowers and made a lovely speech.

Meanwhile, Oestreicher, our producer from New York, called and pleaded: "When?" *Milk and Honey* was now on twofers and falling apart. Yorkin said he could let me go by November 5th and Oestreicher kept saying, "As soon as she can . . . I'd be so happy."

We wrapped up the picture, I took some stills with Frank, and then we celebrated. Frank gave all the women in the cast the costumes they had worn, exquisite clothes. Since I was always in a dowdy black dress, I protested, "Hey, that's not fair." Later that week, when I had sent Frank some copies of my book, he gave me a beautiful gold horn with rubies and diamonds and a great big kiss. As I said, Frank's a gentleman.

CHAPTER ✻ 16

As soon as I reached New York, both Mimi and Weede called, genuinely happy to have me back. Yonkel and I caught Hermione Gingold in my part and we realized why everyone was so anxious for my return. Gingold was utterly wrong for Clara. She was not a Yiddish comedienne, but a lady gifted for funny monologues. Yet, English actors will try anything! So here she was singing "Chin Up" in her slow, throaty style for a musical where the dancing carried more weight than the lyrics! Somehow, the sparkle had vanished from the play.

With the original cast back, everyone tried to tighten and brighten the show. We were having full houses again, and plans were made to extend our run through January, then take *Milk and Honey* on the road.

Meanwhile, I basked in a new light: author. *So Laugh a Little* by Molly Picon was really selling. It was subtitled, "Hilarious Hints on How to Be a Jewish Grandmother" and contained anecdotes Yonkel and I had shared about Mama and my *bubbe*. A celebration was held at Sardi's to help launch it, and I was thrilled to find that my caricature by Gard was still hanging in a respectable position on the wall. The famous illustrator had done my portrait when I first opened at the Palace. At the time, one of the columnists wrote, "Molly Picon is now one of Gard's Chosen People!"

We began auditioning a cast for our road tour and it was clear Mimi would be replaced. A few male singers were also looked at for Weede's part, but the bosses just watched silently. For me, everyone just kept pushing me on and Saturdays were the worst. I had two shows and no throat. So I doctored myself and made it without an ounce of strength left. I was knocked out, but everyone predicted a riot if I didn't go on.

I had been secretly nursing a lot of stomach pain, which I attributed to nerves. Yonkel had also had a bad attack in Famous' Restaurant and I began to worry more about him than me. When the doctors gave him a once-over and said "Perfect," I forgot I had been sick and went back to eight shows a week and bookselling on the side. My pain had gone away. Then, a few days later, I just keeled over.

I found myself in Beth Israel Hospital, flat out. The doctors consulted all day and couldn't figure what was wrong. Then, around midnight, one doctor returned with a drastic decision. He told me he just couldn't sleep because he felt something was wrong. He wanted to operate and I said, "Cut!" He reached my appendix just as it burst, and probably saved my life.

Of all things! I, the big *Knacker* (big shot), was a mean, sick lady. I had a tube through my nose and another from my stomach. I had shots in the derrière and nurses 'round the clock. And this I couldn't laugh off. It would be weeks before I could go back to work and, worse, I didn't know if I wanted to.

I was afraid I had lost all my bravado. No more "Leave it to Molly. She'll do it." Sick is sick and even though the doctors said I'll be out in a few days, I had learned that maybe I shouldn't do *every*thing I was asked. This had been my first major illness and I was scared.

Nineteen sixty-two had been an eventful year: my first Broadway hit, my first Hollywood film, my first book and my first appendectomy! I stayed away from the show and only accepted another "Car 54, Where Are You?" spot. I sneaked in a little dance practice, but it left me winded. Instead, I rested at Chez and watched Sophie Tucker on "The Ed Sullivan Show" celebrating her seventy-fifth birthday. I wondered if she had ever had an appendectomy.

Still, I had promised to rejoin the show on January 14th, so I went back on stage. Shortly after, I slipped and fell during the *horah* and was back in trouble. I was wearing new shoes and feeling a bit unnerved, but I couldn't shake off the pain. The next day, there was blood in my urine, but I still went on and did two shows.

My doctors felt I had passed a stone through my kidney which had caused the blood. They weren't alarmed about it, but (just like the other stars) I found myself out of the show again. I had pills to take and a gallon of water to drink. I was trying to heal but I wasn't working and that got me down.

Yonkel tried to cheer me. He had seen a sneak preview of *Come Blow Your Horn* and was very pleased with my performance. He insisted I looked great, even without makeup, and was natural and funny in my role. So go find an objective critic!

We closed our Broadway run of *Milk and Honey* on January 26th. However, despite its success, the plot was eminently forgettable. Could we survive on tour?

If we were going to succeed on the road, we would have to work the same magic we had created on Broadway: building from one showstopping number to the next while gingerly sliding over our weak plot. Weede, Tommy Rall and I were the only original cast members. I frankly don't remember the various women who played Ruth along the way. What I do remember was that we were joined by a fresh, young gang of dancers who were anxious to whirl up a storm. We would have to sell this show on enthusiasm and it looked like we might do it.

Our first stop was the Shubert Theater in Philadelphia. The snow there had turned to ice and we began our run holding on to each other in the slippery streets. *Abi Gezunt,* I prayed, as long as you're healthy.

The press and photographers greeted us, someone gave me the City Hall Medal, and there was a good deal of fanfare. We then rehearsed from 1:00 in the afternoon 'til midnight with practically a new show: new sets, new scenery and new lights.

We opened to a slow start. A Theatre Guild subscription crowd had the first ten rows and they were as stiff as dried cod. However, we kept coming at them and even wangled an extra curtain call. Our press, thankfully, was unanimously good.

Philadelphia was my home city, and that helped. While

our show ran the public library opened an exhibit called "Molly Picon, the Girl from Philadelphia." There were glass cases full of old pictures, programs and clips and that was exciting for me to see. I guess I got caught up in nostalgia, something I never do, and so I went out to look for pieces of my past: The Columbia and Bijou theaters, the old Northern Liberty School, Orianna Street. All of the buildings were now shacks! So much for memories. They were all down and I was still up. And that was that.

We were doing $71,000 a week, however, and that in bitter-cold weather. So Philly was good to us, and we relaxed and enjoyed her charms. We had the Workmen's Circle Children's Choir in, the Friends of Mt. Sinai, even the Israeli El Al came. And, backstage, Weede was giving us all singing lessons and I was learning. After fifty years, I discovered how to breathe! It was all great fun and we could have stayed another month. But we had advanced bookings pulling us away.

We took the train to Baltimore and found the whole city rebuilt. Only the audience seemed to contain relics. Our houses were good, but with no enthusiasm. I guess Philadelphia had spoiled us. I celebrated my sixty-fifth birthday amid two great shows, but Baltimore let us down. Only $33,000, so we left, gladly.

Those kinds of up-and-down audiences followed us from Pittsburgh to Toronto and Detroit. And when you did your best and the audience didn't respond, you'd lie awake trying to figure it. Am I sagging? Is the show sagging? Or are we off because it's Passover? Maybe the audience was anti-Israel?

A lot of theater guilds were bringing in their subscription crowd almost forcibly. We had to make them like our show, and we often did. But we weren't getting to general audiences and I was tired of opening with strikes against us.

By Detroit, we were down $1,000 and the Jews weren't coming. It was Passover and we made a seder for the cast and crew. Yonkel arranged an intelligent ceremony since most of our guests weren't Jewish. In his delightful way, he clarified for them what the seder was all about, and many outsiders booked dinner just to see what they called "our show."

By the time we got to Washington, D.C., however, *Come Blow Your Horn* had opened to fantastic reviews and brought publicity to us, too. Both the *Washington Post* and the *Star* had big articles on me with pictures, and they helped our business. There were lines at the box offices and smiles all around.

I finally decided it was time I saw my first movie! Yonkel was back at Chez checking on things, so one Sunday afternoon, I went alone to see it. I admit I was apprehensive.

In my one other film, *Yiddel Mit'n Fiddle,* I had played someone very familiar to me. Onstage, in the Yiddish theater, I had done every other part: a madam in a house, a crippled kid, a mama. In all these cases, however, I could always rely on my Yiddish *shtik:* the singing, the dancing, the tricks, which I knew could keep me going on the stage for years.

Film, however, is a lie detector. It magnifies everything you do and if you're not right, you fail in a giant way. So I watched my performance very critically, searching for any tiny flaw. But, I was pleased. I was not a kid up there doing well-worn tricks, I was an actress playing a role in a convincing way. That film gave me the feeling that I had grown as a performer and that I had a future. If I had the chance, I wasn't going to say "no" to movies or television because I saw I could create believable characters on the screen.

My next offer didn't come from Hollywood, but Burbank. We were still on tour and playing at the Biltmore in Los Angeles. Plans were cooking to sell the play for a movie and even bring us back to New York at reduced prices. I was skeptical about both deals. However, I did get a script for "Dr. Kildare" and I loved it. Raymond Massey was the show's big star, with Richard Chamberlain, a newcomer, playing the title role. And both men were great fun to work with. Not surprisingly, after sixty years in what we call the legitimate theater, more people recognized me because of one "Dr. Kildare" TV show than ever could have seen me anywhere else!

After nine months on the road, I said good-bye to Hollywood and flew home. Autumn in the country is spectacular and I didn't want to miss one golden-red leaf. I walked among the trees and just inhaled the air, which smelled like fine wine. It would have been very easy to have just curled myself up and nested right through spring. But let the high-paid analysts figure out why we performers can't sit still. Plans were made for *Milk and Honey* to play in New Jersey and upstate New York in November, and I agreed to go along.

Frankly, if my role hadn't been Clara Weiss I surely would have said "no." (I think!) But, Clara was special. Her exuberance on the stage lifted up the entire show and I loved the feeling I had of pulling everyone with me. What performer wouldn't?

We would open at the Papermill Playhouse in Milburn with William Chapman in Weede's role and Patti Winston playing Benzell's. Burry Frederick directed and Johnny Gringas put even more life into our already spirited dances. The show went very well. We had rave notices and I had great fun with my curtain speeches. It seems many people who couldn't get to Broadway were now coming to see us and we were held over, a complete sellout.

It would have taken some shock to break our spell and we got it. President Kennedy was shot in Dallas while riding in an open car. He died within the hour and the entire country went into a state of mourning which would last for years. Everyone remembers exactly where they were that day and I, also. What a mundane thing: to never forget that I was sitting in a beauty parlor in Mineola, because that was where I heard that J.F.K. was dead.

We've had too many sad assassinations since then, but Kennedy was the brutal first. People just froze in horror, or gathered about in stunned silence.

All the theaters closed down, but they reopened again on November 23rd, and it was too soon. There was no way we could make the audience laugh. People were bewildered. And when Oswald was gunned down, we were more bewildered. I guess we still are to this day. The irony was the stock market went up in support of our new President!

Of course, every life has its own dark clouds and some loomed over us. Yonkel had another fainting attack after a Chinese dinner. He was eating and then just slumped over, the second or third time this had happened. Yet, when we had Yonkel thoroughly checked, they found nothing. So why? we asked, and at seventy-two, you tend to answer the question with "old age." But I never bought that. I'm only sorry that I never challenged the doctors' findings.

Nineteen sixty-four blew in snow, ice and an acting nomination! *The Hollywood Reporter* named me for an Academy Award as best supporting actress. Yonk and I were thrilled. So why ain't I working?

Jerry Herman had a new musical, something called *Hello, Dolly!*, and I guess he learned a few things from his first one with us! It was an exciting night. The costumes, the sets, the dancing were all fabulous, but only a backdrop for one overwhelming star: Carol Channing. Everything about her was larger-than-life: her face, her eyes, her smile, her voice. We went backstage to congratulate her and Jerry and he was pleased to see us.

(By the way, Carol, like Kate Smith before her, is a graduate of the Molly Picon school of Yiddish songs. Many years after her *Dolly* success, Carol came to me because she was setting up a one-woman show and needed help on a song. It was a Romanian number and she wanted me to teach it to her in Yiddish. Now Carol, despite her blond image, was no scatterbrain. She was down-to-earth and worked hard to polish her performance. She did a great job on the song, and gave it her special pizzazz. In fact, my only fear for Carol is that now it will be very hard for her to do anything on a small scale!)

I, however, was bogging down with bus and trucking tours. I was doing *Majority of One* in Paramus and had plans for *Milk and Honey* in Miami. I hadn't planned on Miami, but it happened.

Ella Gerber, a wonderful director, infused great vitality and imagination into our Miami run. We also had a good singing group and a nice, fat bunch of widows. We opened at the Coconut Grove and Miami shared our success.

While in Miami, I finally got to visit a new friend I had made from *Milk and Honey*. Sister Gonzaga had come backstage to see me in New York and we began a delightful correspondence. Once, when *Milk and Honey* was on tour in

Pittsburgh, she had sent a big jar of *matzoh* ball soup! Now we had a car loaded up with goodies to take to Holy Cross Hospital in Fort Lauderdale for Sister Gonzaga and the other nuns. She and her Mother Superior and all the Sisters were waiting for us, and as we got out of the car, they all burst into, "Hello, Molly! It's so nice to see you back where you belong!" What a special day.

Despite those promises I had made to myself when my burst appendix had laid me flat, I was still not learning how to say "No." All my life, people have egged me on, and it became an obsession with me to live up to what other people expected me to do. It started with Yonkel, of course. He was the first one to really push me and, for better or worse, he pushed me into the Yiddish world where I blossomed and did well in my own way. As I got involved in Broadway and films, however, I also began to push myself because I knew I could do even more. As I sat at Chez, with a lawn full of dandelion, I made plans to present a Tony Award, play a ton of Guber tent theaters, *and* start my garden.

After fulfilling an invitation to present Gower Champion his Tony in the award ceremony, I was back at Chez planting twenty-four different annuals, getting my usual batch of spring bites, and trying not to scratch. But my garden was a showplace! We were home for a month, and the place just shone.

Yonkel was undergoing a series of gastrointestonal tests and, again, his doctors found him perfect. (Well, I knew that!) So we laughed and played. My little Aunt Nan was over with Uncle Charlie and we prodded them to take a dip in our pool. Now, Nan's my aunt but she's only a few years older than I. (Mama said Nan was a change of life baby and a big embarrassment to the family. You weren't supposed to be still fooling around at her Mama's age!) She and Charlie got a big kick out of our décor. We had painted three words on the side of the pool: a three-foot *AH*, a five-foot *OY,* and a ten-foot *GEVALD!*

Enough loafing. It was time to go back to work.

We took *Milk and Honey* to every tent that didn't have a boy scout in it. Kansas City, St. Louis, Baltimore. Theater-in-the-round was confusing, it was difficult to find the right ramps to go down in the dark, and it was often hot and sticky and worse. But then, at night sometimes, a full moon would come up over the theater just when I sang my "Hymn to Hymie." So I'd sing to that yellow moon, round as an Edam cheese. And the weeks flew by.

We wrapped our tour at Melody Land in Anaheim in November of 1964 with two good houses and a Johnson landslide. Then Yonkel and I rushed back home and I ended up under the knife.

I had a very bad gallstone which had to come out. It was Operation Beth Israel with Dr. Ginzburg as co-star. I was feeling very low for several days, then Dr. Ginzburg came in and found me dancing, so he sent me home! Yonkel and I cheered the New Year full of health. But we both knew we weren't the toughies we used to be.

We took it easy and wintered in Palm Beach, with both of us working in *Majority of One*. I was now sixty-seven and wanted to stay where it was warm! After Florida, we headed for Phoenix, Arizona, and didn't stray from a thermometer reading less than eighty degrees until April.

Then something crossed my desk and I had a chance to settle down. Jean Pierre Aumont, the great French actor, had a play he very much wanted to produce. It was called *Madame Pounce*, but was translated into the more alliterative *Madame Mousse*. He wanted me to do it with him, so I took the script back to Chez to study.

I didn't like it very much. It seemed too talky and not enough laughs. But, I liked Aumont. He was very intense about this play, which he had written. And I, of course, loved challenges.

Madame Mousse would be something new for me. First of all, I was to be French. Secondly, unlike my other cuddly, *Yiddishe* Mama roles, I was playing a giant pain in the neck! I was such a bothersome mother-in-law, that Aumont and his wife conspire to marry me off so that I'd have a nagging mother-in-law of my own. She would be played by Estelle Winwood, and it all looked like fun.

Meanwhile, until we got rolling, I got digging. Yonkel

and I had Mama's room made larger so two people could sleep there. Maybe us, when we got older. We had new shingles put on the house, and I began to rummage for suitable clothes for Madame Mousse. At our Passover seder (where Yonkel could only find red candles and had to whitewash them), I asked the four questions and there was a feeling of calm and love upon us.

Stanley Gordon, the co-producer of *Madame Mousse*, drove up to tell us he had already booked fifty theater parties, and the costume designer began having me model my wardrobe. At the same time, David Merrick kept saying he wanted me to do *Hello, Dolly!* in Israel, and I wondered if this French farce was such a good idea.

Ward Baker, the man who had steered *The Fantasticks* and Pinter plays to success, would be our director. He talked to me about *Mousse,* and he also listened, and I felt it would work.

With June, my second birthday came around, and I celebrated on "The Merv Griffin Show." I was never comfortable on talk shows, but this time, I felt I was never in better form. Even *I* liked me! I did twenty-five minutes, including a dance and a somersault. I felt light as a feather when I got home, then watched the Gemini astronauts' orbit on TV. It was all very awe-inspiring, and kind of dwarfed my little somersault.

Yonkel also had another stomach attack, and that surely shook me. I couldn't understand why he was sick. He ate some cheesecake and then just conked out. There was no pain, he was just weak and vomited. What could it be? He had passed all his tests perfectly. Worse still, Yonkel wouldn't complain and he wouldn't go doctor-hopping. I was stymied.

He bounced back, as he had done so often, and the two of us flew to Chicago where we had a commitment to do *Majority of One* at the Tenthouse Theater in Highland Park. My contract for *Mousse* also came in, and I signed it at what we hoped was a lucky hour. Yonkel would be playing Asano in *Majority,* and we struggled with a miserable dress rehearsal. I prayed for a miracle and kind critics. (You usually don't get both!) You never know in our crazy profession. No wonder so many of us are nervous. But, things meshed, Yonkel did well and everyone seemed pleased. In one week, we had cars lined up for tickets and promoters clamoring for us to return. I just hoped *Mousse* did as well.

We flew home to Chez, waiting for Aumont to get things in shape, and also tended to our real work. I cut roses, picked beans, washed and hung clothes, cooked up three meals. Then, everyone into the pool! In the middle of all this turmoil, which included an invasion from the *Mousse* cast, I worked up something for "The Mike Douglas Show" and somehow managed to get away and do it.

Mousse, like its name, seemed very light and fragile. Neither Ward Baker nor I seemed to know what we wanted, and Aumont, our author, was equally helpless. Maybe we'd find it in rehearsals?

Aumont, Pierre Olaf, Estelle and I gathered at the Sheridan Square Playhouse for a reading. Baker had most of it blocked and now we had to memorize our lines and find our character's hearts.

Estelle was a delight, even to rehearse with. She weighed about eighty pounds and had to be at least that in years. She was also married to a man who was at least as old, if not older. They had some sort of arrangement where they pretty much lived apart. But, occasionally, he'd pass through and they'd have a quick exchange: "Oh, where have you been, dear," Estelle would ask in her tiny, clipped voice. "Oh, down in Australia for the past year," he'd answer, "and now I'm off to London." And Estelle would chime: "Well, have a good time, dearie!" and go back to her work!

I'd come into rehearsal full of vim and say, "Good Morning, Estelle. How are you today?" And she'd answer: *"Mind your own business!"* She was living with Tallulah Bankhead then, and Estelle would say to me, "Don't try to talk to Tallulah. She's stone deaf and can't hear a word. Just let her talk to *you!"*

I thought it would be very amusing to play mother-in-law with this crew, especially Estelle. But, the more we rehearsed *Mousse,* the less grip everyone seemed to have on it.

Everyone worked hard, but, frankly, I think we were all confused—especially Aumont. At one point, he dropped a real bomb, asking that I finish on a serious note, which I couldn't see at all. *Ça va.*

We had a run-through and it looked pretty bad. Aumont was into blocking and cutting, but I'm afraid we had no show. It was funny in places, then it petered out. But, we persevered.

We opened *Madame Mousse* at the Westport Playhouse on August 16, 1965. We had lots of laughs but they were spotty, and I felt my part just evaporated. Our house was sold out, there was the obligatory champagne, we broke all records, but we didn't have a show. We needed help and I didn't see how Aumont could act, write and translate at the same time.

We all started talking about bringing someone in to save us: George Baxt, Nat Hiken or Goodman Ace. What we really needed was another George S. Kaufman!

We went on to Paramus and more of the same. Nothing worked. We even had a Jewish audience and couldn't get *Mousse* off the ground. I put in my curtain speech which at least sent them out laughing, but it was not enough. A new director, John Berry, came in and he helped. But what we needed was a Play.

The play needed a major rewrite, but with Berry at the helm we opened at the Mineola Playhouse and somehow got away with it. The show was a puzzlement. We had four curtain calls and no show! All of us were tired and we needed time to stop and think.

We ended our tour in September, and limped back home. Yonkel and a play-doctor began rewriting Aumont's script. And, I thought, if we can straighten this play out, we'll deserve medals.

We read our changes to Aumont, Berry, et al., and they seemed happy, but just as confused as to what we should do next. So Yonkel and I picked up some spare change and flew out to the Mill Run Theater in Illinois.

We were scheduled to appear in *Majority of One*, but it looked like our show was a military secret. There was not a word, not an ad, not a sign, nothing. The first night, we played to a half-empty house and the next two nights, to completely empty ones. I guess it was some sort of achievement to keep a show going with sixty people sitting in a house meant to hold 1,600!

I suppose there was a lesson to be learned there, somewhere; but it escaped me. Who needs to know how to play before an absent crowd?

I flew home to catch up on rest, settled into an old chair, and tried to figure out just what was happening to my so-called career. As I pondered, all the lights went out: in New York, Connecticut and the rest of the Eastern coast. We had a blackout, and power outages trapped people in subways, tunnels and elevators. Funny, how relative everything is.

Yonkel finished working on a rewrite of *Mousse* and we brought it back to town to give a reading. Reactions were still mixed, so Yonkel said: "Gentleman, when you have *your* new script, let us know. We'll read it and if we like it, maybe we'll do it. *Au Revoir.*"

Suddenly, we could breathe again. We were glad to get *Mousse* out of our hair.

CHAPTER ✵ 17

MADAME MOUSSE had been a rather sticky, unpleasant dish, but I quickly forgot its disagreeable taste. Yonkel and I always looked ahead and we decided we needed to really get away from show business for a while. It was November and Yonkel's seventy-fourth birthday. We agreed it ought to be celebrated in Israel. It was a trip which would give him one of his heart's greatest wishes.

We landed at Lod Airport and Levy, our old guide, was there to meet us with photographers and the press. Meira, our adopted daughter, was waiting at our hotel with her father and stepmother. She had our room filled with flowers and our reunion was joyful. Meira would be coming back with us to study in New York! It was cause for celebrating.

After our cherished family gathering, Unikovski, Meira's father, drove us to Haifa, and we took a deep breath and plunged in. We walked and walked and walked for hours, just absorbing what was happening.

When a Jew visits Israel, it's very different from a European immigrant returning to his former home. An Italian, Frenchman or Pole can return to a country which had been secure for centuries. A Jew sees an Israel which is still creating itself. Everywhere we looked in 1965, we saw beginnings: the first skyscraper department store in Tel Aviv, new artists' studios out of abandoned Arab houses, more concert halls.

Unikovski, who knew every rock and grain of soil of his beloved Israel, kept us on the go. He took us to Egdod, a new seaport and a completely new city built on sand. We saw the old and new moshavim and the famous Weitzman Institute.

244

Even a Yiddish operetta. But Yiddish theater was a stepchild there, very antiquated and not for us. More up to date was the Sabra Cabaret. Here, homosexuals dressed in female attire, there were acrobats and a French review, all very professional. But gays in Israel? As Mama would have said, It's very modern!

We drove to Jerusalem on a new four-lane highway and checked in to the King David Hotel. The next day, Yoshka, a new guide, took us to Yad Vashem, a shattering monument to our six million dead. Numbly, we moved on to see the miniature Biblical Jerusalem which was being built by an eighty-four-year-old man. From death to life! Then Yoshka invited us to his house for a drink, and it was all so *haimish* (homey).

Chanukah was upon us, and at night, thousands of little children marched with torches to celebrate. And, the next day, a very special light came into our lives.

He was a handsome six-footer, just twenty-one, fair-haired and blue-eyed. Friends had arranged for us to meet, but he was very shy as he stood dressed in a soldier's uniform. He told us his name was Dov Steiner and that his father, who had died recently, had often spoken to him about Yonkel and their hometown in Poland.

The boy's face was beet-red and Yonkel tried to make him comfortable. He asked him what his plans were and he answered, a bit hesitantly, "All my life I dreamed about becoming a doctor, but without my father, it's impossible."

"I'd like to help you," Yonkel said, "in fact, I can be your new father and help you through college. We'll start right now with the financial arrangements."

But, Dov stopped him and said, "First, please tell me about my father."

When Yonkel answered, "I didn't know your father, Dov," the boy's face became ashen. "But I thought you were related to him," he said softly. "This means your money would be charity. No, no, I can't take charity," and he rose to leave. Yonkel stopped him and said, "Look. I'm investing in you and some day I'm sure you'll pay me back. Go home and think it over."

We didn't hear from Dov for over a week. Then, the day before we were to leave Israel, he came to see us and with tears in his eyes, accepted Yonkel's offer. He told us that he would not be able to go to medical school in Israel because spaces were being made for students from the new Black African nations. He had another plan.

"I am going to Siena, Italy," he explained. "They have a wonderful medical school and are accepting eighty Israeli students. I'll be heading up that group!"

Yonkel and Dov kissed like father and son. I got a peck in, too! "My son, the doctor!"

Which reminds me of a story George Jessel used to tell. An actor, carrying a big box, came to see an agent. "In this box," he said, "I have an act that'll be a sensation! It'll make us both rich!" "What is it?" the agent sneered. The actor replied, "A dog! A dog who plays piano!" "Show me," the agent said, whereupon, the actor opened the box and there was a little dog playing a piano! Just then, a big dog rushed in, grabbed the little dog and pulled him out. "Who's that?" the agent asked. And the actor answered, "That's his mother. She wants him to be a doctor!"

Now Yonkel had a son, and one in medicine, too. And his investment proved a good one. Dov finished medical school and with his wife, who is also a doctor, returned to Israel to practice. Dov met his wife in Siena, where she was one of those eighty Israelis. Yonkel and I gladly helped pay for both their degrees. However, neither of them ever asked for anything, but accepted only what we chose to send. Dov wanted to give us something special in return and he did. When he graduated, he gave us his first stethoscope because, he said, we had made him a doctor. Both of them, and their two little children, have truly enriched our lives.

We returned to New York at the New Year with weather in the 60s. John Lindsay was our new mayor in 1966 and with his inauguration came subway, bus and garbage strikes. People were on foot everywhere, including the Mayor, who walked to City Hall. Everything finally got settled, though it cost the city half a billion. Luckily, things started moving just in time for me to get into town and tape another "Merv Griffin Show." I decided to do a mix, so I spoke about Israel and then did a chorus of "Glocca Morra"!

The weather turned white and the snow looked like cake frosting on the windows. I stayed snug in Chez reading Michener's *The Source*, beginning to understand Israel and the Israelis. I was interrupted, however, by a quick call. Could I come and do *Majority* in Miami on February 4th? Seems they were having trouble with Shelley Winters in the role. Temperament! When do we grow up?

Well, I would go. But I had other plans also. Albee Marre, who had directed me in *Milk and Honey*, had been pestering me to do a new play by Ted Allan called *Chu Chem*. I found the story farfetched: it was a musical about a Jewish couple who travel to China looking for Chinese Jews. It was very confused and got more mixed up later. However, Marre had come to Chez and read us his new version, which gave me the star part. Cheryl Crawford would produce it, and Yonkel thought it was a grand idea. After all, hadn't Marre recast it just for me?

Chu Chem (which means "A Wise Man") was in the back of my mind when I agreed to go down to Miami. Whatever happened, I'd have something waiting for me back in New York. Rehearsals started immediately for yet another stint at *Majority*. Funny, at rehearsal, the young people knew their lines but couldn't act. The veterans could act but couldn't learn their lines. Yet, somehow, it looked promising. Then, shocking news. Sophie Tucker and Billy Rose died. And we had just lost Buster Keaton! As Mama used to say, people were dying who never died before.

But those who live and breathe must continue on. And there I was with unfinished sets, shaky lines, sticky co-stars, and God help us. We had a good house, however, and they were with us. At one matinee, in a scene where I pray over the candles, the whole audience said "Amen!"

Meanwhile, Marre had lined up the great comic Menashe Skulnik to co-star in *Chu Chem*. He called Miami all enthused, telling me my name gets money and sells tickets. Everyone wanted to see the *Milk and Honey* star in a new role. Marre wanted rehearsals to start in September, the beginning of the Broadway season, and he was just praising everything to the sky. God help us on this one, too, I prayed.

But, I wasn't complaining. Me, a gal of sixty-eight, and so many irons in the fire. I wrapped up *Majority* in Miami and got a call that Anthony Quinn wanted me back in April to do a film, *Mr. Innocent.* I had just a few weeks of a road show to do and I would be all his.

I was to play an Italian mother and, as in *Horn,* I had another telephone scene. Actually, that was my *only* scene. And I never got to act with Quinn. Instead, I was dressed in a slinky lamé dressing gown and I was filmed talking into the phone to Quinn, my son, while his reaction was being shot elsewhere.

I only got to see Quinn work once, but I'll never forget it. I remember that he insisted on redoing one scene *thirty times.* I just put in my one day and left.

The funny thing is, I didn't even end up in the film. The movie ran too long so they cut out my scene. Still, whenever it runs on television (retitled *The Happening*), I get residuals!

Back at Chez, I found my agents haggling over my getting second billing to Skulnik, while Albee Marre was back on my doorstep chirping about the already phenomenal reaction to the play. He told me over a million dollars had already been booked in advance by theater parties and it would be a crime if I didn't do it. So what if I played second fiddle?

Yonk and I reread Marre's script and we felt, despite my lowered status, there were still parts where I could stand out. Half-heartedly, I agreed to do it.

But I didn't like it, didn't like anything about it. And I resented being wooed with a starring role but being wed to second place. On top of all that, Meira was on her way and suddenly I had responsibility for *Chu Chem* and a daughter. Just leave it to Molly! Ha.

I have always had good friends, thank goodness. I still had road commitments in Chicago and Philadelphia, so I arranged for the Franzblaus to help Meira in New York. She wanted to find a small apartment near NYU, where she would be taking a course in English.

In Chicago, I was to do a brief run of *Dear Me, the Sky Is Falling*. We would play at the Pheasant Run Theater, and I had an interesting experience there.

At one matinee, the audience was made up of young supermarket workers. Many of them were women who had never seen a live stage show and they didn't applaud, as expected, on my entrance. When I asked them later why, they said they didn't know it was permissible to applaud.

In Philadelphia, my stint went much better, But, it always did in my hometown. That particular run, my alumni from William Penn High School came in and we all had tea later at the Belmont. It was very touching. I ran into Mamie Emanuel from Orianna Street. She had taught me to sing "Just Because Your Hair Is Curly" when I was only five years old.

Summer was hot upon us and every chance I had, I raced back to Chez to smell my roses and skinny-dip in our pool. But, so much was happening, or about to happen, that I had trouble relaxing or trying to sleep. My only vice was relying on pills to get some rest. I had been taking them from when I was a youngster, first out on tour. They weren't an addiction in the sense that I had to increase their dose, but I was hooked on them in that I needed the same tiny pills for years. It was only after I was alone, on my own, that I finally stopped taking them.

On June 29th, the thermometer hit 100, so Yonkel and I celebrated our anniversary working in the gardens, then dipping in the pool. We had forty-seven years together to celebrate and we did, with champagne. Meira joined us, a very serious young lady, thin, quiet, but well-dressed. We took her to a play and introduced her to the actors. After dinner, I arranged for her to buy some clothes. I remember she chose only simple things, and said her greatest wish was to begin her studies.

Our summer idyl was interrupted by a theft. Somebody broke into Chez and took mostly poor Mary's things. She was pretty shaken up, we had to have detectives in, and now we had to get someone to stay with Mary. So even in Mahopac we weren't safe! What a world!

We teased Mary, just a bit. Everyday, she was full of the robbery and as she talked, the estimates of her losses rose. We laughed and kept cool in the pool in the nude (no one else was there, of course!).

I was again marking time, waiting for Marre and Crawford and whoever else was involved to get some definite start on *Chu Chem*. All I kept getting were promises, and even those were postponed.

I did more summer stock, and used some of my loot to take care of the "kids." Meira needed money for her new apartment and Dov needed everything else but for Siena. Ah, the joys of Mamahood!

Meira was becoming very much a part of our home life, even our stage life. We were invited on "The Joe Franklin Show" to help boost sales of our book, *So Laugh a Little*, which was now out in paperback. Meira joined us on the air, and considering it was her first TV appearance, she was very calm and intelligent and looked like a little doll. We bought her a lovely coat and found her a nice apartment opposite NYU in Washington Square, and our friends were already calling to play matchmaker with Meira and their sons.

Finally, arrangements were made to begin rehearsals for *Chu Chem* and Marre's double-talk unraveled. I watched as Marre read, the lyricist sang and the rest of the cast followed along. But my part practically vanished into the second act. I was furious!

All the talk about starring me, writing the script for me, needing me, was bull. Marre had rewritten all the comic lines in Skulnik's favor, and I ended up playing straight man with a role which was little more than an unbilled guest appearance.

I wanted out. But Marre talked to me and begged me to have faith in him, etcetera, but I didn't believe a word. I knew I shouldn't have done *Chu Chem*, and three days of rehearsal confirmed my intincts. The only thing that even made me listen to Marre's pleas was that friends of ours had invested money.

It was a mess, and as soon as my threats to Marre hit the papers it got messier. Investors started screaming for their money back and a very incensed Cheryl Crawford called threatening to sue me for half a million if I tried to break my contract.

I was stuck. I begged the Morris office to try and find some other way out, then I went off to Philadelphia to walk through our tryouts. The show should have been called "Gimmicks Unlimited." Suddenly, Marre decided that Skulnik and I weren't a couple in China, only actors playing a couple in a play within a play. But when I would ask Marre how did he want it done, he just said, "Play it tongue in cheek, Molly!"

Poor Menashe was in worse shape. He was a brilliant Yiddish comedian, but Skulnik had less grasp of English than he did of Chinese acting and he was forever saying to me: "What does it mean?" He was completely lost. It was the most vague, muddled script we had ever seen. Yonkel called our first run-through "Amateur Night in Dixie!"

We opened in Philadelphia on November 9th, and I was so humiliated about my performance, I didn't take a bow. The Morris office advised me to play it for one more night while they tried to get my release, and it was agony. Marre insisted on bringing in physical *shtik* to cover the yawning holes in the plot, and I was in pain from pulling this and dragging that.

The Philly notices were equally nasty. The kind critics called it banal and tasteless, without music and dancing, a blintz with soy sauce. Someone said it should have been called "The King and OY!" Marre deserved it. And was I glad I was out!

I was unemployed and happy. We had a big party for Yonkel's seventy-fifth birthday, with Mary making a delicious dinner and everyone drinking lots of wine. For the first time in months, I slept without pills.

Yonkel was well and happy and my own Dr. Katz gave me a clean bill of health. Meira and I took in some theater, and I began introducing her to Rabbi Nussbaum's son, Jerry. Maybe, they'd like each other. (My *Yiddishe* Mama speaking?)

Well, I was reading *How to Be a Jewish Mother* and

learning. Actually, I found the book by Seymour Vall very funny and began thinking it was something I could play. The question was whether or not it could carry an entire evening.

Meanwhile, my friend Rose (Dr. Franzblau) began calling asking about Meira and Nussbaum's boy. So we were two *Yiddishe* Mamas!

Chu Chem lingered on for a few nights without me, then finally flopped. *Variety* wrote that the play made $45,000 in previews with me, and less than half that after I left. It was flattering news for me, but it was sad for the company and for our friends who'd invested.

I comforted them with news of Meira's social whirl. She seemed taken with Jerry, the son of the famous Rabbi Nussbaum who had converted Liz Taylor and Sammy Davis to Judaism. Jerry and Meira began going out and even went to Midnight Mass. So go figure. An Israeli and a rabbi's son!

We celebrated New Year's at my sister Helen's apartment, which was very comfortable for Helen and for us. We had noisemakers and lots of Helen's great food and we watched the ball drop over Times Square with our nice, homey party. A very troublesome year was over. And I felt ready to begin again.

Seymour Vall made it easy for me to jump back into something new. He and I met at Sardi's and we began to talk about bringing *How to Be a Jewish Mother* to the stage. A lot of shows were becoming integrated and Yonkel suggested a Negro co-star. Vall had just the man, Godfrey Cambridge.

Off we went, to the Russian Tea Room, to meet with Cambridge and his agent. We talked about the play and everyone was for it. Yonkel and I went back to Chez settled on *Jewish Mother*. We thought it was novel, something different, but the winter was in, and we'd have to wait and see.

Back at Mahopac, Yonkel and I began gathering some of our memorabilia, which we donated to the American Jewish Historical Society located at Brandeis. We needed three people to come and load a station wagonful of our memories. So now Yonkel and I were authentic museum pieces!

Meira was staying with us and was a delight. She very much wanted to stay in America another year and study at Parsons. She also wanted to get some kind of part-time job, but NYU students were not allowed to work at night and we assured her we'd help her find something during the day. She wasn't the only one looking for work, however. So was I.

I was never comfortable on talk shows, as I've said, but I had an opportunity to do something that turned into great fun. Mike Douglas asked me to come and co-host his show for a week and I joined him on February 13th. Joel Grey and Andy Griffith were among the guests for my first show, and it was just tops working with them. I did a duet with Joel, told stories with Andy, and then made blintzes on the show for everyone!

The second day, I stayed away from the kitchen and came on in tights and boots to do yoga. The rest of the week I sang with Enzo Stuarti, chatted with Muriel Humphrey, danced with Sally Ann Howes. I guess I got carried away because I threw in some somersaults. On the last day, the company made me a birthday cake and Mike presented it to me on camera. Yonkel joined us onstage and we danced together. Quite a lovely week!

My appearance generated all kinds of offers, but we returned home and just stayed put for a while. We introduced Meira to the joys of shopping on Orchard Street on the Lower East Side and even got her a job with Russ & Daughters (purveyors of herring and lox), where she could work on Sundays. Dov wrote beautiful letters to us from Siena; he was learning Italian and polishing his English. Yonkel and I were counting our blessings.

Mamahood seemed to be all around me. Besides waiting for rehearsals to begin in September for *How to Be a Jewish Mother,* I got a script which gave the *Yiddishe* Mama a new twist. The play was called *The Rubiyat of Sophie Klein* by Laird Koenig. There was a very funny part in it for me, and Koenig brought together the novel contrast of a Jewish mama and an Arab sheik. Both Yonkel and I liked it and I planned to do it. Meanwhile, I had to answer the mail I was getting from women all over the country who had seen my Douglas shows. All of them wanted my "formula for life"! And I received the Freedom House Award from Roy Wilkins, who said, "You don't have to be Jewish to know Molly Picon."

Our rehearsals for *Rubiyat* began on April 18th, and the

play still needed work. We were playing in the round, once again, and the entrances and exits involved the usual complications. *Rubiyat* was a new play and it looked like we would have to find it while we rehearsed.

Every actor makes the same mistake. You read a play and you see what you think the play *could* be, not what the play really is. Then, you go into rehearsals hoping the play will improve, mesh, become better than it is, and you're always disappointed when it doesn't.

We would be performing *The Rubiyat of Sophie Klein* at the Westbury Music Fair, a very posh outdoor theater not far from New York City in Westchester. It was rainy and cold in April, however, and the country atmosphere just looked green and damp. We would be following Maurice Chevalier, who was doing a one-man show the week ahead of us. Maurice and I managed to meet briefly. He remembered our shows in Paris in 1937 and we posed together for a fresh set of pictures. We would lose him not too long afterward, and I'm very glad we had a chance to stop and record our meeting.

As for *Rubiyat*, everything was wrong! The props, the furniture, the costumes—all were a shambles. Things were either late, missing, or the wrong size. Thankfully, Chevalier had left his refrigerator stocked full of sandwiches and champagne. We needed them!

I still felt our play had possibilities, however, and when we opened on May 2nd, the audience seemed to agree. We had laughs and color and good reviews. Uonfortunately, it was too late to sell the theater parties and that might hurt. But the show went well and Koenig began rewriting. And a lady at the box office said: "What is this *Rubiyat?* A new hotel in the Catskills?" And her friend answered: "Sophie Klein? Must be the story of Sophie Tucker."

Our struggles at Westbury had diverted our attention from the rest of the world. Suddenly, Egypt was arming along the Israeli border. War looked inevitable. And so it happened! Israel against the Arabs in what was called the Six-Day War. Meira immediately left us to fight in Israel and we sent her money and prayed for her safety. We all watched and waited and, incredibly, Israel was victorious over Jordan and Egypt. The U.N. Security Council voted a cease-fire, Jordan begged for peace, Egypt capitulated, and Israel penetrated the Suez Canal.

It was all a fantasy. Israel was winning the war, Meira had gone to help fight, and Dov wrote that he was sitting on his valise in Siena, waiting to fly home. We felt we were winning and losing all at the same time. Yonkel wired the Bond Office and we pledged all our earnings to Israeli bonds. Yonkel began with a ten-thousand-dollar purchase.

We sent Israel our money, but she had our son and daughter too. We eagerly awaited every letter from Meira and Dov and, with victory, even Yonkel began to talk of moving to Israel. That we had won was miraculous, but it would take a miracle to continue our success. Thankfully, the world leaders today want to prevent another war. And I keep thinking of something Dov said to me just recently: "I don't want another piece of land," he said, "I just want a land of peace."

Yonkel and I threw ourselves into bond sales. I opened *Funny Girl* in St. Louis at the Municipal Opera House with Marilyn Michaels, and Yonk and I sold $200,000 on the side. And that just to 150 sweet ladies. We kept pledging all we made and Yonkel said, "Molly, count your blessings." Here I was, almost seventy, getting $3,500 a week and the audience loved us. And we loved each other.

We played *Funny Girl* for five weeks and I managed to carve out one showstopping number, which I enjoyed. Then, it was on to Philadelphia to begin *Rubiyat* again. Warren Berlinger was in to play the son and I found him cute. We opened in the Playhouse in the Park on August 21st. We had a packed crowd and plenty of laughs, but our press was only so-so. While some people liked it better than *Milk and Honey*, our house was dropping off and so we finished *Rubiyat*. Everyone still thought it was okay for Broadway, but nobody wanted to gamble.

One dud down, two to go? I didn't know for sure, but I was apprehensive. Godfrey Cambridge and I began rehearsals and they were difficult and long. And that week, three shows opened and closed in New York without notice!

Godfrey was refreshingly frank. He couldn't sing or dance and was the first to admit it. "I'm the only Black in creation," he said, "who ain't got rhythm!" All of which meant I would be carrying most of the musical load, and I felt every pound.

Vall had decided to script the book as one narrative play. That kind of stalled the action, but somehow we made it to our first previews in New Locust, Pennsylvania. The show was doubtful, but opening night—*Bang!* Godfrey was up and so was I and, with no critics, we had laughs and applause and, maybe, possibilities. What we desperately needed was more writing help.

We flew to Boston for a pre-Broadway tryout at the Wilbur and a skilled comedy-writing team came in. Renee Taylor and Joe Bologna were rewriting and completely reworked the script. They broke the play down into vignettes where I was always the Jewish mother and Godfrey Cambridge played everybody else in my life: my son, husband, grocer, neighbor.

We had one scene in the first act which was especially good. I was standing in the line at a bank when Godfrey came up in back of me with a drawn gun. I turned toward him, noticed the weapon and said very firmly, "Does your mother know what you do for a living!" In another scene, Godfrey is playing my son, a little boy. I fuss about getting him dressed for school, and list all the horrors that could befall him on his way. I work us both up into such a state that I finally decide to go with him and he ends up helping me on with my coat.

Godfrey was brilliant in both sketches. He may not have had rhythm, but he had great comedy sense and with Renée and Joe rewriting, the play began to come together. What hampered Godfrey was that many of his friends would come backstage and berate him for some of the roles he was playing. One friend criticized Godfrey for helping me on with my coat. He said it made Godfrey look like a servant! These were the sixties and touchy times.

We played Boston to full houses and bad notices. The audience loved us and the critics didn't. I thought with Renée putting more of their skits in, that we were beginning to have something. But the bad word was already leaking to Broadway.

We all flew to Chicago and were now working with a completely new script. The pressure was on and Godfrey blew his top. He was just like a kid with his tantrums so we let him blow off steam and then we went on.

We opened at The Civic Opera House in Chicago and reactions were good. The new scenes were playing well. If only we could get more of Taylor and Bologna into our show, maybe . . . However, as expected, there were unanimous pans for the show, and praise for Godfrey and me. I think these critics were reading the other ones. But our box-office sales were good and Avery Shreiber was also brought in to help out. Together, the writers kept bringing in new scenes for me and I had to ask them to ease up. Godfrey was in the play, too, and I didn't want them to forget him. God (as we called him) was pleased with my concern for him. So, amid all this turmoil, we were getting by.

Shreiber began directing and with new scenes, new comedy and a new director, we began getting screams. God loved me and we were working well together. In many ways, we were trying to do too much too quickly and getting a little muddled, but our audience reaction was terrific. I put in one of the hardest jobs of my life, studying a completely new show while performing the old one. But it looked like we had a chance.

We opened in Detroit, and we began to feel like a success. We were sold out and the reaction was grand. But I was falling back on tricks, my strength was gone. I got by on vitamin shots and grit. We played to a record $82,000 in one week and then winged on to Baltimore. Godfrey was now having health troubles, too, especially with his voice, which had to have been frazzled. We had script changes every day and were dizzy. But, we did $60,000 in sales without any group subscriptions. If we could only keep our strength.

We were inching toward Broadway. One step closer was our previews at the Hudson Theater. Unfortunately, Godfrey just fell apart the first night. He let everyone down and we didn't think we would get off the ground. Yet, the lines were forming at the box office and we couldn't smother just a little bit of enthusiasm. Just maybe? The next few shows were terrific. It seemed we had it, at last. Yonkel brought me home by car and I vowed to just shut my mouth and keep it shut until opening night.

Our final run-through had laughs from curtain to curtain. We opened *How to Be a Jewish Mother* at the Judson on October 20th and I thought we had it all: bravos, ovations— the works! We went to Sardi's and there was applause as soon as we stepped in the door. Everybody's feelings were high.

But the notices were bad. Again, we had a tremendous audience show. The critics raved about Godfrey and me, but they hated the show. I still think they thought they were watching the same one we had performed in Boston, but they weren't. Our friends began calling, incensed that the critics didn't feel the electricity in the audience. Everyone was angry at the critics. So we finished 1967 with a big hit and bad notices, God and I were nursing colds . . . and Happy New Year!

With the exception of *Milk and Honey*, my record on Broadway wasn't too great. I had more flops than hits and you learn to take them in your stride, especially if you know you're in a clinker. But *Jewish Mother* had a lot of good things going; some of the sketches were really first-rate. Once we had an audience inside, we had them laughing from beginning to end. But theater parties read reviews too, and they were staying away.

Worse for me, Yonkel was getting his dizzy spells again and, again, the doctors didn't know why. I took a suite in the Algonquin, which was near the Hudson Theater, so Yonkel could rest there and Helen could come and sit with him while I performed.

Yonkel rested and I wheezed. The theater was freezing cold and a million cases of flu blew across the footlights at us every night. We were on a week-to-week basis, and if we could weather the weather and the critics, we might make it.

But things got hopeless. Cambridge brought us to a screeching halt with one swipe of an axe. The management had begun fixing up my dressing room. They put on a fresh coat of paint and put in new plumbing. Godfrey's room didn't receive the same kind of treatment and he resented it. He had been after the management to fix his sink. When they didn't, he took an axe one night and just hacked up the plumbing. Water pipes burst everywhere and flooded us all out. Everybody hushed it up, of course. Godfrey agreed to pay for the damages so they wouldn't sue. It was all so infantile and only aggravated our already sinking situation. When the fire department came in to bail us out, they took one look at our ancient equipment and wanted the entire theater overhauled! So, in spite of doing better business than many other shows, we had to close. We finished to two full houses and I just couldn't understand why we hadn't clicked.

Godfrey went right from the theater into the hospital. He was operated on at Mt. Sinai for a very damaged throat and spent the entire week recuperating. He had obviously played those last few weeks in nagging pain, which couldn't have helped his disposition. As for me, I had my own patient to worry about. Yonkel was up nights, full of pain and sweat, his stomach upset. He had been too weak even to take me back to Chez. Finally, we got him strong enough to move and we made it to Mahopac, the only place in the world where we could rest.

CHAPTER ✸ 18

Yonkel and I stayed at Chez and both mended: he, his body, and I, my spirit. Whatever was causing Yonkel to faint, once the spell had passed, he seemed to rejuvenate. The doctors came up with various diagnoses, everything from a pinched nerve to earaches. But, since he seemed to continue to bounce back, we all felt there was no cause for alarm. And once Yonkel got better, I did too.

Abi Gezunt. We had our health, and we quickly booked tickets for Israel. Both of us wanted to see Meira and Dov again. We landed at Lod where Meira and her father waited. Her dark eyes sparkled and she was flushed with Israel's victory. Everywhere, the cafés were crowded, people were out walking, talking, laughing—and Israel *es kocht sich* (it's cooking!).

But there were problems galore, of course. The newly conquered lands had to be settled and secured, and Meira wanted to stay and help. She would not be returning to us, to America and Parsons. Her dreams were larger than herself and we accepted that proudly.

Meira had also found love and she introduced us to her fiancé. Together, we walked the jammed streets to see the annual Purim Parade. The children marched in costumes made of paper and spit and imagination. They were part of a new Israel, totally unlike our old ideas of passive Jews. This was a new breed: strong, intelligent and arrogant!

Dov had also returned to Israel during its brief war, but now had returned to Siena to complete his studies. We joined him there and, as with Meira, met another sweetheart, Mariana, who would soon be Dov's wife.

Both of them were studying obstetrics and gynecology. They were preparing for what Israel needed and they were anxious to graduate and begin practicing in Jerusalem. Dov showed us the tiny room where he and Mariana studied from the same book because books cost more than the tuition! Yonkel gave him money for their tuition, plus a little extra. They are two beautiful people.

Yonkel and I went on to Rome and when we arrived, the Italian students were demonstrating in front of the American Embassy: "Yankee Go Home!" And Yonkel thought at first that they meant him!

Poor Rome. The Italians there were mortgaged to their history and their art. The people were poor and the students were rioting. Their world screamed for revolution, but our world was getting it. We flew home to the news that Dr. Martin Luther King had been assassinated and there had been burning and looting in many cities. We had a quiet Passover seder at Chez and listened to the eulogies for Dr. King. We thanked God, once again, for the sanity and love we had there.

My rest was over, however. Robert Merrill wanted me to record an album of *Fiddler on the Roof* in London; Lee Guber wanted me for two weeks of tent duty with *Milk and Honey;* and the huge Milliken Show was upon us.

The latter is something special in Show Biz and needs a little explaining. The Milliken people make fibres and every year they spend over a million dollars to produce a musical which demonstrates their newest fabrics. They make a story about their new line and incorporate the Milliken fabrics into the costumes and sets. The show is always an extravaganza with hundreds of costumes, dozens of singers and dancers and an enormous crew. What's intriguing about all this is that only Milliken's buyers and friends ever get to see the end result. There's no advertising for the show and seating is by invitation only. Yet, Broadway actors love to do Milliken because only the top talent is employed and they get top dollar for fourteen performances. Plus, Milliken pays everyone for rehearsals, the only people in or out of show business to do that.

It's an honor of sorts to be part of a Milliken Show and everyone strives to be in top form. So I threw myself into our rehearsals at the Mark Hellinger Theater from 10:00 to 6:00 while Yonkel held auditions for our *Milk and Honey* tour. We now were booked for eight weeks in the round. Someone asked me if I was doing *Milk and Honey* and I said, "I'm doing Milliken and Money!"

We did our first show on May 27, 1968 at the Waldorf and it was a success. Many young textile students were working with me during rehearsals and my somersaults on stage just shocked them. Not bad for an old lady. And at 8:00 A.M., too. Milliken shows are put on early, which meant I had to be up at 6:00 for exercises and voice warm-ups.

June was upon us and only an Easterner can know how delightful the thought of those next warm months can be. Yet, once again during those frightful years, we had tragedy instead of calm. Bobby Kennedy was shot in Los Angeles and everyone was numb again. People just couldn't believe it. And we were doubly saddened when the suspect was described as a Jordanian immigrant angered because Kennedy backed Israel. So we finished Milliken not with a celebration but In Requiem. We were so grieved that I hardly glanced at our Milliken bonus checks. I thought mine was $500 until Yonkel looked at it and gasped, "*Shmendrick!* It's five thousand!"

We took *Milk and Honey* on the road with Earl Wrightson and Lois Hunt playing the leads. We played flashy spots like Westbury and others nestled into the local shopping center. But, in spite of the heat and other frustrations of working on the road, we had Lee Guber's tent theater chain in smiles. *Milk and Honey* grosses were good and we had done it again.

Touring with Yonkel had whet my appetite for more work. Yet, I still wasn't getting anything worth doing on the stage. The only offers which tempted me were from television and they were too lucrative to turn down. After taping my *Fiddler* album with Merrill in London, I agreed to shoot segments of "Gomer Pyle" and "My Friend Tony." Talk about going from the sublime to the ridiculous. One minute I was in elegant London, singing "Golda" with the Festival

Choir and Robert Merrill, one of opera's great voices. We had a sixty-piece orchestra and everything first-class. Then, the next thing I knew, we were flying over the North Pole on our way to less-elegant L.A. A rather gaudy Lincoln Continental taxied us to our suite, and the next morning I was in mythical Dixie co-starring with a wacky Southern marine.

Sheldon Leonard was the director-producer for both "Pyle" and "My Friend Tony" and he cooked up two very different segments for me to do. After all the zany goings-on with "Pyle," I was to do a very serious dramatic part with James Whitmore, "MFT's" co-star. Acting with Whitmore, an old pro, was a big day for me. The stage crew said I was better than Bette Davis (and I loved it, even if it was a lie).

I had a fire scene in which I had to run into a burning room. Now, on an enclosed theatrical stage we would have used artificial flames, but here it was the real thing. Even the fire department was on hand, just in case. It was a hot scene, no doubt about it. And I spent two days running and screaming into it! But I enjoyed every burning minute.

I flew back to Chez so tired I didn't even unpack. I just caught up on my sleep for a couple of days. Yonkel was writing new narration to be used for the *Fiddler* album, and that was easy work for me. Merrill and I recorded it in New York and then I coasted back home. Halloween was upon us at Chez and all the neighbors' children were at our door. One youngster said, "Are you a millionairess?" And when I said "No," he asked, "Well, are you a thousandairess?" We laughed and loaded them up with apples and candy.

November also brought another birthday, Yonkel's seventy-seventh. We had dinner at Luchow's with our small family and Yonkel looked and felt fifty and it seemed so good. Just one night later, at another dinner, he was telling a joke and just conked out. And it seemed so bad again.

Yonkel said it was like someone just karate-chopped him at the back of his neck. But, if it wasn't a pinched nerve or ear trouble, what was it? Well, now the doctors were saying maybe it was his heart. And that made us scared.

Yonkel went for a cardiogram and the doctors found a bad spot. The spot slowed Yonkel's circulation and a spasm resulted. The condition was curable, we were told, and the doctors all added that Yonkel was basically a healthy man. All he needed was to rest and let the spasm pass. We prayed they were right.

That prescription meant Yonkel and I would sit out Christmas and New Year's in Mahopac and travel to the moon with *Apollo 8*. The astronauts were right on schedule and we had lived through history in the making. Yonkel was also feeling fit and we began thinking about spending our summers in America and our winters in Israel. But Meira's letters discouraged us. She wrote of how beautiful the snow looked in Jerusalem but small mentions of the constant border skirmishes also leaked through. We felt she was sitting on a volcano. And would America help if it began to erupt?

It seems we began each new year sitting amid the snow and contemplating retirement. Nineteen sixty-nine wasn't any different, but as the snow melted, so did our resolve. Suddenly, it was February 28th again, another birthday, and I was feeling fine. Others had to remind me of the years I'd accumulated.

The Museum of the City of New York called and asked for some of my costumes for an exhibition they were doing on theater stars. So I took a sentimental journey through my old stage trunks. I found a stovepipe hat I'd worn in Bucharest in 1923 and realized I had nearly fifty years of outfits stored away. A woman from the museum came and she wanted everything, even the pictures and programs. I made packages and labeled everything, then the Museum people came and took all our things away—a whole lifetime of work and worry and joy, and I regretted to see it all go. But, it would be preserved—and what a glorious life we had in all those old outfits. What a world we covered and conquered.

So how come we're not working?! Every time someone came and reminded me that others saw us as museum pieces, I demanded we go back to work. I agreed to do *Solid Gold Cadillac* in Chicago, but I'd be flying there alone. Yonkel had another dizzy spell and would join me later. So I went to work, as I'd wanted to, but it was lonely. Mentally, Yonkel had the same energetic plans as I, but what was his future physically? His condition seemed to have a mind of its own.

Yonkel toured with me all summer in *Milk and Honey* and I held my breath that he would stay well. I wasn't the only one watching out. Hundreds of our friends gathered at the Commodore Hotel on September 24th, to celebrate our fiftieth wedding anniversary. The Hebrew Actors Union had sponsored the affair, along with the other theater unions, and we were overwhelmed. Robert Merrill sang "Oh Promise Me" and Helen Hayes recited a Shakespearean love sonnet. Yonkel and I both spoke along with our cantor, and my golden dress was a knockout. But the biggest thrill was receiving a huge white leather book, dedicated to us in letters of gold. Inside, were pictures and mementos of our fifty years. After giving so many of our memories away, now we had a compact collection of them. I was delighted, and that book remains on my coffee table today. Very few people in our profession ever have such a day, or such a book, in their lives.

Broadway had remembered us and was thinking of me still. I allowed myself to get conned into doing another play. I was dubious, as always, but "Leave it to Molly, she'll do it." Why? I don't know.

The play started out with the rather discouraging title, *Will It Last?* However, shrewder minds prevailed and we eventually took it to Broadway as *Paris Is Out*. The plot involved a husband and wife who have very different ideas. The man refuses to budge from his home, he is happy where he is. The wife, on the other hand, wants to see the world before she dies. On such skimpy threads, even successful plays are woven. I began rehearsals in Paramus, with Jack Somack as my co-star, and we enjoyed some quick laughs. Yonkel still didn't think we had a fat enough plot, but out in New Jersey everyone said it was a sure-fire Broadway play. We'd have to wait and see.

I had an opportunity to step into Helen Hayes' role in *Front Page*, then doing very well on Broadway, and I took it. The producers gave me a free hand with the part, Helen left a lovely note, and all the ads in the papers sang out: "Hello, Molly!" I opened on December 1st at the Barrymore and got cheers from the start.

It was fun for me to step in in that way, rather than have

to struggle with a play whose future lay in doubt. And I was getting a chance to meet a newer audience. Publicity from *Front Page* brought about talk show offers and I joined Muhammad Ali on "The David Frost Show," was the mystery guest on "What's My Line?," did "Merv Griffin," and others. On each I talked about *Front Page* and myself. Frost even coaxed me into my song and somersault from *Milk and Honey,* and now a new generation of people still stop me on the street to "OOH and AAH" over it. I welcomed 1970 in great shape, although I was two years older than the year itself.

I started the New Year closing *Front Page* and beginning rehearsals for *Paris Is Out.* Sam Levene was now my co-star and I hoped our combination was half as good as what I'd just left behind.

It wasn't. The play still had a lot of it which was *Yech,* but my biggest problem was Levene. Sam was a rude, uncouth man offstage with a needlessly sharp tongue. Since he was replacing Jack Somack, my co-star in Paramus, I began our rehearsals by feeding Levene a line. "What d'ya wanna do, my part?!" he snapped at me and I knew here was a man I was going to leave alone. Even the taxi drivers cautioned me that Sam had a reputation for being difficult. I resolved never to bother with him offstage, and I didn't. Eventually, Levene thawed a bit toward me, but I never felt comfortable with the man. I still don't.

But, besides Sam's frosty bite, I wasn't too hot about the script, either. It seemed everyone had a funny part but me. Yet, in the first preview performance, the play got laughs from curtain to curtain, so perhaps I was wrong. We were playing to sellout preview crowds. If the critics didn't kill us, *Paris Is Out* would be in.

The management had not allowed any reviewers in, which meant that they weren't sure that the audience reaction could be trusted. And when we finally opened, the concern was proved legitimate. According to the critics, what we had wasn't too bad. But it wasn't too good, either. We'd just have to see which side of the coin the ticket buyers would read. Meanwhile, our publicists would help them along with big newspaper ads and selected quotes from our critics.

I had no idea how this play would do or how long it would last, and I shared my feelings with Florence Klotz, our costume designer. She and I had met for lunch during the first few weeks of our Broadway run, and during my complaining I mentioned that Yente, the matchmaker in *Fiddler on the Roof*, was more the kind of part I liked. I knew Norman Jewison was starting to film it and I commented that I should have played Yente. Obviously, Klotz agreed because she conveyed my feelings to Jewison, who called me shortly afterward.

"You're a natural for the part," he said, "why didn't I think of you!" He invited me to read for him and immediately signed me to do Yente on film. It would be some time, however, before Jewison would actually start shooting, and I wondered if Paris would sustain the wait. We were now into our fourth week and holding.

I drummed up business any way I could. I did the Johnny Carson show, celebrated my birthday on stage, even showed up to pick the New York State Lottery winner.

The political climate didn't help. Bomb scares were everywhere and we had our share. The audiences for *Hair* and *Last of the Red Hot Lovers* found themselves out on the street. There were 137 threats in one week. The city was frightened and the stores and theaters were emptying. This was the time that New York as "Fun City" took on a very different meaning.

Yet, despite snow, sleet and the lunatic fringe, we kept going right into April. Sam Levene even went on while sick, much to the distress of his understudy, Jack Somack! Well, the fates were kind to Jack. Levene went on and made himself really very sick, so Jack took over the very next day. Somack knew his part from when he had co-starred with me in Paramus. We got all our expected laughs and nobody took their money back.

But, with Sam out, we weren't long for the street. We closed after our hundredth performance, which was not a bad run considering what we had to run with!

I retired to spend spring at Chez. I wanted to watch every bud break out in bloom and make the theater seem a million miles away. I just sat back and enjoyed. A pony strayed onto our property and his owner rushed over to take back our uninvited guest. The man brought me a lovely plant and apologized, saying the pony had just come over to get my autograph.

I celebrated my second birthday of the year in June and Mary, our housekeeper, on her first trip abroad to Italy, mailed me a lovely rosebush which the local nursery delivered. Yonkel, meanwhile, had presented me with a fancy antique plate. He got all dolled up in a tux and an old top hat he'd bought in London in 1914. Then he grandly presented me the plate, which he'd wrapped in fancy toilet paper! What a guy! (It was the only thing handy.)

I would start filming *Fiddler on the Roof* in London, in July, so Yonkel and I drew up new wills, sent our bags and baggage to Fun City, then left New York behind. Just before we flew, I learned that Menashe Skulnik had died. Our ranks were growing thinner still and our Yiddish theater seemed doomed. Now Hollywood was doing *Fiddler,* and I only hoped I could bring my very best to this rather foreign interpreter of one of our great Yiddish tales.

London was clean and quite green. We were staying at the Grosvenor House, in a lovely room, and I would be squired to Pinewood Studios by Rolls-Royce. This was a strictly first-class operation!

Our Tevye, the part made famous on Broadway, would be played by Topol, the internationally famous Israeli star. I met him and Norma Crane, who would play Golda. Jewison wanted us to gather in London to pre-record our lines. Then, we would move on to Yugoslavia to actually shoot the film footage. Yonkel would also be joining us for a small role. Jewison took one look at him and gave him a part, providing Yonkel would grow a beard.

It was after our first taping that Jewison realized he had a small problem. Norma and I had absolutely the same voices —tone, timbre, etcetera. Jewison was afraid the audience wouldn't know which one of us was speaking if they heard our voice off camera. I offered a solution.

Yenta had been played on Broadway as a big, buxom woman with a loud, brassy voice. I offered to play her, instead, as a whining old crone who would speak in a higher, more frightening voice. Since Yenta was the woman responsible for making—or breaking—people's lives with her matchmaking, I saw her more as a little old witch. Jewison was delighted with the idea.

Yenta, to me, was a kind of Baba Yachna, a richer, funnier character much like the ones I had played in the Yiddish theater. Vincent Canby, the major film critic of *The New York Times,* called my portrayal the only authentic Yente he had seen. Pauline Kael, on the other hand, wondered why Jewison didn't step in to put a stop to my "obviously wrong" interpretation. Now you know why an audience should make up its own mind!

There would be a short break between our London and Yugoslavian stints, and Yonkel and I hopped over to Israel for a brief visit. The Unikovski family, including Meira, were waiting along with her boyfriend, a nice, young Sephardic boy who was anxious to marry her. We found him delightful and only asked that we be sure to be invited to the wedding. What a country. Israel had war on three frontiers, yet took the time for a Music Festival Week! We heard Beethoven's *First* and *Ninth Symphonies* with Zubin Mehta conducting, the Philharmonic Choir singing, and tenor Richard Tucker soloing.

Dov and Mariana had been accepted at a hospital in Haifa and we journeyed there to see them. They had two years of residency ahead, but they wanted to marry and we gave them our blessing. While at Rambam, we also visited the Tel Izchak Kibbutz where 250 men, women and children were housed. Eighty American teenagers were also working there, and when one of them heard my name, she shouted, "My mother will just faint!" Old and New Jerusalem were equally exciting—from the Bible to the Beatles.

We left Israel once again renewed, all aglow, happy for Dov, Mariana, Meira and her beau. We were off to Vienna. We hadn't been there since 1921.

It felt strange to be back, so much had happened since our last visit. We found the people in Vienna clean but poorly dressed, and still playing *The Merry Widow.* We walked the streets looking for the Stephanie Theater where we had performed *Yonkele* nearly fifty years before. But Vienna was only a stopover. The cast would be gathering in Zagreb, an hour's flight from Vienna. At the airport we met teenagers from Springfield, Illinois, and their big complaint? *If only we could get a McDonald's hamburger!!*

Yonkel and I checked into the Esplanade Intercontinental Hotel, full of big, old-fashioned rooms with exaggerated baths. Very Viennese. The streets reminded us of Poland before the war, but the young people in mini-skirts and the Rolling Stones graffiti on the walls meant that modern times had come.

Time only stopped, and then briefly, at the little village Jewison had found as the location for our film. It was very much like the town of Chabovka where Yonkel had been born and where his mother had lived until we had gotten her to move to Lodz. Everything was authentic: the unbelievable Kazimierz houses, the peasants, the geese, the mud. And in our *Fiddler* clothes, we fit right in. I even wore my *sheitel*, but we did no work.

It was typical film scheduling: sit around and wait. Lights and camera angles were fussed over and we sat in the mud (there were no dressing rooms on location). I watched peasant women washing clothes in a creek, then broke for lunch. Everyone got in line, even Jewison. Then it was back to work for a while, before our tea break at 4:00 P.M. Then more lights, cameras—and no action.

Finally, after two days of waiting in *sheitel* and shawl, I was on. I wanted the character I created to stand out and as soon as I stepped into Tevya's house, the whole crew and cast laughed their approval.

I managed to get a few lines in (and hoped they didn't end up on the cutting room floor). The next day, all they filmed was my walk. Things were moving very slowly. But Jewison gave me a mezuzah and a lovely note on that first day: "You'll always be one of the Chosen Few."

It was August in Yugoslavia, hot and very sticky amid all that mud. Topol had rented an old, so-called mansion in the hills and we went to join him and escape the heat. The place was shabby but homey, and we enjoyed Topol's gang: his wife, three children, a nana and a tutor. They enjoyed simple, homemade meals, then sang, all of them together. It was a family full of love and understanding for each other. We celebrated Sabbath with them, not an Orthodox one but honestly Yiddish!

I had one day on, another day off. The costume designer saw the rushes and told me I was very funny in my walk. Other than that, however, I had no idea *wit wot*. Then, we had a bout of rain, and *Poof!*—a week had gone by and we were somehow four days behind.

The Franzblaus arrived from America, all smiles and eager to see us in action. We chirped: "So are we!" Nevertheless, we arranged for them to come on location and see *Fiddler* in the making.

We were on what was called "Will Notify." It's another version of "Don't call us, we'll call you." So I spent my time roaming the city. The young people were very well-dressed and the parks were full of their rock 'n roll. And, finally, we met a few Jews.

A Mr. Nash from America was in the country to buy lumber and he had recognized me. He took us to a Zagreb *shul* (synagogue). It was nothing more than a large stone house with no sign or mark outside. There, in a small room on the second floor, was their temple with Torahs, a pulpit and a Sephardic cantor. Yonkel read the Sabbath service and then we met the members. None of them had ever seen or even heard of me, although the cantor showed us pictures of himself in a film. So, for the first time in a long time, I made new friends among Eastern Europe's Jews.

One of their number was a Mrs. Yelenik, who was Mrs. Tito's dressmaker. She took us to her villa in her own car. And this was a Communist country?

We took a rather strange impression from our visit to Mrs. Yelenik. Both her parents were deaf and mute, and Mrs. Yelenik had taken over the household as a child. She had lost two brothers in the war and worked as a seamstress to get by. Now she was a top couturière, doing business with Bergdorf's and Saks. She was divorced, with two grown children, and preferred to live in Zagreb and work for Tito's wife. It was a strange community of Jews. They had a club and card players and no one asked us, *"Fin vamen kumt a Yid?,"* an old Sholom Aleichem phrase: *"Where does a Jew come from?"*

We walked in the gardens, watched the women rake, waited. Then, finally, we were "notified." We were up at 7:00 A.M. for Mala Gorica. Hundreds of people, horses, carts, hay wagons, cows, geese, chickens, fruits and vegetables were all on the set. I did a funny thirty-second bit.

There was Yonkel in his beard and I in my *sheitel* and we had nothing else to do that day. We wheedled our Yugoslavian porter to take us for a ride and we ended up seeing *Fiddler* performed by the National Theater. To us, everything in their portrayal was wrong, but it was still a great play. To them, Tevye was only one Yugoslavian farmer with Yugoslavian problems. Tradition, children, intermarriage, rebels—even God—were all local concerns for this man.

We really couldn't fault those Yugoslavians for their performances, not when we were wondering when *we'd* work. Then, at last, Yonkel made his film debut.

He appeared in the pouring rain and portrayed a *melamed* (teacher) working with children. When he finished, Jewison ran over to him and kissed him. Only three takes! A genius! And Yonkel said he was going to change his name to Barrymore or play Tevye's horse, which he thought was a better part.

Everyone who saw Yonkel's rushes said the goodness in him shone through in his face. So Norman added another scene and Yonkel got a royal welcome from the entire crew. He got up at 6:00 A.M. for Mala Gorica now, and I slept!

I didn't make another appearance until the huge wedding scene. Then the whole town turned out with the peasants as extras. Hundreds of candles were lighted and as the sun set, it was all quite touching. We then worked on the close-ups of the wedding canopy and—suddenly—Jewison decided he wanted Yonkel to play the best man. Everyone hurried to get him dressed and standing next to Topol under the canopy. After only eight weeks, Yonk was already third man on the totem pole.

Yonkel was loving every minute, too. During one day, Yonkel and I reported for shooting even though we were both feeling ill from some fish we'd eaten. It was cold and damp and Yonkel was overdressed. The heat and lights got to him, and he fainted. Jewison ran over to Yonkel and helped him come to. "I'm sorry, Norman," Yonkel explained. "I ate some bad fish, I guess, but I can do the next scene." And Jewison said, "You're not in the next scene, Yonkel." To which Yonkel, stretched out on the ground, answered, "That's why I fainted!"

The weather was continually bad, which didn't help. I bought Yonkel and me some long-johns for working at night in the bitter cold. In one scene, Yonkel had to work again in the rain and mud and when Jewison asked him if he was all right, Yonkel said, "For a close-up, I'm fine!" And, meanwhile, I sat in a trailer from four in the afternoon 'til two in the morning. So this was how films were made?!

Soon, my memories of the picture was not about Tevye or Yente, but Yonkel. He had a scene in the synagogue with Zvi Scooler, who played the rabbi. It was terribly warm under the lights, and Yonkel said, "It's hot to be a Jew!" He had everyone laughing and he brightened up what could have been a long, tiresome job.

We spent the Day of Atonement in Zagreb, and their little *shul* was so depressing, we stayed in our hotel. We counted our blessings, the main one being our passports. We, at least, are free to roam and free to go home.

By our tenth week in Zagreb, the biggest news was that I had made the *Times* crossword puzzle. But, by the eleventh week, I had plenty of work to do and my twenty-hour days began. We worked in a very congested space full of lamps, cameras, and about twenty other people. But, I worked hard and Jewison was pleased. He kissed me for being "so real."

I had one week's work and one week "Will Notify." Yonkel was back in front of the camera and he took me along to watch. Yonkel spent about an hour doing another synagogue scene and when they were finished, he asked Jewison if he was getting a close-up. Jewison looked stunned until Yonkel added, "If not, I'll faint again." And, of course, Jewison broke up.

Because the weather had put us behind time, Jewison was pushing to make up and he was tired and tense. But we had the first part in the can and hoped to do more. Mainly, however, it was a crazy sort of rushing about only to wait and wait.

Everybody tried to break the tension. We even decided to give a concert in the Jewish Community Center despite the fact that the people only understood Serbo-Croatian. Some people did their act in French, others in English, and Zvi Scooley in Hebrew. Yonkel and I decided to do a medley in a mixture of English and Yiddish and somehow they understood.

Yonkel's seventy-ninth birthday was also duly celebrated. We had Bernie, our food man, bring in cake and champagne and I sang "It's Not the Tower of London, John" and everyone howled. We desperately wanted to keep our spirits up.

We spent sixteen weeks in Yugoslavia, all told. It was several weeks too many. We returned to London on a cloud. Hurrah! Civilization! Yonkel and I caught Robert Morley in a new play and immediately invited him out to the nearest pub for a drink. Then we walked and walked along Piccadilly viewing the Christmas decorations.

Everyone of the cast was happy to be there. We journeyed to Pinewood Studios and there was a complete replica of our Yugoslav village. Everyone agreed this London version was more pleasant than the original.

We were filming the wedding dance and I finally got my first close-up. I had to react to all the young girls dancing and I was glad to show any kind of expression after hours of just sitting in corners.

We had about two weeks of work, interrupted by an electrical workers strike, but we finally wrapped it up. We celebrated Christmas in Paris, a treat, then returned to London for some final looping, then good-bye. It was an interesting episode in our lives, but we were happy it was over!

We had chalked up another colorful, eventful year: handsome Yonkel with his lovely beard and me in my feather-white hair. We had stood up to a tough job and we were ready to go again.

CHAPTER ✳ 19

A FOOT OF SNOW buried Chez as 1971 began. We dug out just to get to the New York Museum's exhibit of theater costumes from 1870 to 1970—one hundred years of brocade, satin and sparkle except for one raggedy *Yonkele* outfit, circa 1923. It stood out like a beggar at a fancy-dress ball.

The year's good news was that Meira and Shlomo were getting married and they wanted us to come. This would be the first family wedding I would be attending. Technically, I was Meira's great-aunt. Emotionally, however, I felt like Mama of the bride. And Mama was nervous. But I flew to Israel vowing not to cry, too much.

Meira wanted to get married in a white gaucho suit and the two of us went shopping for white boots to match. I wanted to go along with whatever her wedding plans were, but I also asked her to go along with a small plan of mine.

It is traditional for the Jewish bride to undergo a ceremonial cleansing, to be purified before her wedding. Meira allowed me to take her to the *mikva* (the ritual bath) and there a huge Romanian attendant dunked her three times and I watched her emerge a kosher bride. Since the bride is not allowed to carry money, I was to pay. I asked Meira how much and she said two pounds would do. All I had was a five-pound note, so I asked the huge Romanian lady if she had the change. She took a fast look in her bag, folded her hammy arms over her bosom, and said, *"Nu."* Now *Nu* in that tone is a Yiddish word which means "So what are you going to do about it, big spender?" Naturally, I let her keep the five-pound note.

Meira looked like glazed Dresden in her white suit and

boots and Spanish veil. It was a lovely, simple wedding, although the young rabbi performed the Orthodox ceremony sort of tongue-in-cheek. Afterward, there was rock and roll music on the stereo and two hundred young people in and out. We joined them in dancing and *kvelling* all night and made Meira and Shlomo very happy.

When we returned home, it was time for me to go back to work. The Milliken people were on the phone and had rewritten their script four times, coming up with a very funny part for me. Helen Gallagher was also signed on. I started to limber up, ready to sing and dance again.

Yonkel and I got our feet wet with a few B'nai Brith concerts and then I threw myself into a round of Milliken conferences. Our biggest problem was how to do eighteen minutes of dialogue around forty minutes of dancing and singing about Acrilan.

I was so enmeshed in Milliken that I wasn't aware that Yonkel was undergoing some X-ray tests. He had recently gotten a perfect bill of health and I wasn't expecting anything less from these. However, the doctors at Beth Israel found an obstruction in his bladder which might also affect his kidneys and prostate. They wanted him in the hospital immediately.

I met with the Milliken choreographer and showed him my bag of tricks. I packed for a "Mike Douglas Show" and put in a happy appearance. But my heart wasn't in any of it. I was anxious about Yonkel. The doctors were in and out of Yonkel's room explaining how the exploratory operation would work. Yonkel was sure it was just prostate trouble and even the doctors were cheerful. They stroked his beard and said everything was fine. But I was worried.

Yonkel came through the first operation without a mishap. In the recovery room, he smiled at me and said, "It's a fake." When Helen and I came to see him, he was sitting up and talking a mile a minute. Dr. Schack, his internist, was in to tell us the biopsy would take forty-eight hours, but so far everything looked hopeful.

We waited and Yonkel had a little dizzy spell and I was still worried. I got Yonkel comfortable, sat near him and we both fell asleep. Dr. Schack came in and found us that way.

He left a little note: *"Shluft, meine kinder"* ("Sleep, my little ones").

Yonkel awoke joking. "If the President can *pish* (urinate), so can I!" But Dr. Schack's news wasn't good. There was a mass on Yonkel's kidney and he needed a major operation. It might be malignant, but catching it now would give him a good chance for recovery.

Reluctantly, I left Yonkel with those words in my ears, to do a Milliken rehearsal. I went through it, then raced right back to Beth Israel. I continued to race back and forth and then Yonkel stopped me for a small lecture.

He said I should take all this lightly and just face the facts. I had a life to live, he said. But I couldn't, wouldn't, even think of life without him. I kept right on working, trying to find funny lines in a dull, stupid script.

Yonkel was operated on on May 10th. I got the news the operation was over and Yonkel was okay while I was at rehearsal. I left immediately for the hospital. Dr. Schack was waiting for me with the details. The mass was malignant and the doctors had been forced to remove the entire kidney. Now, their only hope was that hormones and radiation might cure the prostate so Yonkel wouldn't have to undergo any further surgery. Yonkel was still under sedation so I spent the next four hours pacing the floor until he was brought up to his room. When he saw me, he smiled and said, "Sorry I kept you waiting." What a guy.

Yonkel rested, felt better and told me to go on and do my job. The Milliken Show was a flimsy story loaded with showy numbers. And each number led up to a new synthetic material. I just hoped Stanley Prager, our director, could make it all mean something as he'd done with the last one.

Yonkel took his first walk and all the patients and nurses gave him an ovation. The doctors said his recovery was miraculous. Yonkel called to tell me that one doctor said if he felt any better, they'd put him on exhibition. It was raining and I said, "Rain makes people feel bad." And Yonkel said, "Not me!" He was eating and walking and joking and I prayed, "Please God, make him all well and send him back to me."

Dr. Schack warned us Yonkel had undergone a major operation, but he released him and I was overjoyed. Yonkel was home, looked beautiful, and life was worth living again. We babied Yonkel and he loved it. He needed time and care and we gave him all we had of both. I was relaxed enough to get back to my Milliken rehearsals, and after much, much work, it got pulled together. We rehearsed all day and as my Italian mason used to tell me, "Missa Pick, everyting she's a getta done!" We opened at the Waldorf at 4:00 P.M. and we had a fast, furious show full of gimmicks and tricks. Everybody was happy.

For the next two weeks, I slept at the Waldorf, did my two shows a day at 8:00 and 4:00, and kept in touch with Yonkel by phone. He was healing but tired easily. Our only worry was his enlarged prostate, but we hoped the hormone treatment would work.

I danced every number with so many other things on my mind, but Yonkel knew how to ease my worries. One afternoon, he surprised me by showing up with Helen for our afternoon show. He had to be practically carried backstage, but I cried and thanked God he was starting to live again.

Yonkel also joined me for the last Milliken show and they sent us home in a limousine with my $7,500 bonus. Later, one of the Millikens sent me a thank-you note for being such a pro and not bringing my sorrow with me to the show. He quoted one of my lines from Milliken: "What you got, we need!"

I had agreed to do *Hello, Dolly!* in Beverly, Massachusetts, a commitment I had made months before. I didn't want to go, but Yonkel and I rested in the country and he seemed to bloom. We had a joyous fifty-second wedding anniversary, no parties, no hoohah, just walking hand in hand and thankful for each day.

When Yonkel's doctors checked him and said they didn't think he'd need more surgery, I began packing for Beverly. But I knew Yonkel wouldn't be coming with me. He was up all night, urinating every half-hour. He decided to stay with Helen and urged me to go on to Beverly alone.

I opened *Hello, Dolly!* with Mickey Deems (Judy Garland's last husband) playing Vandergelder. We worked long hours and it was a *shvitz* (sweat) show. I wore heavy costumes, hats and wigs, but still did my somersault on the last bow. We got good notices but Yonkel's were even better. He called me and sounded twenty years younger. I had hope.

By the end of July, I was back home, trying to tempt Yonkel to eat. Something was wrong. It was three months after his operation, but the aftermath seemed worse than the surgery. He wasn't eating or sleeping. But he didn't like my fussing over him and he urged me to go back on the road.

I was torn, but I went ahead with a commitment I'd made in Philadelphia. I had promised to give *Paris Is Out* another whack and I opened at the Playhouse in the Park.

The reaction was bizarre, again. We had twice as many laughs as on Broadway, and, as far as our audiences were concerned, we were a smash. The press, however, universally panned us. At least in New York we had gotten some good reviews. Here, it was all thumbs down. Yet, because the audiences loved us so, we played to packed houses and I finished the week feeling wonderful.

I returned to Chez and Yonkel couldn't disguise the fact that he was glad to have me back. The doctors still didn't think he needed more surgery, but Yonkel just wasn't bouncing back like before. His slow recovery soon depressed him, and one day, while we were sitting quietly together, he made a terrifying request. He wanted me to put him in a nursing home! First he listed his nagging ailments: the pain from his incision hadn't abated; he was having trouble swallowing solid food, especially meat; worst of all, his bowel movements were becoming excruciatingly difficult. "I can't be a burden to you," he told me, "I don't want you to be constantly upset about me. A nursing home would take good care of me."

The very idea was ridiculous. I wouldn't hear of it. We were home together, and there we'd stay until he was better. I turned down every offer, and took a new role: Florence Nightingale.

My loving care worked. Soon, Yonkel was well enough for a short trip to Boston and another to New York City for the premiere of *Fiddler on the Roof*. We thought the film looked better than its previews and thought I came off well. Canby, of the *Times*, agreed despite an otherwise negative review.

Yonkel loved traveling with me. Surely, we had reason enough to keep him home, but he felt better being on the road. We flew to Cleveland and Cincinnati to do various benefits and Yonkel gave small speeches and did his Hymie Kaplan monologue and generally kept on performing. It kept him going.

Our future was parceled out in good moments and bad. And, measured on a yardstick, most of life's inches lay behind us. The American Jewish Historical Society at Brandeis asked for more of our memorabilia, and I began 1972 once again going through piles of papers and records. I loaded twenty-one cartons of our life, from Buenos Aires to Africa, and sent them along.

It was so joyful looking back. It was the uncertainty which lay ahead that frightened me. I was all set to go to Los Angeles for a television show, when Yonkel's X rays revealed that his enlarged prostate was blocking both his bladder and only remaining kidney. He would have to have more surgery.

Yonkel took the news calmly. Outwardly, I did, too. Inside myself, however, I was absolutely hysterical. I got out of the TV commitment, got Yonkel back into Beth Israel and stayed with him. Dr. Schack was afraid Yonkel's testicles were also affected, but he told me not to worry until he told me to. Ha! None of them could know what Yonkel meant to me. I stayed near him until they threw me out, then spent several sleepless nights being near him in spirit.

The doctors decided to operate on the testicles to relieve pressure on Yonkel's only kidney, but they had to wait until he was fit. What irony! waiting to get well enough to go under the knife! Yonkel was worn out and weary but he quoted the Israeli *kine brera:* "You have no choice."

He came through this second operation better than anyone expected. The doctors just flipped. He was awake and smiling and even called his doctors to thank them for their good work. They told me no patient had ever done that before.

Yonkel kept fighting back and that kept our spirits up. We took him home and he blossomed. The doctors said his kidney was clear and his prostate was shrinking. Meira had sent news of our newest grandchild's birth: Roni, an eight-and-a-half-pound baby girl!

I allowed myself a little extra leash, went for a rehearsal, and left Yonkel alone in the apartment. He got dizzy, fell, and had a huge gash on his forehead and nose.

Yonkel and I were frightened. He had had brain X rays and all kinds of monitoring, yet none of the doctors could solve the mystery of these attacks. All we could do was go easy. I bathed him, made him rest on his recliner, got him to eat better.

And he did well; other than these sudden spells, he was getting better. But these attacks came without warning. He'd be talking or eating or just sitting and he'd drop. Naturally, they made him leery of walking so Helen and I stayed close by.

Dr. Schack suspected a nerve in Yonkel's neck was the culprit, and he came up with some medication we hoped would arrest it. Operating on sheer optimism, I tried to pick up my career. Throughout the summer, I played *Dolly* and *Milk and Honey* all over the East and Midwest. Yonkel's new medication was working—so could I.

The brain scans, the graphs, the X rays, all the reports on Yonkel were good. He was relieved and we started to breathe freely again. So many things were providing a lift.

Dov had written that he and Mariana had been accepted to practice medicine in Haifa and Yonkel glowed as any father would for a real son. We were able to celebrate Yonkel's eighty-first birthday with a few close friends and he was in top form. What a relief after a year and a half of fear.

Yonkel felt so good, he began making plans to tour with me. Two delightful young people, Stockton Briggle and Steven Willig, wanted us to do *Come Blow Your Horn* at the Hotel Carillon in Miami Beach and we agreed.

We ushered in the New Year with new plans! Yonkel took the trip well and we opened January 7, 1973, to an enthusiastic SRO crowd. Our only problem, of all things, was a cold spell, and I had to wear a fur coat. But Yonkel was fine, the pet of the beach. He was beaming and we began adding extra chores. We did Jack Eisen's radio show with Don Rickles' mother, and she's funnier than Don!

We had such a fantastic engagement that we only rested a few weeks before flying off again. This time, to Israel. What a joy for us both to see Meira, Shlomo and little Roni. We felt right at home but didn't overdo. We walked a bit and then just sat in the outdoor cafés and watched the Jews go by—all young, unlike Miami!

I celebrated my seventy-fifth birthday in Tel Aviv with a huge cake. But I had my wish. He was by my side.

We spent one wonderful month there and I was the only one who needed a doctor. It was a rather funny experience. I was having pains in my neck and an old German doctor came and gave me an injection. He said I had a crink in my neck and sent Yonkel to fetch some Swiss medication. Yonkel returned and gave the doctor the bottle. The doctor began reading the label. "Umm, very good, very good," he said, then added to me, "Don't take it." And he left!

We left Israel and returned to Chez determined to build our strength up and start to live again. Yonkel was still having little spells, but they were manageable. I think it was because he felt somewhat better that he spoke to me for the first, and only, time about dying.

Yonkel gave me a long lecture on how to behave when the end came, for either of us. He didn't speak about dying in terms of how he wanted to be buried or what kind of funeral he wanted to have. He just said that when the end came, I shouldn't become hysterical or throw fits. We both agreed that we were grown-ups and would act grown up. But dying was very far from our minds. We both had checkups and Yonkel came off better than I. So we prayed for more good years together and went on living.

Yonkel spoke at the Putnam County Hospital Drive, where we were honored guests, then he joined me in town to see the new Milliken show and everyone fussed over him. And we fussed over Chez Shmendrick. I'd go shopping and watch the prices soar. The pump needed fixing, the pool needed draining, and all the gardens needed weeding.

Meanwhile, Yonkel created a new attraction. He made an arch out of two evergreens to enclose a huge rock on which he had me paint: "Here Lies Our Dearly Departed Money." Another laugh for visitors.

We now had a new helper, Tor Osmundsen, a fine Norwegian boy who did everything. His coming to us eased my still shaky nerves enough so that I decided to take another plunge into movies.

Peter Yates was doing a new movie with Barbra Streisand called *For Pete's Sake*. They had a different kind of part for me, a madam, and I found it more amusing than offensive. Yonkel liked it too, and we decided I should do it.

Meira and Shlomo were visiting with little Roni, the Israeli bombshell. We settled them in and began making plans. Even Yonkel had a script to consider, a cameo part in *Harry and Tonto,* which Art Carney was about to make.

I journeyed to New York ready for work. John McGiver, Paul Michael Glaser, Streisand and I sat around and read, but I felt down. I didn't like my reading, there were no laughs, but Barbra was very helpful and tried to give me extra lines. She and Yates were pleased and I hoped they'd be as nice to work with.

Yonkel was also in town to read for *Harry and Tonto.* Paul Mazursky, the producer, knew us and he thought Yonkel gave a beautiful reading. Emotionally, it would be so good for him to have this part. The only snag was that shooting would begin while I was in Los Angeles with Streisand. But we'd see.

I had four days of work in Hollywood and it was typical film-flam. Yates was nervous, Barbra was late, and the studio work tiring. Barbra was a strange girl to work with. She was a very private person, never outgoing or warm. When she finished a scene, she'd go right to her dressing room without so much as a "so long." However, when she was acting, she was intensely professional. Too intense, in fact, and that led to some needless hysterics.

In one scene, we were in a junkyard and I had to drive around with Streisand as a passenger. Someone had told Barbra that I didn't do much driving, so she was afraid to drive with me. She insisted that my stand-in do the driving and she made that poor little lady one nervous wreck. "Barbra's a lunatic!" my stand-in told me afterward. "She kept saying I was driving too slow, then too fast, and then she just kept saying 'You're gonna kill me!'" The lady walked off the set shaking like a leaf.

We had a break in our shooting and I flew right back to Yonkel. He had flowers from our garden already picked and waiting for me. I wanted him to come back to Hollywood with me. He had gotten the part in *Harry and Tonto*, but wasn't well enough to do it and that had really let him down. I asked him to come back with me and he said he didn't think he should risk it. And then he started to cry.

I had never seen Yonkel in tears and it stunned me. We went for a little walk and we talked. We decided he should go. I thought the warm climate would be good for him, and he agreed. It was now October and cool in the East and I had shooting to do at Marietta Springs, a hot sulphur bath.

I kept my fingers crossed and we made it to Hollywood. We were together and everyone was glad to see us. I had one more scene to do and couldn't wait to finish. This production looked *farblonzet* (lost) to me. Barbra had changed everything, including cutting out every scene in which she had nothing to do. They were looking for a new name, a new last scene, and heaven knows what else. I did my work and left. Barbra was already gone. She never came to say good-bye.

Yonkel and I stayed at the hot, lovely spring and took mineral baths. We had a whirlpool, a restful lake and no pressures. We celebrated his eighty-second birthday there, and we were so happy just to be together.

It's funny how just when things finally go good that all the bad things you've been suppressing rise up to hit you. We were back home, Yonkel's doctors said "dramatic recovery!" and I went to bed full of the shakes. I got up in the middle of the night trembling over every inch. I had to wake Yonkel and Mary and they called Dr. Schack. He prescribed some sedatives and I finally slept a little. That's what we call in Yiddish, *kaduchas!*

But Christmas was upon us and we made merry. Barbra

Streisand sent me some of her records as a gift with the note, "For Molly, You were perfect, Love, Barbra." I was surprised she'd remembered my name. Our neighbor, Bill Griffis, gave a big Christmas party and Yonkel entertained with his stories. I wore a new green suit and Bill said I was pretty enough to hang on the Christmas tree. And me a kosher Jewish girl!

We were up, and we were down. Yonkel would be fine, then he'd fall and feel weak. He was also getting pains in his back and arms and lived on Tylenol and heating pads. I christened the new year with a visit to his doctors. They were pretty succinct. If it is cancer, they can't help. If it's rheumatism, they can't help. And if it's old age, they still can't help. So we kept Yonkel quiet and just hoped.

Dr. Schack had said there was still no sign of malignancy and, even if there were, other people seemed to be living with it. Stockton Briggle and Steven Willig, our young friends from Miami, came to visit us in New York and we learned that both of them had cancers. Steven had lymphatic cancer which was bad, but he was fighting. (He called us much later, convinced he was cured of his cancer and about to wed. Unfortunately, he didn't make it. Stockton, however, did conquer a similar cancer and is still with us, thankfully.)

Stockton talked us into coming back to the Carillon to do *Majority*. He had a very good cast with George Gitto playing Asano. Yonkel felt fine and the warm weather helped. We enjoyed great harmony and the actors seemed in awe of me. Stockton worked to bring out the confrontation between cultures in the play and relied less on the comedy. Yonkel watched me work in this new interpretation and for the first time he told me I had grown as an actress. That was a word he rarely used. Over the years, he had praised me for my singing and dancing and comedic touch. But he had never really praised my acting, and I was thrilled. I think Stockton was on the right track. He cut out laughs to achieve sympathy and get to the point of the play: intolerance. After some disastrous rehearsals, we had a great opening night success. Yonkel said I was a Miami attraction, just like the Dolphins!

I celebrated my seventy-sixth birthday onstage at the Carillon and Sister Gonzaga provided a cake. Wires came from Mayor Beame and Senator Javits of New York and President and Mrs. Nixon. We read the wires to the audience and they applauded. When we came offstage, George Gitto said, "You know, Yonkel, we just heard that Nixon is going to resign." And Yonkel said: "If he does, I'll send him back his telegram!" Could this man be sick?

Very sick. And much sicker than we ever knew. He went for some physiotherapy in Miami and had a bad night. The doctors did a bone scan and the results were the worst. He had more cancer and it had spread to his ribcage and spine. Yet, they thought cobalt treatment might arrest it, and so we flew back to Beth Israel to begin. Yonkel would be getting five treatments a week, and the pain was severe. One doctor told us he had patients who had lived thirty years with cancer. So Yonkel took it and smiled.

And they seemed to work. The pain left and Yonkel got much steadier on his feet. We had Passover at home, and hoped all illness had passed us by, too. We had a simple seder, just Yonkel, Mary and I. But we all dressed up, including Yonkel. Golda Meir resigned that day and she looked so old and worn on television. God help her and Israel. There were wars and kidnappings and "Impeach Nixon" signs. Everything seemed corrupt and it was all incomprehensible. We just sat tight and tried to enjoy our home.

Nixon resigned and Ford was our President. When Ford held his first press conference, Yonkel said, "Watch how he'll soft-pedal Nixon." And that's just what he did. And Yonkel said, "You see? I'm a Jewish Kissinger!" The President gave Nixon a complete pardon! And now, we asked, will he pardon those already convicted and in jail, or the draft evaders?

We worried with the rest of the world, but our own problems also came back to demand our immediate attention. Yonkel was starting to lose his battle to get well, and it was now clear that he was just fighting to stay alive.

The first bad sign was when he began urinating blood. And the tests all showed him very anemic. He needed transfusions and more tests and I was amazed how he could stand it. Yonkel was in and out of the hospital, fed intravenously, and weakening. At one point, he just gave up and said he wanted to die.

I told the doctors what Yonkel had said, and they agreed that he had the right to decide. But first, Dr. Schack said, we must give the doctors a chance to look for what's causing all the pain. So I told Yonkel the truth, that the doctor's can't guarantee recovery, that he might only gain a day, a month, a year, but that he would need a very big operation to survive at all. And he answered: "To see your face again for a day, it's worth it."

The doctors wanted to perform another operation. This one involved attaching a tube to Yonkel's intestine and diverting his body wastes so that they emptied into a bag which he would wear on the outside. Yonkel had had so much trouble with his bowels, that every time he put pressure on his kidney he would bleed. The operation would relieve the pressure and the excruciating pain which went with it.

Yonkel survived the operation, but as a very, very sick man. I was desperate and ragged and worn out. Here he was at eighty-two, with a nephrostomy, and I had let him go through with it. I just hoped we had done the right thing.

My chore was to handle the bags, and when one of our friends told Yonkel that Roy Wilkins wore one and cleaned it himself, Yonkel chirped, "Sure, he's black!" Mentally, Yonkel was alive again. And, he had his dignity. He was so ashamed when he couldn't control his bowels and I'd have to clean up his sheets. Then, he would try to joke and call it his picassos. Now he didn't have to worry.

On November 18th, 1974, Yonkel had his eighty-third birthday and we never thought he'd make it. The cancer was spreading, and we knew it, but every day he lived was another day for me as well. My heart went out to him, because he ate practically nothing and was very tired. I would leave my bed in the middle of the night to sit by his side and he'd ask, *"Vie lang noch?"* ("How much longer?").

Yonkel knew there was no hope. He would try to walk and fall into a faint and Helen and I couldn't lift him. Help would come and we'd put him to bed and then we'd just feel helpless. And I'd look at this person whom I loved who was obviously dying, who felt such shame at losing his faculties, and I asked myself, Should I have sanctioned his last grueling operation?

And there was—is—no answer! Had I said no, he would have died then and there and I never would have forgiven myself for not trying to save him. So I said yes, and had to sit by and watch his life ebbing away. I saw him grow weaker and weaker and he'd try to smile and joke the whole horror away. All my days were alike: we'd wash, clean, bandage and feed Yonkel and try to make him comfortable. Then he'd have another painful movement and faint into a heap. He had no strength and we had no hope.

Jack Benny died of cancer at eighty, and there was no cure anywhere. We said good-bye to one old sick year and said hello to another. Yonkel started 1975 back in Beth Israel for a week of blood transfusions. He could barely talk between pain killers and it was all so sad, so sad. When he tried to tell me something, and I didn't understand, he shouted from his groggy soul, "God, are you dumb!" And I asked Dr. Schack what was next? What's the answer? And he said, "I have no answer."

The doctors all agreed Yonkel would be better off home at Chez, so we took him back by ambulance. We hired a nurse, bought a commode and a bed with aluminum bars so he couldn't fall out at night.

I arranged for the nurse to stay up all night because I was just too tired and afraid I'd collapse. Yonkel was so terribly confused from all the pain killers and medication, it was impossible to communicate with him. Yet his humor was intact! At one point, I chided him that he was confusing and he said, "So deconfuse me!"

He stayed at the Mahopac Hospital for just a brief set of transfusions, and I stayed at home. I was seventy-seven and it was the saddest birthday of my whole life. Yonkel was in the hospital but he had no chance of recovery and what was my life going to be without him?

We were preparing for the last effort. We had Yonkel home, and I set up the living room like a hospital. We put his bed there and I arranged to sleep nearby on the couch. Yonkel and I had always slept in separate beds, but they were always close together in the same room. I wasn't going to change that now.

Our neighbors came in to say hello, and Yonkel brightened up with each visit. I engaged an intelligent, congenial nurse, Jacqueline Hahn, and she fell in love with Yonkel right away. We vowed to do all we could, but we knew the end was near. I tried to give him something to drink, and he couldn't even hold the glass. So I tried again and then kissed him. He blurted out: "Kisses and kisses and you don't let me drink!" And I just cried.

He was semi-conscious, taking no food and no pills. His face looked gray and I watched and died a little with him. But, at least, there is some dignity in dying; there was no pain and Yonkel just slept. It was unreal. I watched him breathe, listened to his quiet moan, and laid out a suit for his burial.

Around 2:00 A.M., on March 16th, I got up to see if he needed to be covered. I touched Yonkel's face and saw he was dead. No pain, just sleep, and he was gone.

I went through the aftermath as if playing a role. I remember that Yonkel looked beautiful and peaceful in the casket, that Abe Franzblau gave a moving eulogy, that the sun came out just as I threw flowers on his grave. Those aspects of saying "Good-bye" were not tragic.

But accepting the loss is something else. I had had Yonkel for fifty-six years. Every corner of my life reminded me of that and made me empty inside. I didn't know how I would face the future.

I was on my own, for the first time. I was a widow and, suddenly, I noticed how many of us there are in this country. And when I saw an old couple holding hands and helping each other across the street, I ached with envy.

But, I couldn't let Yonkel down. I had to make a life of my own. I began by making a "Yonkel" album. In it, I put his obituary notices, wires, pictures, condolences, and our love letters. I answered over three hundred sympathy notes, then gathered up all of Yonkel's clothes and asked the Yiddish Theatrical Alliance to come and take them and give them to other performers. Day by day, I became a little more accustomed to living again.

One of my biggest hurdles was financial. Yonkel handled

all our business affairs. With him gone, like too many other women, I had to acquaint myself with wills, taxes, savings accounts and trusts. All of which I knew nothing about but had to learn, fast.

I also needed to get rid of anything that might make me cry. I gave away knickknacks and posters and other mementos in the hopes that it would help me adjust.

I wanted to rejoin the human race. I called my agent and begged to be sent out to work immediately. Visits from our dear friends had helped, but they couldn't sustain me. I needed to perform.

My first appearance was at the 100th Anniversary of the Yiddish theater held at the Museum of the City of New York. They showed a scene from our film *Yiddel Mit'n Fiddle* and when they introduced me, I joked, "I don't know whether it's the Yiddish theater's 100th anniversary or mine." Everyone laughed and I just choked up and ran out. So my first "Molly, you can do it!" didn't do so good. It was just so hard to accept the finality. Oh how I missed him!

CHAPTER ✸ 20

YONKEL USED TO SAY, *It's no trick to drink from a full bottle. It's a trick to drink from an empty one.* And that was just how I felt in the months which followed Yonkel's death: an empty bottle with nothing to drink from. I didn't feel like singing or dancing or acting, but I had to do it. And I couldn't allow myself to brood.

I began by attacking Chez's gardens with a vengeance. Pruning and weeding were tiring, but it kept me from self-pity. I also rented a Ford Pinto and began learning how to drive again. And I signed contracts to perform in Miami and Cleveland and Carnegie Hall.

Four months after Yonkel died, I opened in *Come Blow Your Horn* at the Showplace Theater in Cleveland. I had a good cry for Yonkel and then I went on. It was good for a starter, and I knew I could continue.

Of course, I had help. It came from somebody I had shared my life with even before Yonkel: my sister, Helen. She was a widow too, and I begged her to come and live with me. She couldn't say no and she was a comfort. Returning to Chez was always a sad event in those early months, but Helen understood and would let me cry it all out.

Away from Chez, I was much better and so I tried to get work on the road. My first big offer was also great fun to do.

Twentieth Century-Fox was making a movie for television called *Murder on Flight 502*. Joining me would be Ralph Bellamy, Walter Pidgeon, Robert Stack, Theodore Bikel and a newcomer named Farrah Fawcett-Majors. They would be shooting in Hollywood and Helen and I were eager to go.

The cast was very relaxed and we had a lot of time to

laugh and joke. It was typical film work: one day of work, then five days off. Helen and I took a bus to Hollywood and Vine and it looked just like our 14th Street—*Yech!* We did the Brown Derby and the Cultural Center and even got to see the Mexican section of town.

Then it was back to work. All the action took place on board this plane with all kinds of plots and subplots going on among the passengers. I think Walter and I stole the show as we played two "Senior Citizens" who meet on the plane and fall in love. I gave Walter a rather funny line which broke the cast up. We decide at the end of the flight to spend the night together. Pidgeon's line was, "Do you think it's seemly we share a room?" That sounded too stuffy for me, so I got him to say with a knowing smile, "Do you think it's kosher for us to share a room?" The director loved it and Pidgeon confessed it was the only Jewish word he'd uttered in his entire career!

Pidgeon was very warm and witty. Poor Ralph Bellamy was playing a doctor and having a very difficult time with some of the medical terminology. On about the twentieth take, Pidgeon shouted out: "I told you to get Marcus Welby for the part!" Theodore Bikel sang and played his guitar, everyone told stories, and we just had fun. The only one I don't remember well was Farrah. She was truly an unknown then and didn't attract much attention.

Back home, I began working on my concert for Carnegie Hall and really felt I had a challenge on my hands. I tried dancing: I had no legs. I tried singing: and didn't have a voice. An empty bottle, *nu?* So I decided to make slides of myself starting with pictures of me as a baby and then going through my plays and movies. The last slide would be my birth certificate—big and clear—born February 28, 1898. What a sneaky way of getting a sympathetic reaction!

I didn't believe it would be, but the concert was one of the most exciting evenings of my whole life: October 12, 1975. After the slides, I came on to a standing ovation and there I stayed for an hour without a dull moment. I found the breath and legs and I sang and danced for a cheering young audience. Yes, Yonkel, I can do it!

So, I began a new chapter in my life, something that I have continued to do. Now I play one-night concerts just like the rock 'n roll stars and I just love doing them.

Something else I tackled was the TV soap opera. Don Appel, the author of *Milk and Honey*, was doing a new day-time show called "Somerset." Don initially conned me into doing a few weeks' work, but I stayed on for seven months and sixteen episodes. It was lucrative work but incredibly boring. First of all, I was playing a sickly old lady so that meant I didn't have too much physical stuff to do. And, of course, with all the pregnant pauses on those shows, your facial expressions are usually limited to two: happy or sad. I really don't call that acting as much as it's re-acting. Frankly, I was glad when they finally finished me off. It gave me the time for two important things.

First, I wanted to see Yonkel's monument put up at Mt. Hebron. Nearly a year had passed and I still couldn't believe that anyone so alive could be dead. But when I saw how many other theater greats rested nearby, I felt Yonkel was in good company.

Secondly, I now had the hours I needed to spend with my tax accountants to straighten out my assets. Women should know about these things when their husbands are alive, but we are so afraid to discuss dying! We let other people take care of things and then we don't know how to take care of ourselves. Worst of all, if our assets are only in our husband's name (as mine were) we often have to wait an uncomfortably long time to have things probated. I, thankfully, could earn money to get me by, but what about those poor women who don't have a penny in their names?

I didn't want Helen ever to have to wait for my will to be probated, as I was waiting for Yonkel's. So I closed out one of my bankbooks and deposited a good chunk of it in her name, just in case.

Then Helen and I flew to Israel for a special memorial service. It was her first trip and my fifteenth, but we were equally thrilled. In Tel Aviv, the Municipal Hall was showing *Yiddel* and there was a beautiful eulogy for Yonkel. The movie was in Yiddish but with Dutch subtitles, because the woman who had brought the film to Israel had found it in Holland. That night, an elderly man came up to me with an ancient copy of one of my songs: *"Oy Vet Mich Der Rebi Schmeisen"* (Oh, the Rabbi Will Whip Me). He had kept it for fifty years, even through the Holocaust. Now, it remains in Tel Aviv, a fitting resting place.

We went to Paris and then Brussels, where George was waiting for us. Our first foster child, whom we once knew as a frightened war orphan, had grown into an important professor of physics. His two little daughters were now young ladies, and they showed us Belgium at its best: Waterloo, Bruges, Ghent. It is always a joy to me to know we had a part in his life and achievement.

We journeyed to London on the boat train and jerked in the sleeper all night. In the morning, we had what the waiter called a typical British breakfast: one sloppy fried egg, bad bread and worse coffee, all for ten bucks!

I wanted to take Helen on a sentimental journey to where Yonkel and I had lived when we performed there over the years. We even visited Jermyn Street and the little flat we'd lived in when I was doing *Majority* with Robert Morley. Then we flew home to Kennedy, where there was no one to meet us.

We were constantly reminded we were ladies alone, but we grew very comfortable in the role. And I had somebody to share some of my show biz shenanigans with.

One classic snafued case involved a "Dinah Shore Show." Dinah was doing a tribute to Raymond Burr and she asked me to sneak into town to appear as a sort of mystery guest. I flew to Los Angeles, got to the studio and waited for my cue. Dinah and Burr were on the air and she worked around to his Korean War tour. She asked him if he remembered the lady who had joined him, then he said my name, and I came on stage. There was lots of applause and then the stage darkened and I sang a medley of the songs I'd done in Korea. It was the end of the show, and as I finished my song, I looked around and everyone was gone! No Dinah, No Burr. Just me and the technicians! I was all alone and full of the flu and had to ask a stagehand to take me to the airport.

Naturally, the plane was late, so I sat, alone, with a sandwich and a limp cup of coffee. Ten hours later, we were in the air but a blizzard in New York prevented us from landing at Kennedy. We were diverted to Dulles Airport in Washington, D.C., where after more hours of waiting for flight clearance to New York, I took a train into the city. There, I stepped out into the blizzard still dressed in my "Dinah Show" gown and open-toed shoes. I got plenty soaked trying to find a taxi in the snow and ended up taking two buses to Helen's apartment. It had taken me twenty-six hours to get home! My whole body ached and I missed a taping for "Somerset" the following morning.

The irony of it all was that Burr never thanked me for coming. So I had no glory, no money, and a bad case of the flu! That's the big time?

I guess that's why even though I still do television and movies, I return again and again to my people who've known and loved me for generations.

After that "Dinah" mess, I went to Miami for a round of concerts and it was like going home.

I was playing the various condominiums, which is grueling, but the audiences were adoring and it was a joy to hear them laugh. And a man from New York saw me on the street and said: "Molly Picon! Even though you're not dancing, it's a pleasure to see you walking!"

One thing I did learn, however, from both Miami and L.A., was that I wasn't going to be able to shuttle back and forth to Mahopac. I would have to sell Chez.

It was something I approached with many mixed emotions. On the one hand, I didn't want to rattle around in that huge house in my Golden Years. Helen had a small apartment she rented, and I felt it would be better if I got something similar. On the other hand, the thought of dismantling Yonkel's fabulous library, of shutting down Mama's room, of abandoning all our gardens and walkways was very painful to consider.

So I asked for a fabulous price and half-hoped it wouldn't be met. In the meantime, I was distracted by a new play of Henry Denker's called *The Second Time Around*.

Hans Conreid, a super actor and gentleman, would join me in the cast and so I signed on. We were to perform first up in Sarasota and then Atlanta, Georgia. (Don't ask me why these two spots!) But we desperately wanted the play to come alive.

Hans and I played a widow and widower who fall in love. Our romance, however, shocked Hans' stage children, who were aghast that he would want to marry with his wife not a year in her grave. The plot involved first the children's efforts to prevent our marriage and then their dismay when we decide to live together. Then, they can't wait to "sanctify" our union.

There were enough twists and turns in the story to keep the action going, and the busy lines were just what I needed. Unfortunately, Denker was also a lawyer (and the author of the hit, *Case of Libel*). Often, he wrote lines for us which sounded more like a summation to a jury than natural speech. Hans and I worked to get our dialogue more casual and funny. And Denker clocked 300 laughs during our first audience previews.

The Atlanta audiences (Southern *goyim?*) gave us a tremendous reception and the stage managers threw a giant party. We had several smash weeks and everyone said, "On to Broadway." Only Conreid thought the New York critics wouldn't like the play, and he began to convince me he was right.

But, as always, you operate on momentum. Adela Holtzer must have needed a tax writeoff because she was determined to bring us to Broadway. It wasn't the first time someone would take on a production which was ready to fail.

So I waited for new rehearsals to begin and began to wrap up Chez's loose strings. I was offered $102,000 for the house and I told my lawyer to accept. It was way below what I felt Chez was worth, but I wanted out. I signed the contract for the sale, then sat back and watched Jimmy Carter nominated for President. A Southerner in the White House? And someone else in mine. The world was a-changing all around me.

What followed was a month of physical and emotional

trauma. I literally had to dismantle fifty-six years of my life and put it into boxes. Thankfully, YIVO (the Yiddish Institute and Library) came and took every picture, plaque and book I cared to give away. Still, the more I packed, the more I seemed to have left.

September 27, 1976, was my last day at Chez and I said "Good-bye" to every bush and tree and stone. They had been a part of my life for nearly thirty years. Now, I thought of the Bible: A time to reap, a time to sow, a time to travel on.

I had found a house to rent in Cortland, which was much closer to New York City. Rent and utilities for it and an apartment in New York would cost me over $15,000 a year, which meant I'd have to earn at least $45,000 to have enough to pay for everything, after taxes. Was I being a *shmendrick* to think, at seventy-eight, that I could handle such a task? Well, maybe if I just had to rely on myself, I would have been a fool. Thankfully, however, Yonkel had left me a little cushion to fall back on, just in case.

The Cortland house sat on a lake and had a wonderful terrace and balcony overlooking the water. We christened it right away with a wedding.

Mary, our wonderful housekeeper, was about to get married again. She had been the wife of Angelo, our genius gardener who had been incapacitated with a stroke. Mary had moved in with us and worked to pay for Angelo's care. Now, he had passed on and she had found a new love. We were sorry to lose her, but we insisted on catering the affair. *Salúd* to Mary and Rocco!

I guess I just got carried away with playing Cupid. When I asked Tor Osmundsen to move into Cortland with me, he agreed but wanted to bring his sweetheart along. Only if you get married, I insisted. So we had our second wedding out on the terrace, down by the lake!

Rehearsals for *The Second Time Around* were beginning on October 12th. We had a new director, Bob Livingston, and a new name: *Something Old, Something New.* It seems there was a song out called "The Second Time Around" and Adela Holtzer felt people might think we were doing an old play instead of a new one.

Hans and I were the only holdovers from the Atlanta cast, so the first rehearsal was rather a sloppy affair with a lot of new people trying to get a feel for their roles. With the emotional drain surrounding selling Chez, I was down and dispirited and just grouchy about my part. A peculiar apathy had crept over me. I didn't feel like eating, didn't feel like sleeping, and always seemed on the verge of hysteria. I kept going through rehearsals by rote alone, hanging in by my fingernails.

I think what was happening to me is common among widows. My entire psyche was finally accepting that Yonkel was gone, that I was alone, that I had to carry on for just my sake and no one else's. Of course, my heart didn't accept that. I thought of Yonkel all the time. I still do, each and every day. But, I didn't really, completely, say "Good-bye" to him until after Chez had been sold and I was really on my own.

We traveled to the Shubert Theater in New Haven for our out-of-town tryouts. Our rehearsals were no fun because many of the young actors were green and confused, our author was unsure about new lines, and our director was adamant for change. I thought Livingston was cutting too many of the laughs out of the play and Conreid agreed. Yet, at our first New Haven opening the audience seemed to really enjoy the show, so we got more optimistic.

Holtzer was especially up, even though the morning papers had praise for me and for Hans, but not for the play. (Molly, Molly. How many times have you heard that!)

We opened in Philadelphia and the notes were flying adding lines and cutting others. We had a fair house, but the first act was dull until Hans and I got on and sweated to pick things up. And Livingston lectured the cast—Hans and me, too—that we weren't giving our all to the play! I told him and Denker that if they could get someone else, I'd gladly step out. They were shocked.

They were in a jam, and Denker, in desperation, thought he would bring in a new scene where I would do a cartwheel. A cartwheel?! She and Hans are respectable senior citizens. This lady doesn't do cartwheels. I called Robbins, my agent at William Morris, and he backed me up: Ridiculous! So we all went back to work, fed up with being over-rehearsed.

Still, Adela was serious about bringing us to New York. She brought in a new gag writer to brighten the dead spots and maybe a miracle would happen. We had more rehearsals to work on the new material and I couldn't tell if any of it was good or bad. Lines came in and lines went out. It would take all my guts and stamina to get through Boston and then Broadway.

We moved on to the Wilbur Theater and—surprise—we had a good house and a tremendous audience response. But, I was so depressed with the whole venture, I didn't care. That is, I didn't care until Livingston tried to cut out my bow. Then I really tongue-lashed him! We old-timers have our pride!

Despite our big reception in Boston, the critics really destroyed the play. They were especially merciless to Livingston and Denker, the author. Once again, the audiences loved a show but the critics didn't and from experience, I know you can't beat them.

Hans Conreid and I begged Denker to close the play in Boston. We had one day I shall never forget. We had forty people in at the matinee and one hundred that night. How we gave performances, I'll never know. That was rock bottom.

What I didn't understand, of course, is that some people can lose a lot of money without it personally affecting them. Backing a sure-fire flop is just one more way to balance out their ledgers. And it's just too bad that small investors and innocent actors get ground-up in the process.

We had gotten bad reviews in Atlanta, in New Haven, and in Boston. Yet, we would open in New York just the same.

Our previews at the Morosco Theater were only lukewarm, but Adela seemed pleased. We had a good matinee and a better evening, but Bob insisted on taking my bow out and I told him off amid hysterics. Denker and the rest of the company were with me, but I was all shaken up. The next night, the audience gave me a standing ovation and shouted, "Molly, we love you!" Livingston then sent me flowers and an apologetic note and I hoped our feud was over. We had two fantastic performances that Saturday and the love that greeted me and the standing ovations had us all in tears. This was definitely an audience show. But the critics? Forget it.

We opened on January 1, 1977, and Hans and I took it all in our stride. Denker was panicky and Holtzer didn't even show up. No one, in fact, from the show's management was there so we did our best, then made our own party at Sardi's later on. Hans Conreid picked up the bill.

Tor drove me back to the country and I collapsed into an exhausted heap. When was I going to follow my instincts from the start when I was skeptical about a play? Our notices were disastrous and Holtzer closed the play. Denker called that he wanted to do the play in Miami, but I was too tired to care.

The ironic twist of this sad story is that the play did go on to achieve success. Not on Broadway, but in tent theaters around the country. It was returned to its original name, *The Second Time Around,* and both Broderick Crawford and Pat O'Brien have toured with it to terrific reviews. It's still playing in Miami! So who can figure it?

I had been burned on Broadway, again, so I stopped to take stock of things and while I was waiting, I got talked into doing this book. "You ought to write a book, you should write a book, you must write a book." That's what friends had been telling us for years. And Yonkel started, time and again, to comply with their advice, but never finished. So I've undertaken it and that takes a little bit of *chutzpah,* I guess.

Chutzpah is something our Israelis are blessed with. For example, a young Israeli company developed a perfume which they hoped would compete with Chanel No. 5. To make sure it was perfect, they called in French perfume experts to test it. They told them it was quite good, but would take two or three years to be ready for the market. Whereupon the Israelis answered, "We want to put it on sale next week." The Frenchmen gulped, *"Quelle chutzpah!"* So the Israelis named their fragrance *"Chutzpah"* and the next time you're in Israel, you can buy it!

And it's never too late to begin a life or a book. Helen and I packed up my things from Cortland not too long ago, and now the two of us are living in a brand-new, swank apartment across from Lincoln Center in the heart of the apple: New York City. I'm thrilled with the lights of this magical place and the energy they give me.

Old age? It doesn't bother me much. Except once, in a Tel Aviv hotel. The chambermaid had seen me in Romania fifty years before. She took one look at me and said, "Molly? It can't be you! I remember when you had black hair." Then she held her head in her hands and, shaking it from side to side, said, *"Oy, vus es vert fin a menchen"* (Oy, what happens to a person!)

Another old lady was asked to come to the funeral of her next-door neighbor and she answered, "Why should I go to her funeral? She won't come to mine."

Fanny Brice's mother, who was a widow, also had some thoughts on age. She was prodded by her friends to get married again, to feel young again, and she said, "I don't want to be young. I did that already."

Mama, on the other hand, often said, "I don't give you five cents for old age." And the truth of the matter, of course, lies somewhere in between.

Which reminds me of one more story before I close.

An old couple came to a rabbi for a divorce. They had been married for sixty-five years. The rabbi, astounded, asked the wife, "Why, after sixty-five years, would you want a divorce?" And the old lady answered, "Because enough is enough!"

So maybe enough is enough for me, too, and it's time to sign off. And, once more, I must quote one of my lovely old ladies who, after a concert, came backstage and said to me: "How can I tell you how I love you?"

I quote her and ask: how can I tell all the people who have laughed and cried with me through my seventy-five years in the theater, all over the world, when I was up and when I was down, and especially now when I'm on my own, how can I tell you how much your love for me has gladdened my heart through a wonderful life?

All I hope is that I have gladdened your hearts too, and brightened your lives as you have mine.

INDEX

Chicago Palace, 54
Children's Fund, 125
"Chin Up, Ladies," 220, 222, 224, 231
Christenburg, General, 158
Chu Chem (Allan), 247–52
Chutzpah perfume, 300
Circle Amical, 107
Circus Girl, The, 44
Citizen Kane, 87
City Theater (New York), 87
Civic Opera House (Chicago), 257
Clayton, Jackson and Durante act, 45, 146
Club Cinq (Paris), 107
Coates, Paul, 160
Cobb, Lee J., 225, 228
Coconut Grove (Miami), 214, 237
Cohan, George M., 78, 85
Cohen, Myron, 213, 222
Cole, Nat King, 229
Colette, Sidonie G., 36
Colonial Theater (Boston), 220
Colonie Summer Theater (Latham, N.Y.), 216
Columbia Artists, 142
Columbia Yiddish Theater (Philadelphia), 15, 16–17, 18, 74, 234
Come Blow Your Horn, 88, 212, 233, 248, 281, 291
    casting of, 225–26, 228
    Jewish roles in, 227
    reviews of, 235
Comédie Française, 61
concentration camps, 106, 107
    concerts for survivors, 109–10, 113, 117–18
    Jews' treatment of each other in, 107, 110
Conreid, Hans, 296, 298–300
Coolidge, Calvin, 28
Cooper, Gladys, 198, 201, 207, 225
corazones particulos, 156
Cornell, Katharine, 63
Country Girl, The, 151–52
Coward, Noel, 203, 222
Crane, Norma, 268
Crawford, Broderick, 300
Crawford, Cheryl, 247, 250–51
Criterion Theatre (London), 205

Daniel Frohman Memorial radio program, 84–85
Daughters of Israel, 104
"David Frost Show," 266
Davis, Bette, 263
Davis, Peter, 192
Davis, Sammy, Jr., 252
"Day in the Life of a New York Woiking Goil, A," 98, 157
Dean, Ivor, 205
Dear Me, the Sky Is Falling, 249
Deems, Mickey, 278–79
Denker, Henry, 295–96, 298–300
Deslys, Gaby, 66
Diamond, Selma, 160
Diamond Brothers, 78
"Dinah Shore Show," 294–95
Douglas, Melvyn, 128, 161
Douglas, Mike, 253
Douglas, Paul, 154–55
Downs, Hugh, 215
"Dr. Kildare," 235
Dubinsky, David, 150, 161
Dudley, Bide, 83, 93
Duncan Sisters, 54, 78
Durante, Jimmy, 45, 146
Du und Dort (Here and There), 124
Dybbuk, The, 99

"East Side Symphony," 63, 75
Edelstein, Mr., 13, 43–44, 51, 147
"Ed Sullivan Show," 152, 224, 232
Edward, My Son, 206
Eforie Theater (Teater Carl al Marre) (Bucharest), 41
8th Street Playhouse (Chicago), 180
Einstein, Albert, 45, 55
Eisen, Jack, 282
Eisen, Max, 212, 214–16, 218
Eisenhower, Dwight D., 206
Elena, queen of Greece, 208
Ellstein, Abe, 57, 66, 76
Elman, Mischa, 146
Emanuel, Mamie, 15, 249
Empire Theater (Johannesburg), 73
Enlightenment, Jewish, 35
ethnic theaters, in New York, 46–47
Ettinger, Solomon, 35
Exodus, 205